FUNCTIONAL PROGRAMMING WITH HOPE

ELLIS HORWOOD SERIES IN COMPUTERS AND THEIR APPLICATIONS
Series Editor: IAN CHIVERS, Senior Analyst, The Computer Centre, King's College, London, and formerly Senior Programmer and Analyst, Imperial College of Science and Technology, University of London

Abramsky, S. & Hankin, C.J.	ABSTRACT INTERPRETATION OF DECLARATIVE LANGUAGES
Alexander, H.	FORMALLY-BASED TOOLS AND TECHNIQUES FOR HUMAN–COMPUTER DIALOGUES
Atherton, R.	STRUCTURED PROGRAMMING WITH BBC BASIC
Atherton, R.	STRUCTURED PROGRAMMING WITH COMAL
Baeza-Yates, R.A.	TEXT SEARCHING ALGORITHMS
Bailey, R.	FUNCTIONAL PROGRAMMING WITH HOPE
Barrett, R., Ramsay, A. & Sloman, A.	POP-11
Berztiss, A.	PROGRAMMING WITH GENERATORS
Bharath, R.	COMPUTERS AND GRAPH THEORY
Bishop, P.	FIFTH GENERATION COMPUTERS
Bullinger, H.-J. & Gunzenhauser, H.	SOFTWARE ERGONOMICS
Burns, A.	NEW INFORMATION TECHNOLOGY
Carberry, J.C.	COBOL
Carlini, U. & Villano, U.	TRANSPUTERS AND PARALLEL ARCHITECTURES
Chivers, I.D.	AN INTRODUCTION TO STANDARD PASCAL
Chivers, I.D.	MODULA 2
Chivers, I.D. & Sleighthome, J.	INTERACTIVE FORTRAN 77
Clark, M.W.	PC-PORTABLE FORTRAN
Clark, M.W.	TEX
Cockshott, W. P.	PS-ALGOL IMPLEMENTATIONS: Applications in Persistent Object-Oriented Programming
Colomb, R.	IMPLEMENTING PERSISTENT PROLOG
Cope, T.	COMPUTING USING BASIC
Curth, M.A. & Edelmann, H.	APL
Dahlstrand, I.	SOFTWARE PORTABILITY AND STANDARDS
Dongarra, J., Duff, I., Gaffney, P., & McKee, S.	VECTOR AND PARALLEL COMPUTING
Dunne, P.E.	COMPUTABILITY THEORY
Eastlake, J.J.	A STRUCTURED APPROACH TO COMPUTER STRATEGY
Eisenbach, S.	FUNCTIONAL PROGRAMMING
Ellis, D.	MEDICAL COMPUTING AND APPLICATIONS
Ennals, J.R.	ARTIFICIAL INTELLIGENCE
Ennals, J.R.	BEGINNING MICRO-PROLOG
Ennals, J.R., *et al.*	INFORMATION TECHNOLOGY AND EDUCATION
Filipič, B.	PROLOG USER'S HANDBOOK
Ford, N.	COMPUTER PROGRAMMING LANGUAGES
Guariso, G. & Werthner, H.	ENVIRONMENTAL DECISION SUPPORT SYSTEMS
Harland, D.M.	CONCURRENCY AND PROGRAMMING LANGUAGES
Harland, D.M.	POLYMORPHIC PROGRAMMING LANGUAGES
Harland, D.M.	REKURSIV
Harris, D.J.	DEVELOPING DEDICATED DBASE SYSTEMS
Henshall, J. & Shaw, S.	OSI EXPLAINED, 2nd Edition
Hepburn, P.H.	FURTHER PROGRAMMING IN PROLOG
Hepburn, P.H.	PROGRAMMING IN MICRO-PROLOG MADE SIMPLE
Hill, I.D. & Meek, B.L.	PROGRAMMING LANGUAGE STANDARDISATION
Hirschheim, R., Smithson, S. & Whitehouse, D.	MICROCOMPUTERS AND THE HUMANITIES: Survey and Recommendations
Hutchins, W.J.	MACHINE TRANSLATION
Hutchison, D.	FUNDAMENTALS OF COMPUTER LOGIC
Hutchison, D. & Silvester, P.	COMPUTER LOGIC
Koopman, P.	STACK COMPUTERS
Kenning, M.-M. & Kenning, M.J.	COMPUTERS AND LANGUAGE LEARNING: Current Theory and Practice
Koskimies, K. & Paaki, J.	AUTOMATING LANGUAGE IMPLEMENTATION
Koster, C.H.A.	TOP-DOWN PROGRAMMING WITH ELAN
Last, R.	ARTIFICIAL INTELLIGENCE TECHNIQUES IN LANGUAGE LEARNING
Lester, C.	A PRACTICAL APPROACH TO DATA STRUCTURES
Lucas, R.	DATABASE APPLICATIONS USING PROLOG
Lucas, A.	DESKTOP PUBLISHING
Maddix, F. & Morgan, G.	SYSTEMS SOFTWARE
Matthews, J.L.	FORTH
Millington, D.	SYSTEMS ANALYSIS AND DESIGN FOR COMPUTER APPLICATIONS
Moseley, L.G., Sharp, J.A. & Salenieks, P.	PASCAL IN PRACTICE
Moylan, P.	ASSEMBLY LANGUAGE FOR ENGINEERS
Narayanan, A. & Sharkey, N.E.	AN INTRODUCTION TO LISP
Parrington, N. & Roper, M.	UNDERSTANDING SOFTWARE TESTING
Paterson, A.	OFFICE SYSTEMS
Phillips, C. & Cornelius, B.J.	COMPUTATIONAL NUMERICAL METHODS
Rahtz, S.P.Q.	INFORMATION TECHNOLOGY IN THE HUMANITIES
Ramsden, E.	MICROCOMPUTERS IN EDUCATION 2

Series continued at back of book

FUNCTIONAL PROGRAMMING WITH HOPE

ROGER BAILEY
Department of Computing
Imperial College of Science and Technology
University of London

ELLIS HORWOOD
NEW YORK LONDON TORONTO SYDNEY TOKYO SINGAPORE

First published in 1990 by
ELLIS HORWOOD LIMITED
Market Cross House, Cooper Street,
Chichester, West Sussex, PO19 1EB, England

A division of
Simon & Schuster International Group

© Ellis Horwood Limited, 1990

All rights reserved. No part of this publication may be
reproduced, stored in a retrieval system, or transmitted,
in any form, or by any means, electronic, mechanical,
photocopying, recording or otherwise, without the prior
permission, in writing, of the publisher

Printed and bound in Great Britain
by Bookcraft (Bath) Limited, Midsomer Norton

British Library Cataloguing in Publication Data

Bailey, Roger
Functional programming with HOPE. —
(Ellis Horwood series in computers and their applications).
1. Computer systems. Programming languages:
HOPE language. I. Title
005.13'3
ISBN 0–13–338237–0

Library of Congress Cataloging-in-Publication Data

Bailey, Roger.
Functional programming with HOPE / Roger Bailey.
p. cm. — (Ellis Horwood series in computers and their
applications)
ISBN 0–13–338237–0
Functional programming (Computer science).
2. HOPE (Computer program language). I. Title.
II. Series: Computers and their applications.
QA76.62.B35   1989
005.1'1–dc20   89–24815
                                              CIP

Contents

Preface xi

Chapter 1 Expressions 1
  1.1 About computers 1
  1.2 Mechanised arithmetic 2
  1.3 High-level languages 2
  1.4 Hope as a notation for writing expressions 3
  1.5 The priority of operation 4
  1.6 Manipulating expressions by rewriting 5
  1.7 The Hope Machine 6
  1.8 The concept of types 7
  1.9 Numbers 8
  1.10 Truth values 10
  1.11 Characters 12
  1.12 Conditional expressions 14
  1.13 Rewrite rules for conditional expressions 15
  1.14 Review 17
  1.15 Exercises 18

Chapter 2 Abstraction 20
  2.1 Abstract expressions 20
  2.2 Defining new operations 21
  2.3 Using functions 22

vi CONTENTS

2.4 Functions over other types of object ... 23
2.5 Rewrite rules for function applications ... 24
2.6 More about equations ... 25
2.7 Program order ... 26
2.8 The scope of names... ... 26
2.9 Functions with more than one argument ... 27
2.10 Another way to use functions ... 28
2.11 More about names ... 29
2.12 Functions with more than two arguments... ... 30
2.13 Reduction strategies ... 30
2.14 Non-strict functions ... 32
2.15 Recurrence relationships ... 33
2.16 Computational cost ... 36
2.17 Qualified expressions ... 38
2.18 Another kind of qualified expression ... 40
2.19 Multiple qualification ... 41
2.20 More about name scope... ... 41
2.21 A word about programming style ... 44
2.22 Review ... 45
2.23 Exercises ... 46

Chapter 3 Data Structures ... 48
3.1 Different types of pair ... 48
3.2 Tuples ... 49
3.3 Operations on tuples ... 50
3.4 More general functions ... 51
3.5 Defining tuples recursively ... 53
3.6 Programming style again ... 56
3.7 Lists ... 57
3.8 Operations defining lists ... 59
3.9 Other operations on lists ... 61
3.10 Functions which define lists ... 62
3.11 Functions over lists ... 64
3.12 More functions over lists ... 67
3.13 Constructors ... 68
3.14 Patterns ... 68
3.15 Patterns matching other data types ... 69
3.16 Ambiguity and completeness ... 71
3.17 More specific patterns ... 72
3.18 Patterns in qualified expressions ... 73
3.19 Pattern synonyms ... 74
3.20 Review ... 75
3.21 Exercises ... 75

Chapter 4 New Kinds of Data ... 78
4.1 User-defined data types ... 78
4.2 Data structures containing user-defined types ... 79
4.3 Constructors with parameters ... 80
4.4 Using constructors to disguise data ... 82
4.5 Constructors with more than one parameter ... 83
4.6 Floating-point numbers ... 84
4.7 Constructors with different argument types ... 85
4.8 Types containing user-defined types ... 86
4.9 Constructors as infix operations ... 87
4.10 Recursive data types ... 88
4.11 Indirectly recursive types ... 90
4.12 Mutually recursive types ... 91
4.13 New names for old types ... 92
4.14 Non-linear data structures ... 93
4.15 Searching binary trees ... 95
4.16 Building a balanced binary tree ... 97
4.17 Flattening a balanced binary tree ... 98
4.18 Evaluating expressions using trees ... 99
4.19 Choosing the best data structure ... 101
4.20 Delaying the decision ... 102
4.21 An abstract data type example ... 103
4.22 Review ... 105
4.23 Exercises ... 106

Chapter 5 More General Types ... 108
5.1 Why lists are powerful ... 108
5.2 Constructed types ... 109
5.3 Universal type declarations ... 109
5.4 User-defined polymorphic data types ... 110
5.5 Data structures with polymorphic components ... 111
5.6 Spot the deliberate mistake ... 112
5.7 Less general data structures ... 113
5.8 Non-linear polymorphic types ... 115
5.9 Ordered binary trees ... 115
5.10 More general trees ... 118
5.11 More manipulations on trees ... 121
5.12 More powerful functions ... 122
5.13 User-defined polymorphic functions ... 123
5.14 More polymorphic functions over lists ... 124
5.15 More powerful polymorphic functions ... 125
5.16 More deliberate mistakes ... 126
5.17 Not all mistakes are deliberate ... 128
5.18 Polymorphic functions over non-linear data types ... 128

viii CONTENTS

    5.19 Overloading ... 130
    5.20 More powerful abstract data types ... 131
    5.21 Review ... 133
    5.22 Exercises ... 134

Chapter 6 More General Functions ... 136
    6.1 More about abstraction ... 136
    6.2 Common patterns of computation ... 136
    6.3 More general higher-order functions ... 140
    6.4 Fully general higher-order functions ... 141
    6.5 Reducing applications of `map` ... 142
    6.6 Realising the full power of `map` ... 143
    6.7 Non-linear higher-order functions ... 145
    6.8 Another common pattern of recursion ... 146
    6.9 Making `combine` fully polymorphic ... 147
    6.10 Reducing applications of `reduce` ... 148
    6.11 Realising the full power of `reduce` ... 150
    6.12 Specifying the base case ... 152
    6.13 Left-associative consolidation ... 154
    6.14 Consolidating non-linear data structures ... 156
    6.15 Variations on a theme ... 158
    6.16 Polymorphic sorting revisited ... 159
    6.17 Higher order functions over abstract data types ... 162
    6.18 Review ... 164
    6.19 Exercises ... 165

Chapter 7 Creating New Functions ... 167
    7.1 Anonymous functions ... 167
    7.2 More complex bodies ... 168
    7.3 Finding the type of a lambda expression ... 169
    7.4 Programming style again ... 170
    7.5 Partial application ... 171
    7.6 Why lambda expressions are powerful ... 172
    7.7 Multi-rule lambda expressions ... 174
    7.8 Functionals ... 176
    7.9 Programming style revisited ... 178
    7.10 Generalising functions ... 178
    7.11 Recursive lambda expressions ... 181
    7.12 Analogues of `listify` ... 182
    7.13 Functions in data structures ... 183
    7.14 Using functions in data structures ... 185
    7.15 Programming style yet again ... 186
    7.16 True functional programming ... 187
    7.17 Generalised functional composition ... 188

7.18	Functions as alternatives to data structures	189
7.19	Review	192
7.20	Exercises	192

Chapter 8 Lazy Evaluation ... 194

8.1	How long is a list?	194
8.2	Infinite lists	195
8.3	Lazy evaluation	196
8.4	Lazy constructors	197
8.5	Patterns matching lazy constructors	197
8.6	Practically infinite lists	198
8.7	Solving problems with infinite lists	200
8.8	Using infinite lists safely	202
8.9	Infinite lists and non-strict functions	203
8.10	Packaging infinity	205
8.11	Saving space with infinite lists	206
8.12	Approaches to a limit	206
8.13	Visualising infinite lists	208
8.14	Unbounded problems	209
8.15	Review	211
8.16	Exercises	212

Chapter 9 Input and Output ... 215

9.1	Saving the results of programs	215
9.2	Retrieving the results	216
9.3	Special files	218
9.4	Delaying the input	218
9.5	Controlling the output layout	222
9.6	Control sequences	224
9.7	Analysing the input	225
9.8	Discovering the input layout	227
9.9	Controlling interleaving	228
9.10	Formatting infinite lists	231
9.11	Review	232
9.12	Exercises	233

Appendix 1 Solutions to Exercises ... 235

Chapter 1	235
Chapter 2	238
Chapter 3	240
Chapter 4	243
Chapter 5	246
Chapter 6	249
Chapter 7	253

x CONTENTS

Chapter 8 256
Chapter 9 261

Appendix 2   Language Summary 269
  A2.1   Character classes 269
  A2.2   Words 269
  A2.3   Program structure 270
  A2.4   Program order 277

Appendix 3   Standard Facilities 278
  A3.1   Reserved words 278
  A3.2   Predeclared names 278
  A3.3   System commands behaving as functions 279
  A3.4   Top-level system commands 280

Appendix 4   Ordinal Values of Characters 281

Index 282

Preface

This is primarily an introductory textbook about computer programming, but it is written with the secondary aim of demystifying the new technology of Functional Programming. Many previous treatments of the topic have been rather theoretical, with a bias towards implementing functional languages rather than using them. This has tended to obscure the fact that they are first and foremost convenient programming tools. This book aims to redress the balance by presenting Functional Programming as an entirely unexceptional and practical activity requiring no theoretical background.

The unifying idea behind Functional Programming is very simple. Programs are based on the evaluation of expressions, suitably generalised to allow complex data structures to be specified. The description "functional" arises from their use of side-effect-free functions as the main program structuring and abstraction device. Side effects are a major source of errors in programs, and their absence from functional languages gives the software engineer a powerful tool for rapidly developing reliable modular programs. Removing side effects also reduces the normal dependence of program meaning on evaluation order and makes functional programs especially suitable for executing on parallel machine and easy to reason about informally.

The book has its origin in notes written for an advanced workshop held in the Department of Computing at Imperial College in 1983, sponsored by the Science and Engineering Research Council. The material was later expanded and formed the basis of a number of functional programming courses given in subsequent years to second and third-year undergraduate and master's degree students. Many of those students contributed to the development of the material, particularly the exercises.

During this period, the need for a comprehensive textbook became increasingly apparent, and I have taken this opportunity to try and write one which is suitable for students with no previous experience of computing. The recursive functional style has been successfully taught for several years in elementary programming courses at Imperial College, and the idea of teaching a purely functional language as a first programming language is now widely accepted.

The book emphasises systematic program design and analysis, using term rewriting as an execution model. It also encourages informal complexity analysis of programs and addresses other important software engineering concepts, such as abstract data types. Whilst presented as a first programming text, it is also intended to be a straightforward introduction to the ideas of functional programming suitable for the practising programmer; it is hoped that the exercises and their solutions will make it suitable for self study as well as for classroom use.

Functional languages have a much longer pedigree than conventional ones, and owe their origins to Alonzo Church's Lambda Calculus of 1941. John McCarthy's LISP of 1962 is essentially a mechanised version of the Lambda Calculus, and can be regarded as the grandfather of all functional languages. Hope itself was originally developed at Edinburgh University in 1980 by Rod Burstall, David MacQueen and Don Sanella, and incorporates Robin Milner's work on strong polymorphic type checking. Hope was introduced to Imperial College by John Darlington in 1981 for use in the ALICE parallel machine project and the first portable implementation was written in Pascal by Victor Wu Wai Hung. Later versions were written in Hope itself by Ian Moor and by Keith Sephton and Nigel Perry for the Alvey Directorate's fifth generation Flagship project. None of the work of the Functional Programming Group at Imperial College would have been possible without their efforts.

I must also acknowledge my gratitude to many other individuals who have contributed directly and indirectly to this book by reading through early drafts, by giving their time to discuss obscure points and offer advice, and by providing a generally supportive framework in which to write it. My special thanks for this help go to Alison Surry, Gavin Bierman, Stuart Cox, Tony Field, Gordon Gallagher, Chris Hankin, Brian Meek and Sue Wright.

Roger Bailey
Imperial College
December 1989

Chapter 1

Expressions

1.1 About computers

The classical stored-program digital computer consists of two parts: a *processor* and a *store*. The processor contains a small set of *accumulators* (often only one), each capable of holding a single number known as a *data item*. The processor can perform a wide variety of different arithmetic and logical operations on data items held in accumulators. Operations are specified by *instructions* which are also numbers. The store contains a large set of numbered cells which can hold data items or instructions, and instructions are provided to copy data items from store cells to accumulators and vice-versa. A set of instructions in successive store cells is called a *program*. The computer *executes* the program by copying instructions automatically and in sequence from the store to the processor, obeying each one before transferring the next.

Special instructions are also provided to vary the orderly fetching and execution of instructions from the store. A *branch* instruction causes the next instruction to be fetched from a specified location rather than the next in sequence. If the new instruction is one which occurred earlier in the program, the machine will *loop*, or execute a group of instructions repeatedly. This feature gives the computer the power to perform repetitive calculations. More powerful still are the *conditional* instructions which are executed only under special conditions such as an accumulator containing zero. By combining these with branch instructions, the machine can be made to select *alternative* actions according to the results of earlier calculations.

Finally, by employing suitable conventions, the numbers in the store cells and accumulators may be given other interpretations, allowing the computer to be used for processing many kinds of non-numeric data such as text and formulæ.

1.2 Mechanised arithmetic

From their inception, digital computers have been used for performing numerical calculations. The primitive nature of the basic machine operations means that a fairly simple calculation may require quite a long program to perform it. As an example, consider the calculation specified by the arithmetic expression:

(113 + 6) - (2 + 85)

where the symbols have their usual mathematical meanings. Suppose that we wish to evaluate this on a computer with a single accumulator and the following fairly typical repertoire of instructions: **insert** which places a specified data value into the accumulator; **save** which copies a value from the accumulator into a specified store cell; **move** which copies a value from a store cell to the accumulator; **add** which adds a copy of the value in a store cell to that in the accumulator; and **subtract** which subtracts a copy of the value in a store cell from that in the accumulator. In each case the new value placed in the accumulator or in a store cell destroys its original contents. The sequence of instructions required to evaluate the expression will be something like this:

insert	the value 113 into the accumulator
add	the value 6 to the contents of the accumulator
save	the contents of the accumulator in store cell 1
insert	the value 2 into the accumulator
add	the value 85 to the contents of the accumulator
save	the contents of the accumulator in store cell 2
load	the contents of store cell 1 into the accumulator
subtract	the contents of store cell 2 from those of the accumulator

In this example the program has been written in an English-like notation (sometimes called *assembly language*) to make it more self-explanatory; inside the store of the machine, the instructions are represented by numbers which are indistinguishable from data items. After the last instruction in the program has been obeyed, the accumulator will contain the number 32, the value represented by the original expression.

1.3 High-level languages

It is not easy to be certain that the program shown above computes the value of the arithmetic expression correctly. All the instructions work by changing the *state* of the machine (the accumulator and store cell contents), so the order in which the operations are specified is very significant. To convince ourselves that it works, we would probably need to simulate the operations using a pencil and paper, checking that the intermediate values are calculated, stored, and retrieved correctly.

When we attempt to use the computer for a realistically sized numerical calculation (*i.e.* one which is too large to do by hand), the task of specifying the operations in the correct order and taking care of the intermediate results becomes very time-consuming and it is easy to make careless clerical errors. The effect of an individual instruction depends on the state of the machine, but it also changes the state. To understand the effect of any instruction, we may need to examine all previously executed instructions; in the worst case this may mean examining the *entire program*. The difficulty of writing and of understanding larger programs increases in proportion to the *square* of the number of instructions they contain.

This observation has led to the development of *high-level languages* which allow calculations to be specified directly as expressions like the one above. The meaning of an expression is usually much clearer than that of an equivalent program to compute its value because the expression is a *static* description of the way in which values combine together to define a result. The meaning of an instruction in a program depends upon the state of the machine, and thus on all previously executed instructions, but the meaning of a term in an expression is *independent* of the context in which it occurs. This property is called *referential transparency* and allows us to understand the meaning of parts of an expression in isolation. Expressions let us concentrate on specifying *what* value is calculated, rather than *how* it is calculated.

The *functional languages* are a class of high-level languages which extend the idea of programming with expressions to its logical conclusion. Practical programs need to calculate large numbers of values; functional languages simplify the organisation of this task by allowing an expression to specify a whole collection of values. As well as expressions which specify numerical values like the example above, they also allow expressions to specify other types of value, such as text. An entire program is effectively written as a single large expression, with certain simplifications to make it easier to read. The property of referential transparency applies throughout such an "expression-program", so that the meaning of any of its parts (terms) can easily be understood without having to examine the whole program.

1.4 Hope as a notation for writing expressions

The functional language Hope is a notation for writing programs in the form of expressions. Programs are usually entered into a computer from a typewriter-like keyboard, and the notation therefore makes an allowance for the fact that the keyboard lacks many common mathematical symbols, and cannot easily cope with notational conventions like subscripts and superscripts. Here is a complete Hope program which performs the calculation in the example above:

```
( 113 + 6 ) - ( 2 + 85 ) ;
```

The expression is shown in a typewriter-like typeface to emphasise that it is a real Hope program. We shall adopt this typographical convention throughout the book, both for complete examples, and for referring to parts of programs in the text. This will occasionally result in sentences which appear rather cryptic at first sight, but careful attention to the typefaces used will always reveal them to be unambiguous.

Hope expressions are constructed from a vocabulary of basic symbols; in the example above, the symbols are +, -, (,), 113, 6, 2, 85 and ;. Symbols formed from more than one character (*e.g.* 1 1 3 and 8 2) are regarded as indivisible. Symbols are classified as *operations* (also called *operators*), *operands* or *punctuation marks*; thus + and − are operations; 1 1 3, 6, 2 and 8 5 are operands, whilst (,) and ; are punctuation marks. The ; marks the end of the program and the other symbols have their usual mathematical meanings. Within an expression operations are said to be *applied* to their operands. For this reason, functional languages are sometimes known as *applicative* languages.

1.5 The priority of operations

In elementary mathematics, certain operations (such as multiplication and division) are considered to have a higher priority than others (such as addition and subtraction) and are evaluated first in an expression. Hope associates a numerical priority with every operation in an expression, and evaluates the operations with the highest relative priority first. It also obeys the mathematical rule that any parts of an expression enclosed in parentheses are evaluated first, irrespective of the priority of other operations. Addition and subtraction have priority 5. Multiplication and division are also provided, using the symbols * and div respectively. These have priority 6, so the program:

    2 + 3 * 4 ;

evaluates to 1 4 rather than 2 0 because it is treated as if it had been written:

    2 + (3 * 4) ;

When adjacent operations are of equal priority, they are treated as though the leftmost operation has the higher priority, so the program:

    9 − 5 + 3 ;

is treated as though it had been written:

    (9 − 5) + 3 ;

and evaluates to 7 (rather than 1). Equal-priority operations are said to *associate to the left*. As we saw in the first example, we may override the normal priority of operations and force any part of an expression to be evaluated first by explicitly placing it in parentheses. Thus the program:

    (2 + 3) * 4 ;

evaluates to 2 0 rather than 1 4.

1.6 Manipulating expressions by rewriting

A powerful feature of mathematics is that it not only provides us with a notation for writing expressions, but also with a set of rules for manipulating these expressions into different forms without changing their meanings. Hope expressions have many of the properties of mathematical notation and many of the same manipulations may be applied to them. Substituting expressions by different but equivalent expressions is called *rewriting* and the rules which tell us which substitutions are valid are called *rewrite rules*. In the case of expressions consisting of arithmetic operations, the rewrite rules are the familiar rules of arithmetic.

Rewriting may increase or decrease the complexity of an expression. Rewrite rules which simplify expressions are particularly useful, for by using them we can discover the simplest expression with the same meaning as the original. Here "simplification" means removing operations and may not always result in an expression which has less terms than the one we started with. Simplifying expressions by rewriting is also called *reduction* and the rewrite rules *reduction rules*. An expression or part of an expression which can be reduced is called a *redex* and an expression which contains no redexes is said to be in *normal form*. As an example of reduction, consider again the program:

(113 + 6) - (2 + 85) ;

A rewrite rule for an expression consisting of + and two numbers is to rewrite the expression with the sum of the two numbers. There are two redexes of this form in the the example above, and we can choose either one to reduce first, giving two ways of performing the first two reduction steps:

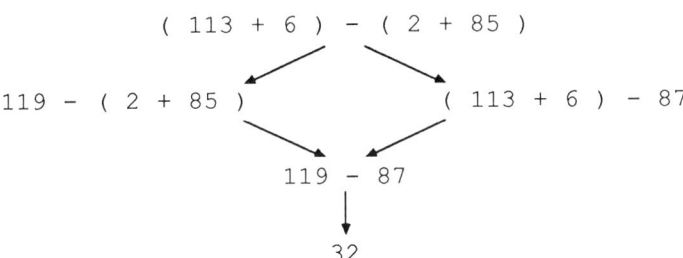

A rewrite rule for an expression containing - and two numbers is to rewrite the expression with the difference of the numbers. There is one such redex in each of the intermediate expressions, and one in the final expression, which can thus be rewritten to 32. There are no rewrite rules for numbers, and the expression is now in normal form. The normal form of an expression may be regarded as its *value*, and rewriting as a way of evaluating the expression.

In this example there were initially two redexes and hence two possible routes for reducing the expression, although these converged to a single route after one further reduction step. It is not obvious that this will happen in a more complex expression with many redexes, suggesting that there may be more than one normal form of the same expression. Fortunately, an important logical theorem called the *Church-Rosser Theorem* implies that every expression has effectively a single normal form. Not all expressions actually have a normal form however, because some rewrite rules may lead to *infinite* reduction sequences. A second theorem called the *Standardisation Theorem* gives us a strategy for choosing redexes so that the reduction sequence will terminate with the normal form if it exists. Reduction strategies are discussed further in §1.13 and again in §2.13. We shall see an example of an infinite reduction sequence in §2.15.

1.7 The Hope Machine

By using a special auxiliary program called an *interpreter*, a computer may be made to evaluate Hope programs directly and behave as though it is a machine whose basic operations are those of Hope. We shall assume throughout the rest of this book that we are using such a "Hope Machine".

At the simplest level, the Hope Machine behaves like a calculator, accepting expressions typed in at the keyboard, evaluating them and displaying their results on the screen. The screen normally displays the symbol >: which is called a *prompt* and indicates that the machine is expecting an expression to be typed in. The layout of expressions is quite flexible; in general, adjacent symbols may be separated by any number of blank, tab or newline characters to make the expression more readable (as in the example above), but these are usually optional. Occasionally a layout character is obligatory when two adjacent symbols are both formed from the same class of characters (such as all letters), and might otherwise be confused as one symbol. The full rules are given in the language summary in appendix 2.

If we evaluate the arithmetic expression in the example above using the Hope Machine, it will appear as follows on the screen:

```
>: ( 113 + 6 ) - ( 2 + 85 ) ;®
>> 32 : num
>:
```

The parts which are underlined were typed in by the programmer. ® represents the newline character, sometimes labelled *return* on the keyboard. The Hope Machine has evaluated the expression and displayed the result (32), together with the annotation : num, which is explained in §1.8. The final prompt shows that the machine is ready to evaluate another expression.

The Hope Machine examines each line as soon as the newline has been entered. Any typing mistakes within a line can be corrected before it is entered by backspacing over the incorrect characters and retyping them. If a mistake is discovered in the part of the expression entered so far, the Hope Machine displays a pointer (^) under the last line at the point the error was discovered and then displays an informative error message, for example:

```
>: ( 113 + 6 ) - ;®
              ^
ERROR-10 Incomplete expression
>:
```

When this happens, the whole expression must be retyped. Some versions of the Hope Machine may have more elaborate correction facilities.

Not all errors in programs can be discovered immediately they are typed in; some may only be discovered during the evaluation of an expression. For instance, division by zero is a mathematically undefined operation, and causes evaluation to stop if attempted. We express this with a rewrite rule for expressions formed from a number, `div` and 0 which is to rewrite the expression with the value **error**. Whenever the error value is generated, the Hope Machine displays a message and the value of the *whole program* reduces to the error value. For example:

```
>: ( 3 + 4 div 0 ) ;®
Run time error : division by zero
>:
```

For the remainder of the book (except for chapter 9) we shall adopt a slightly simpler convention when showing examples of Hope programs as they might be evaluated by the Hope Machine. We shall omit the prompts and distinguish the result of the evaluation by printing it in *italics*, for example:

```
( 113 + 6 ) - ( 2 + 85 ) ;
```
32 : num

1.8 The concept of types

The annotation `: num` which follows the result in the examples above indicates the *type* of the value. The symbol `:` may be read as "is of type ..." whilst `num` is short for *number*. Types are a way of classifying values according to their properties, and type information is used by the Hope Machine to check that the programmer does not try to specify an inappropriate operation on an operand.

Every object in a Hope program has a type; in particular *operations* in expressions have types as well as their operands. The type of an object is described by a *type expression*. For operations, this takes the following form:

type of operand(s)   ->   *type of result(s)*

where the symbol `->` is read as "yielding a ...". For example, the standard arithmetic operations which we have seen so far all have the type:

```
num # num -> num
```

The symbol # is read as "and a ...". This type expression states that an arithmetic operation is an object which has *two* numbers as its operands and yields a single number as its result. An operation of this type may only be applied to two numbers (or expressions which define numbers) and the whole expression may only occur in a larger expression where a number is required. The Hope Machine checks every expression *before* attempting to evaluate it, to ensure that the operations and operands have the specified types. We shall see examples of this in §1.10 when some different types of operand have been introduced.

Hope provides three basic (or *primitive*) types of object which may be used as operands in expressions. In addition to numbers which we have already seen, there are two other types of value called `truval` (short for *truth value*) and `char` (short for *character*). We shall now describe these three types of value in more detail.

1.9 Numbers

Values of type `num` are *integers* (whole numbers) and are represented in expressions as sequences of digits. There is an upper limit to the size of a number which depends on the particular Hope Machine used to evaluate the program. This is usually at least nine digits although it may occasionally be less. Larger numbers appearing in expressions are rewritten *modulo* the maximum permitted number, for example:

```
9999999999 ;
1410065407 : num
```

This unfortunate feature (known as *integer overflow*) arises from the way that numbers are stored and manipulated in the real computer which is used to simulate the Hope Machine. The reason is explained more fully in §4.2. Hope provides five standard operations on numbers:

+	addition
-	subtraction
*	multiplication
div	integer division
mod	remainder after integer division

These operations are all of type `num # num -> num`. Addition and subtraction have priority 5; the remaining three operations have priority 6. When `div` and `mod` are used in expressions, they must be followed by a layout character unless the next symbol in the expression is an open parenthesis. There is no direct representation for negative numbers in expressions, but they can be generated as a result of subtraction operations. An expression may thus be used to denote a negative value, for example:

```
0 - 5 ;
-5 : num
```

The operation `abs` yields the absolute value (magnitude) of a number. This has a single operand and is known as a *monadic* operation, in contrast to *dyadic* operations which have two operands (such as +, -, *, div and mod). The type of `abs` is:

    num -> num

For example:

    abs (0 - 5) ;
    5 : num

All monadic operations have the same priority, which is higher than that of any dyadic operation. Without the parentheses, the expression above would be interpreted as:

    ((abs 0) - 5) ;

and evaluate to -5. Because of the general rule in Hope that equal-priority operations associate to the left, an expression containing two successive monadic operations must have extra parentheses to make sure that it is interpreted correctly, for example:

    abs (abs (0 - 5)) ;

Without the parentheses, this is interpreted as:

    (abs abs) (0 - 5) ;

which will be reported as a type error because the first `abs` operation is applied to an object of type num -> num (the second `abs`), rather than to a num.

The arithmetic operations do not quite behave like the corresponding operations from elementary mathematics because of the way in which numbers are represented inside a computer. Addition may cause integer overflow, hence we cannot assume that two expressions such as:

    x + y - z   and   x - z + y

are equivalent as they would be in mathematics. Since numbers may have only integral values, the `div` operation is defined to ignore the fractional part of its result in cases where the result would not be a whole number, for example:

    3 div 2 ;
    1 : num

    (0 - 100) div 55 ;
    0 : num

The second example is especially counter-intuitive, because truncation is always towards zero, so the sign of the result changes. Pairs of expressions which are mathematically equivalent, such as:

$$x \cdot y/z \qquad \text{and} \qquad x/z \cdot y$$

will not necessarily be equivalent when written in Hope. The `mod` operation is even more counter-intuitive than `div` when its arguments are negative:

```
10 mod 3 ;
1 : num

10 mod ( 0 - 3 ) ;
1 : num

( 0 - 10 ) mod 3 ;
-2 : num

( 0 - 10 ) mod ( 0 - 3 ) ;
-4 : num
```

1.10 Truth values

The second primitive type provided by Hope is the *truth value* or `truval`. A value of type `truval` represents the truth of some logical assertion (*e.g.* "it's raining outside"). Assertions in programs may be constructed from a *comparison operation* and two values of the same type, such as two numbers. Hope provides the following primitive comparison operations:

=	equal to
/=	not equal to
<	less than
=<	less than or equal to
>	greater than
>=	greater than or equal to

All these operations have priority 6 and may be considered to be of type:

```
num # num -> truval
```

There are only two possible truth values, which are represented by the symbols `true` and `false`. Here are some examples of comparison expressions involving numbers as they might be evaluated by the Hope Machine:

```
( 3 + 4 ) = ( 4 + 3 ) ;
true : truval

( 22 + 33 ) < 50 ;
false : truval
```

In these examples the arithmetic subexpressions are in parentheses because + has a lower priority than any of the the comparison operations. Without the parentheses the second expression would be interpreted as:

```
22 + ( 33 < 50 )
```

which is invalid because the operands of + are the wrong type. The Hope Machine can detect this error before evaluating the expression, and reports it as follows:

```
22 + 33 < 50 ;
ERROR-63 Wrong operand type for +
Expression    : ( 22 + ( 33 < 50 ) )
Expected type: ( num # num )
Actual type   : ( num # truval )
```

The type of the operation < is num # num -> truval, hence the operands of + are num # truval and not num # num as required. These examples may seem rather unnatural, since no reasonable person would write programs to evaluate relations formed from constant values such as (3 + 4) = (4 + 3). However, we shall see in §2.5 that expressions like this may arise naturally as the result of rewriting.

Truth values may be combined together using the operations and of priority 5 and or of priority 4, both of type:

```
truval # truval -> truval
```

For example:

```
( 3 + 2 ) < 4 or ( 3 - 2 ) > 0 ;
true : truval
```

Truth values may be inverted (or *negated*) using the monadic operation not of type:

```
truval -> truval
```

For example:

```
not true ;
false : truval
```

Truth values may be compared using the = and /= operations, for example:

```
false = false ;
true : truval
```

This expression is valid because the comparison operations are also considered to be of type `truval # truval -> truval`. Both operands must have the *same* type however, and an expression such as:

```
3 = false ;
```

is incorrect and results in a type error. The operations are not considered to be of type `num # truval -> truval` (or `truval # num -> truval`). Since numbers and truth values are fundamentally different kinds of object (like ravens and writing desks), it would never make sense to write such an expression in a program. The concept of types formalises this idea and lets the Hope Machine check that expressions are formed from the correct types of object before it attempts to evaluate them.

1.11 Characters

The remaining type of object provided by Hope is the *character* or `char`. A character value consists of any single printable character (including blank) enclosed in single quotation marks. The comparison operations described in §1.10 are also considered to have type `char # char -> truval` and can be used to compare characters. As well as testing for equality with = and /= we can use the other comparison operations to determine the lexical (alphabetical) ordering of two characters, for example:

```
'A' < 'B' ;
true : truval
```

Appendix 4 lists the complete set of characters recognised by the Hope Machine, and gives their lexical ordering. Two monadic operations are provided to relate characters to their positions within the ordering:

```
ord       of type       char -> num
chr       of type       num -> char
```

`ord` gives the position of a character within the ordering and `chr` gives the character at a given position in the ordering. The character ordering defined in appendix 4 exhibits a number of useful properties:

(a) The lower-case letters have consecutive ordinal values such that comparison results in alphabetical ordering. For any arbitrary character c, the expression:

```
c >= 'a' and c =< 'z'
```

evaluates to `true` if `c` is a lower-case letter and `false` if it is not.

(b) The upper-case letters have consecutive ordinal values such that comparison results in alphabetical ordering. For any arbitrary character `c`, the expression:

```
c >= 'A' and c =< 'Z'
```

evaluates to `true` if `c` is an upper-case letter and `false` if it is not.

(c) The ordinal value of a lower-case letter is less than the ordinal value of the corresponding upper-case character by a constant difference. For any arbitrary lower-case letter `l`, the expression:

```
chr ( ord l + ord 'A' - ord 'a' )
```

evaluates to the corresponding upper-case letter. Conversely, for any arbitrary upper-case letter `L`, the expression:

```
chr ( ord L - ord 'A' + ord 'a' )
```

evaluates to the corresponding lower-case letter.

(d) The characters representing numeric digits have consecutive ordinal values such that comparison results in numeric ordering. For any arbitrary digit character `d`, the expression:

```
d >= '0' and d =< '9'
```

evaluates to `true` if `d` is a numeric digit and `false` if it is not. The number which corresponds to `d` is given by the expression:

```
ord d - ord '0'
```

whilst the character representing a number `n` (where $0 \leq n \leq 9$) is given by the expression:

```
chr ( n + ord '0' )
```

We shall see later how these properties can be exploited in Hope programs.

1.12 Conditional expressions

Much of the power of the digital computer arises from the conditional instructions, which allow a program to choose between alternative actions according to the results of earlier calculations. This feature is reflected in Hope by an expression which has two possible results. The construction is called a *conditional expression* and has the following form:

```
if truval-valued expression
   then expression of any type
   else expression of the same type
```

The three symbols `if`, `then` and `else` constitute an indivisible two-way *choice operation* with three operands, called the *predicate, consequent* and *alternative* respectively. Operations which are represented using more than one symbol with operands between them are called *distributed fix* or *distfix* operations by analogy with the dyadic *infix* operations which appear between their operands and the monadic *prefix* operations which precede their operands. When talking about distfix operations, we shall use ellipses (...) to show where the operands go. Thus, `if ... then ... else ...` signifies a distfix operation with three operands which follow the symbols `if`, `then` and `else` respectively. Here are some examples of conditional expressions as they might be evaluated by the Hope Machine:

```
if ( 3 + 4 ) = ( 4 + 3 )
  then 'e'
  else 'u' ;
'e' : char

if 'a' < 'z'
  then 3 * 4
  else 3 div 4 ;
12 : num
```

Except in very simple cases, we shall adopt the convention of laying out conditional expressions over several lines with the consequent and alternative indented as in the examples above. This enables the three operands to be easily identified in more complex programs.

It is important to note that the consequent and alternative expressions must both have the *same type*, which is also the type of the whole conditional expression. Thus we are not allowed to write:

```
if ...
  then 3
  else 'a' ;
```

since this might evaluate to either a number or a character depending on the value of the predicate, and the Hope Machine insists that the types of all objects in expressions are known *before* they are evaluated. Provided that this requirement is observed, the consequent and alternative can be any valid Hope expressions, including further conditionals, for example:

```
if ...
   then if ...
           then 0
           else 1
   else if ...
           then 2
           else 3 ;
```

In this example both the consequent and alternative are themselves conditional expressions. Since they must both have the same type, all the lower-level consequent and alternative expressions must also have the same type, in this case num.

Since conditional expressions represent single values like the arithmetic and logical expressions which have been introduced above, they may also appear as components of larger expressions provided that they have the correct type for the context in which they are used, for example:

```
9 - if 3 > 4
       then 3 - 4
       else 4 - 3 ;
8 : num
```

The symbols if, then and else are considered to represent an indivisible choice operation; however, this operation has a *lower* priority than any of the arithmetic or logical operations, and the expression above is interpreted as though it had been written as:

```
9 - ( if ... then ... else ( 4 - 3 ) )
```

rather than:

```
9 - ( if ... then ... else 4 ) - 3
```

and thus evaluates to 8 (rather than 2).

1.13 Rewrite rules for conditional expressions
There are two rewrite rules for conditional expressions. The first can be applied to an expression of the form:

```
if true
   then consequent expression
   else alternative expression
```

and causes it to be rewritten to:

consequent expression

The second rewrite rule can be applied to a conditional expression of the form:

```
if false
   then consequent expression
   else alternative expression
```

and causes it to be rewritten to:

alternative expression

The three operands of the conditional are all redexes, and the Church-Rosser theorem tells us that we may reduce them in any order. We can see from the rewrite rules above that either the consequent or the alternative expression will disappear when the choice operation is reduced, so reducing either of them before the conditional or the choice will be wasted effort. A more important reason for postponing the reduction of the consequent and alternative expressions is illustrated by the following example:

```
if 0 = 0
  then 3 * 0
  else 3 div 0
```

This expression initially contains three redexes: *(1)* the predicate 0 = 0; *(2)* the consequent 3 * 0; and *(3)* the alternative 3 div 0. Once the predicate has been reduced, the choice operation *(4)* becomes a redex. Once again the example is slightly unnatural because an expression such as 3 div 0 would never be written directly in a program; however, we shall see in §2.5 that it may arise as a result of an earlier reduction. The diagram below summarises the possible reduction sequences. The arrows indicating the reduction steps are numbered to show which of the four redexes has been reduced at each step. It is clear that a normal form (0) exists, but only reduction sequences which reduce the choice operation before the alternative lead to it; all others terminate with **error**. Since an error could equally well arise when reducing the consequent, the only safe strategy is to reduce the choice operation before either the consequent or the alternative. It is also the only sensible strategy to employ if we want to use conditional expressions to *avoid* potential errors in programs, which is of course the real reason for writing the program fragment shown above.

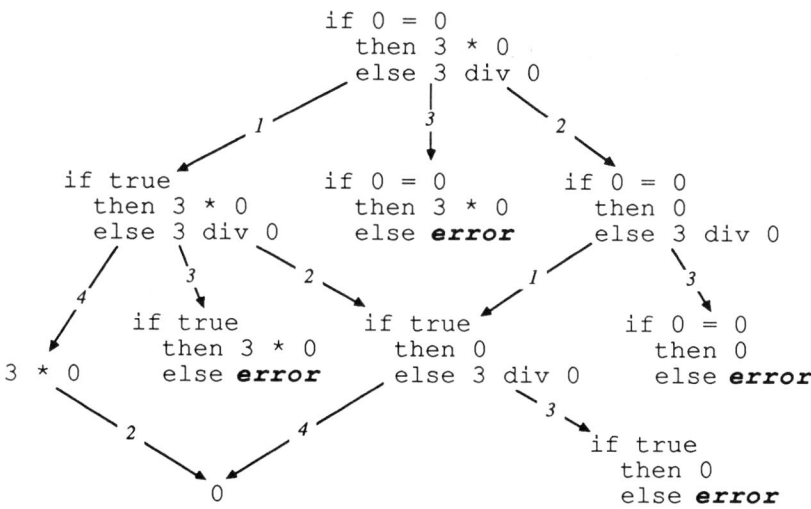

Erroneous operations are not the only reductions which can prevent us discovering the normal form of an expression. In §2.15 we shall see how infinite reduction sequences may occur, and how the conditional expression may be used to avoid them.

1.14 Review
Here is a summary of the main points introduced in this chapter:

- Computer programs may be written in the form of expressions.

- Hope is a notation for writing such expressions.

- The Hope Machine is a computer which directly evaluates Hope expressions.

- The objects in expressions are classified into types according to their properties.

- The primitive types of data object are numbers, truth values and characters.

- A set of basic arithmetic, relational and logical operations is provided to operate on the primitive types of object.

- The Hope Machine uses type information to detect incorrect expressions before they are evaluated.

- The conditional operation allows a choice between alternative values for an expression.

- Expressions may be simplified by rewriting and their meanings discovered.

18 EXPRESSIONS [Ch. 1

- Rewrite rules have been introduced for the basic arithmetic, relational and logical operations, and for the conditional operation.

1.15 Exercises

1. Evaluate the following Hope expressions (see appendix 4 for the ordinal values of characters):

    (a) 2 - 3 - 4
    (b) 2 - (3 - 4)
    (c) 100 div 4 div 5
    (d) 100 div (4 div 5)
    (e) (3 + 4 - 5) = (3 - 5 + 4)
    (f) chr (ord 'a' + 1)
    (g) 2147483647 + 1
    (h) 2 * (2147483647 + 1)

2. Give Hope expressions which correspond as closely as possible to the the following mathematical expressions:

    (a) $\dfrac{-100}{3}$ (b) $\dfrac{100}{-3}$ (c) $\dfrac{2/3}{4}$ (d) $\dfrac{2}{3/4 + 1}$

3. Write Hope expressions to find the values of the following:

    (a) The last digit of the number 123.
    (b) The penultimate digit of the number 456.
    (c) The eighth lower-case letter of the alphabet.
    (d) The "middle" upper-case letter of the alphabet.
    (e) The minimum number of 13 gallon barrels needed to hold the entire contents of an 823 gallon vat.

4. Write a Hope expression to calculate the distance covered by a rocket in 24 hours if its initial speed is 1000 km/h and its acceleration 50 km/h/h. The distance covered in time t by a body moving in a straight line with initial velocity u and acceleration f is given by the formula $ut + 1/2 ft^2$.

5. Write a Hope expression to calculate the temperature in °C corresponding to 98°F. The conversion rule is to subtract 32 from the temperature in °F and then multiply the result by $5/9$.

6. Write down expressions which evaluate to true if:

    (a) 100 is exactly divisible by 10.
    (b) 22 is even.
    (c) The penultimate digit of 139 is different from the last digit of 55.
    (d) The letter 'z' is the 26th lower-case letter of the alphabet.
    (d) The letter 'c' is either the 1st or the 3rd lower-case letter of the alphabet.
    (e) The letter 'b' is neither the 1st nor the 3rd lower-case letter of the alphabet.
    (f) As for (e) but this time do not use the not operation.
    (g) 100 lies between 50 and 200.
    (h) 10 does not lie between 50 and 200.
    (i) As for (h) but do not use the not operation.

7. State the types of the following expressions where they are correct, and identify those whose types are incorrect:

    (a) 2 * 3 = 6
    (b) 6 = 2 * 3
    (c) 2 + 3 = 5
    (d) not 2 * 3 = 10
    (e) 3 = 4 = true
    (f) true = 3 = 4
    (g) if 3 = 4 then ord 'a' else ord 'b'
    (h) ord if 3 = 4 then 'a' else 'b' + 1

8. Assuming that the expressions with incorrect types of in problem 7 were a result of the programmer accidentally omitting parentheses, suggest where they might be added to make the types of the expressions correct.

9. Write down the possible sequences of reductions which may occur when the following expressions are evaluated:

    (a) if 0 /= 0 then 2 + 1 else 2 - 1
    (b) 3 + 4 + 5 + 6
    (c) ord 'x' + ord 'y'
    (d) (3 = 4) = (4 = 5)
    (e) ord 'a' = (ord 'b' - 1)
    (f) chr (ord 'a' + 1)

Chapter 2

Abstraction

2.1 Abstract expressions

We often use a calculator to perform the same calculation repeatedly, entering different numbers at each repetition, but pressing the function keys in the same order each time. We can use the Hope Machine like this, entering the "same" expression each time, but varying the values in it. For instance, to convert a series of temperature readings (*e.g.* 40°, 65°, 103° ... *etc.*) from degrees Fahrenheit to degrees Celsius using the formula which we saw in exercise 5 of chapter 1, we could enter:

```
( 40 - 32 ) * 5 div 9 ;
4 : num

( 65 - 32 ) * 5 div 9 ;
18 : num

( 103 - 32 ) * 5 div 9 ;
47 : num
```

and so on. Here the only "variable" value in each expression is the first one in each case (40, 65 and 103 respectively) which represents the Fahrenheit temperature we wish to convert; the others are the same in every instance of the expression.

Converting a whole series of temperature readings in this way is obviously very tedious, and the chance of mistyping one of the expressions is quite high. A feature of the stored-program computer is that the same program may be used to process several sets of data items without having to reload the instructions into the store each time. This is reflected in Hope by a mechanism which relieves us of the need to reenter the whole expression each time we want to perform the same calculation.

The first step is to construct an *abstract expression* which conveys the form of the required calculation, but which uses a *symbolic representation* for the values which differ in particular instances of the expression. The following abstract expression conveys the form of the Fahrenheit-to-Celsius conversion:

```
( f - 32 ) * 5 div 9
```

In this expression, the as yet unknown Fahrenheit temperature is referred to by the symbolic name f. Symbolic names in expressions are called *formal parameters*, and the process of replacing the variable parts of expressions by names in this way is called *abstraction*. We have already used the idea of abstraction informally in §1.11 to write expressions in terms of arbitrary (*i.e.* non-constant) characters.

We shall generally use sequences of upper and lower-case letters to form symbolic names in examples. The full rules for constructing names are more lenient; they are elaborated in §2.11 and given in full in the language summary in appendix 2. Names must be different from any words which have predefined meanings for the Hope Machine (such as if and div). Appendix 3 contains a list of these *reserved words* which may not be used as names.

2.2 Defining new operations

The abstract expression above contains all the details of the Fahrenheit-to-Celsius conversion, except for the actual value of the Fahrenheit temperature. We can regard it as an *operation* which is applied to a number representing a Fahrenheit temperature and which yields a number representing a Celsius temperature. The type of the conversion operation is:

```
num -> num
```

This type expression is read as "an object which converts (or *maps*) a number to another number". The next step is to give the abstract expression a name, which allows us to refer to it without entering it into the Hope Machine every time we need to use it. The rules for constructing this name are the same as those for formal parameter names; we shall name the conversion operation Celsius to remind us of its purpose when it is used later. The named expression will be used as an operation, and the Hope Machine must therefore know its type so it can check that expressions using it are correctly formed. This information is conveyed by entering the following *declaration* into the Hope Machine:

```
dec Celsius : num -> num ;
```

The symbol dec is short for *declare* and is a reserved word. The symbol : is read as "is of type" in the usual way. Declarations are different from expressions because they are not evaluated and do not specify any kind of value; instead, they are used to convey information about expressions which will be entered later.

The final step is to attach the name Celsius to the abstract expression which we wrote in §2.1. We do this by entering the following *recursion equation* into the Hope Machine:

```
--- Celsius f <= ( f - 32 ) * 5 div 9 ;
```

The symbol --- introducing the equation can be read as "the result of ...". The expression Celsius f is called the *left-hand side* of the equation and introduces f as the name of a formal parameter. The symbol <= is read as "is defined as ..." and the expression following it is called the *right-hand side* of the equation. We can read the whole equation as: "the result of applying the operation Celsius to an arbitrary value f is the value of the expression (f - 32) * 5 div 9".

Although the recursion equation contains an expression, this is not evaluated immediately, but is stored by the Hope Machine until Celsius is used in some other expression. The declaration and the equation together constitute the *definition* of the Celsius operation. Operations which are defined in this way are known as *functions*, giving rise to the term "functional language" as a description of Hope. In general the terms "operation" and "function" are interchangeable, but we usually refer to primitive objects (such as * and div) as operations, reserving the term function for objects like Celsius which are defined by recursion equations.

2.3 Using functions

We can now use the Celsius function to perform the required series of Fahrenheit conversions with the minimum of typing:

```
Celsius 40 ;
4 : num

Celsius 65 ;
18 : num

Celsius 103 ;
47 : num
```

The Celsius function behaves in all respects like a primitive monadic operation (such as not). For instance, it has a higher priority than any dyadic operation and in expressions which contain both, applications of Celsius will be reduced first; for example:

```
Celsius 40 + 25
```

Sec. 2.4]   FUNCTIONS OVER OTHER TYPES OF OBJECT   23

is interpreted as:

```
( Celsius 40 ) + 25
```

and evaluates to 29 (rather than 18).

The type information provided in a function declaration is used to check that expressions using the function are correctly formed. In the case of `Celsius`, this means that its argument must always be a number, and that it must only be applied in a context where a number is expected. Type errors usually occur when an expression has been incorrectly or insufficiently parenthesised, as in the following examples:

```
not Celsius 40 = 3
```

Here the two monadic functions `not` and `Celsius` have highest equal priority but associate to the left, so `not` is incorrectly applied to the `Celsius` function itself, rather than to a truth value as required.

```
not ( Celsius 40 ) = 3
```

In this version of the expression `Celsius` is applied first yielding a number, but the monadic `not` has a higher priority than the dyadic `=` and is incorrectly applied to this number rather than to a truth value.

```
not ( Celsius ( 40 = 3 ) )
```

The dyadic `=` is first applied to two numbers yielding a truth value, but `Celsius` is incorrectly applied to this rather than to a number. A correct version of the expression would be:

```
not ( ( Celsius 40 ) = 3 )
```

`Celsius` is first applied to a number yielding a second number. The dyadic `=` is next applied to two numbers yielding a truth value. Finally, the monadic `not` is applied to this truth value yielding another truth value. The inner parentheses are not strictly necessary as the application of `Celsius` has a higher priority than the relational operation; hence the expression could equally well have been written:

```
not ( Celsius 40 = 3 )
```

2.4 Functions over other types of object

The `Celsius` function defines one numeric value in terms of another. The set of all possible values on which a function may operate is known as its *domain* and the set of all possible results as its *range*. We often characterise functions by their domain, saying that `Celsius` is *a function over numbers* (or more strictly, numbers greater than –459, which represents *absolute zero*, the lowest attainable temperature). The range and domain of Hope functions are not limited to numbers; the following function determines whether a number is odd. Its domain is the set of numbers but its range is the set of truth values:

```
dec odd : num -> truval ;
--- odd n <= n mod 2 = 1 ;
```

The following example of a truth-valued function has the set of characters as its domain. It uses the properties of the character ordering which we saw in §1.11 and evaluates to `true` if its actual parameter is a lower-case letter and `false` if not:

```
dec LowerCase : char -> truval ;
--- LowerCase c <= c >= 'a' and c =< 'z' ;
```

When reading this example, care should be taken to distinguish the "is defined as ..." symbol (<=) from the "greater than or equal to" operation (=<).

2.5 Rewrite rules for function application

The rewrite rule for applications of functions defined in this way is the *reverse* of the abstraction process used to create the definition. The application is replaced by the right-hand side of the recursion equation which defines the function, but the formal parameter is substituted with the value to which the function is applied, which is called the *argument* or *actual parameter*. Substitution of the formal by the actual parameter is called *instantiation*. Consider the application:

```
Celsius 40
```

Here the actual parameter is the number `40`. The reduction takes place in two separate steps. First the occurrences of the formal parameter `f` in the recursion equation defining `Celsius` are instantiated by replacing them with the actual parameter of the application. The equation was:

```
--- Celsius f <= ( f - 32 ) * 5 div 9 ;
```

so instantiating `f` to `40` gives:

```
--- Celsius 40 <= ( 40 - 32 ) * 5 div 9 ;
```

which can be regarded as a specific equation for the case when `f` has the value `40`. It can be read as follows: "the expression `Celsius 40` is equivalent to the expression `( 40 - 32 ) * 5 div 9`". This statement effectively says that the expressions are interchangeable. If occurrences of the former are replaced by the latter, it may be regarded as a *rewrite rule* for the application Celsius 40. The second reduction step uses this rule to replace the application by the expression, giving:

    (40 - 32) * 5 div 9

The original recursion equation containing the formal parameter name can be regarded as a general rewrite rule for *all* possible applications of Celsius.

As soon as the formal parameter has been instantiated, the right-hand side of the recursion equation will contain only constant values as operands. This is how the relational expressions containing constant values which we saw in §1.13 can arise in Hope programs. A example, an application of the function odd from §2.4 will be reduced in four steps as follows:

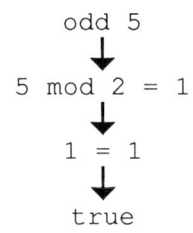

$$\begin{array}{c} \text{odd 5} \\ \downarrow \\ \text{5 mod 2 = 1} \\ \downarrow \\ \text{1 = 1} \\ \downarrow \\ \text{true} \end{array}$$

When a function application forms a term in a larger expression, parentheses are added when it is reduced to ensure the correct interpretation of the result. Thus:

    1000 div Celsius 212

will be rewritten to:

    1000 div ((212 - 32) * 5 div 9)

to yield the expected result (10) rather than:

    1000 div (212 - 32) * 5 div 9

which would be interpreted as:

    ((1000 div (212 - 32)) * 5) div 9

and evaluate to 2.

2.6 More about equations

The formal parameter may appear any number of times on the right-hand side of the equation which defines the function. For instance, here is a function which calculates the square of its argument:

```
dec square : num -> num ;
--- square n <= n * n ;
```

Applications are reduced by instantiating *each* occurrence of the formal parameter with the actual parameter from the application.

The expression on the right-hand side of the equation may also contain applications of functions which have been defined previously. Thus we can use `square` to define a function for calculating fourth powers:

```
dec FourthPower : num -> num ;
--- FourthPower n <= square ( square n ) ;
```

Applying a function to the result of an earlier function application is called *functional composition* and is another way of using functions as "building blocks" to construct large programs. Here we use `LowerCase` (from §2.4) to define a function which "folds" a lower-case letter into the corresponding upper-case letter without affecting any other characters:

```
dec fold : char -> char ;
--- fold c
    <= if LowerCase c
       then chr ( ord c + ord 'A' - ord 'a' )
       else c ;
```

To make the definition more readable, the recursion equation has been laid out slightly differently from the earlier examples, but this does not affect its interpretation.

2.7 Program order

When functions are used to define other functions, the order in which the definitions are entered into the Hope Machine is important. The rule is that the declaration of a function must be entered before its name appears in any equation, and that the equation defining a function must be entered before trying to evaluate an expression containing an application of it. In the `fold` example of §2.6, the declarations of both `fold` and `LowerCase` must be entered before the equation defining `fold`, but they may appear in either order since they do not depend on one another. The equation which defines `LowerCase` cannot be entered until after its declaration, but need not be entered before the equation defining `fold`. However, the equation for `LowerCase` must be entered before attempting to evaluate an application of `fold`.

2.8 The scope of names

If we look again at the definitions of `FourthPower` and `square` we see that name `n` is used for the formal parameter in both. Similarly, the name `c` is used for the formal parameter in both `LowerCase` and `fold`. However, no confusion will arise because a name used as a formal parameter is considered to be completely *private* to the equation it appears in and *distinct* from any other object in the program with the same name. We say that the *scope* of a formal parameter name is limited to or *local to* the recursion equation in which it appears.

A name used for a function behaves differently, and once defined can be referred to anywhere in the program; thus the names `square` and `LowerCase` in the equations defining `FourthPower` and `fold` refer to the `square` and `LowerCase` functions defined earlier. We say that the scope of function names is *global to* the entire program, and it means that all function names within a program must be unique, and may not be used as formal parameter names.

2.9 Functions with more than one argument

The functions which we have seen so far have a single argument and correspond to the primitive monadic operations. We may also define functions with more than one argument. As an example, we shall define of a function to find the greater of two numbers. First we declare the type of the function, which we shall call `greater`:

```
dec greater : num # num -> num ;
```

In order to use the function, its arguments must be combined together into a single object called a *pair*. We do this using the dyadic operation , (comma) between the individual argument values. If we enter an application of , into the Hope Machine:

```
3 , 4 ;
3 , 4 : num # num
```

we can see that the expression is already in normal form, and may be regarded as the *representation* of the pair. The components of a pair may be defined by any valid Hope expressions. The `greater` function is applied like a monadic operation by writing its name in front of the argument pair. The pairing operation has a lower priority than any other operation (including conditional) and will generally be reduced last in any expression. This means that the application:

```
greater 2 , 3
```

will be incorrectly interpreted as:

```
( greater 2 ) , 3
```

and must be written as:

```
greater ( 2 , 3 )
```

The recursion equation which defines `greater` looks like this:

```
--- greater ( i , j ) <= if i > j then i else j ;
```

Once again the left-hand side of the equation looks like an application of the function, except that two *different* symbolic names are used for the two formal parameters. The right-hand side is a conditional expression evaluating to the larger of the two. When an application of the function is reduced, each occurrence of i and j is instantiated with the corresponding element of the pair which is supplied as the actual parameter:

```
         greater ( 2 , 3 )
                 ↓
         if 2 > 3 then 2 else 3
```

This is how a conditional expression containing constant values can arise. It will be reduced in the order predicate, choice, consequent-or-alternative as described in §1.13:

```
         if false then 2 else 3
                  ↓
                  3
```

Applications of greater may be composed together just like those of square; thus we can find the largest of three numbers by writing:

```
  greater ( 2 , greater ( 3 , 4 ) ) ;
  4 : num
```

2.10 Another way to use functions

The primitive dyadic operations are applied by placing them between their arguments and are consequently known as *infix* operations. Infix operations are completely equivalent to functions with two arguments, except for the way they are applied, and we are allowed to use functions we have defined ourselves as infix operations. As an example we shall define an operation under to perform *inverse* division, so that:

```
  5 under 10
```

will evaluate to 2. The type declaration takes the usual form:

```
  dec under : num # num -> num ;
```

To introduce the function as an infix operation, we require an additional declaration, which also gives its relative priority:

```
  infix under : 6 ;
```

Here, `infix` is a reserved word. When the function name is used on the left-hand side of a recursion equation, it must appear *between* its arguments:

```
--- i under j <= j div i ;
```

When the new operation is used in expressions together with other operations, the interpretation will depend on the relative priorities of the other operations in the expression. For example:

```
3 + 4 under 5 * 6
```

is interpreted as:

```
3 + ( ( 4 under 5 ) * 6 )
```

and evaluates to 9. Notice that when an application of `under` appears next to the operation * it obeys the usual Hope rule for equal-priority operations and associates to the left. Even though we have defined *inverse* division, left association will cause the expression:

```
2 under 3 under 4
```

to be interpreted (possibly against our intuition) as:

```
( 2 under 3 ) under 4
```

and to evaluate to 4 (rather than 0).

2.11 More about names

Functions are often defined as infix operations to enable programs to be written more concisely, and to allow them to resemble mathematical notation more closely when this is appropriate (*i.e.* when writing mathematical programs). As a further aid to this end, Hope does not restrict names entirely to upper and lower-case letters, but also allows them to contain numeric digits, provided that they start with a letter. A third possibility is that a name may be constructed entirely from *sign* characters. These include the characters used in the primitive infix operations (+, -, =, /, *etc.*), together with a number of others, which are listed in appendix 2. There is no restriction on the characters used to form a name for any particular purpose, and it is quite legal to use -/- as the name of a function, or +++ as the name of a formal parameter. However, it is recommended that this style of name is reserved for infix operations. This makes programs easier for the reader to understand, because they follow the conventions of mathematical notation more closely.

2.12 Functions with more than two arguments

In §2.9 we defined the function `greater` to find the larger of two numbers and saw how two applications of `greater` could be composed together to find the largest of three numbers. If we need to find the largest of three numbers frequently, it may be more convenient to define a special function for the purpose. It will have *three* arguments and be of type:

```
num # num # num -> num
```

We shall call the function `greatest`; its definition will be an abstract form of the expression in which two applications of `greater` were composed together and will contain three formal parameters:

```
dec greatest : num # num # num -> num ;
--- greatest ( i , j , k )
    <= greater ( i , greater ( j , k ) ) ;
```

The new function is applied like this:

```
greatest ( 2 , 3 , 4 )
```

After the formal parameters have been instantiated, the application will be rewritten with the right-hand side of the defining equation in the usual way:

```
greater ( 2 , greater ( 3 , 4 ) )
```

The idea may be extended in the obvious way to allow functions of four or more arguments if required. Functions with more than two arguments may not be used as infix operations, and must always be used as prefix operations like `greatest`.

2.13 Reduction strategies

When the actual parameter of an application is itself an expression, both the application and the parameter expression are redexes. The Church-Rosser theorem allows either to be reduced first, giving two possible reduction routes. For example:

```
                    Celsius ( 10 + 30 )
    Celsius 40                          ( ( 10 + 30 ) - 32 ) * 5 div 9
                    ( 40 - 32 ) * 5 div 9
```

In the left-hand route, the actual parameter expression has been reduced first using the rewrite rule for the + operation. The resulting expression is then reduced as described in §2.5. The right-hand route is more interesting, because the *application* has been reduced first by instantiating the formal parameter of Celsius with the *entire actual parameter expression* (parenthesised to ensure correct interpretation of the resulting expression). However, after one further reduction step the expression is the same as that resulting from the left-hand route.

The left-hand route is known as *applicative-order* or *innermost* evaluation, and the right-hand route as *normal-order* or *outermost* evaluation. Both reduction strategies yield the same normal form in almost all cases, but normal-order reduction may require more steps. For example, in §2.6 we defined the function square by the following equation:

```
--- square n <= n * n ;
```

Notice that the formal parameter n appears *twice* on the right-hand side. If we apply square to an expression and reduce the application in normal order, we obtain:

$$\text{square } (2 + 3)$$
$$\downarrow$$
$$(2 + 3) * (2 + 3)$$

Because the formal parameter appears twice on the right-hand side of the defining equation, the actual parameter expression is *duplicated* by normal-order reduction, and must now be reduced twice. This is a trivial example, but the number of duplicated terms can sometimes grow in an unexpected way, for instance:

$$\text{square } (\text{square } (2 + 3))$$
$$\downarrow$$
$$(\text{square } (2 + 3)) * (\text{square } (2 + 3))$$
$$\downarrow$$
$$((2 + 3) * (2 + 3)) * ((2 + 3) * (2 + 3))$$

The unconvinced reader should examine the effect of normal-order reduction on:

```
square ( square ( square ( 2 + 3 ) ) )
```

Using applicative-order reduction, no unnecessary reduction steps are performed:

$$\text{square } (\text{square } (\text{square } (2 + 3)))$$
$$\downarrow$$
$$\text{square } (\text{square } (\text{square } 5))$$
$$\downarrow$$
$$\text{square } (\text{square } (5 * 5))$$
$$\downarrow$$
$$\text{square } (\text{square } 25)$$

```
              square ( square 25 )
                      ↓
              square ( 25 * 25 )
                      ↓
              square ( 625 )
                      ↓
                   625 * 625
```

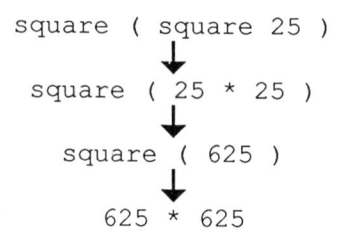

Although it is actually possible to avoid generating and reducing multiple copies of expressions during normal-order reduction, the extra complications required in the Hope Machine mean that normal-order reduction is generally more expensive than applicative order. For efficiency reasons, the Hope Machine always reduces function applications in applicative order.

2.14 Non-strict functions

In most cases applicative-order reduction yields the normal form of an expression less expensively than normal order; however, a normal form may sometimes exist which cannot be reached by applicative-order reduction. Consider the following function:

```
dec incr : num # num -> num ;
--- incr ( n , m ) <= 1 + m ;
```

The result of `incr` depends only upon the value of its second argument, which is incremented by one; the value of its first argument is *ignored*. Functions which do not use the values of all their arguments are said to be *non-strict*. More specifically, `incr` is said to be *strict in its second argument*. Now consider how the following application might be reduced:

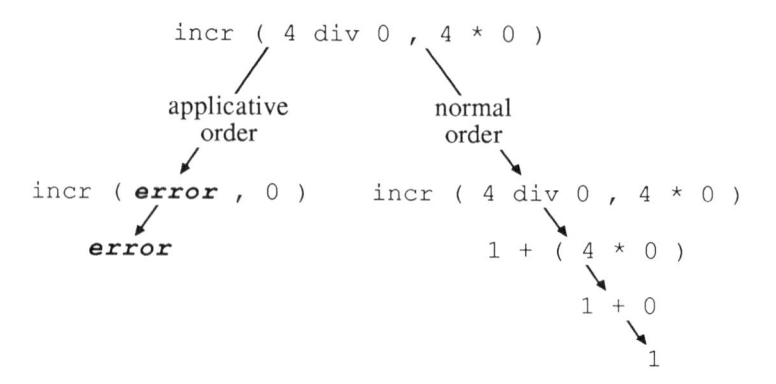

```
                    incr ( 4 div 0 , 4 * 0 )
                   /                        \
           applicative                    normal
             order                         order
              ↓                              ↓
       incr ( error , 0 )         incr ( 4 div 0 , 4 * 0 )
              ↓                              ↓
            error                        1 + ( 4 * 0 )
                                             ↓
                                           1 + 0
                                             ↓
                                             1
```

Here, normal-order reduction has yielded the normal form 1, whilst applicative order has failed. Since Hope uses applicative-order reduction, some applications of non-strict functions which have well defined values will fail like the example above. In spite of this, non-strict functions are still useful in practical programs. Hope allows us to emphasise non-strictness by using the symbol _ to represent any formal parameter which is not used on the right-hand side of the recursion equation. Using this, the definition of incr can be written as follows:

```
--- incr ( _ , m ) <= 1 + m ;
```

This version is to be preferred to the original, because the appearance of _ on the left-hand side is an explicit statement to a reader of the program that the value of the first parameter is not used on the right-hand side; this fact may not be immediately obvious when the right-hand side is a complex expression.

There are two cases where the Hope Machine does not use applicative-order reduction. The most important is the conditional expression where the consequent and alternative expressions are not reduced until after the choice operation (*cf.* §1.13). In addition, the applications of certain operations are reduced using a strategy known as *lazy evaluation*. This is described in greater detail in chapter 8.

2.15 Recurrence relationships

In §2.6 we defined a function to find the square of a number. We might define an analogous function for finding the cube of a number:

```
dec cube : num -> num ;
--- cube n <= n * n * n ;
```

We also defined a function to calculate fourth powers in §2.6. Here is an alternative definition of FourthPower which resembles the definitions of square and cube shown above:

```
--- FourthPower n <= n * n * n * n ;
```

It is clearly impracticable to define a separate function for every possible power we might want to find. The solution is to define a function of *two* parameters, in which the second parameter specifies the exponent. We shall call the new function power and we shall consider only non-negative exponents. Its declaration will be:

```
dec power : num # num -> num ;
```

A difficulty appears when we try to construct an abstract expression to capture the form of square, cube, FourthPower and other functions which we have not yet written. This can be seen by abstracting only the first argument, and writing out a *partially* abstract recursion equation for different values of the exponent:

```
(1)   --- power ( n , 2 ) <= n * n ;
(2)   --- power ( n , 3 ) <= n * n * n ;
(3)   --- power ( n , 4 ) <= n * n * n * n ;
```

34 ABSTRACTION [Ch. 2

The problem is that the number of terms in the right-hand side expression depends on the value of the exponent; since this is not known until power is *applied*, it appears impossible to write a single expression for all exponent values. However, there is a simple relationship (called a *recurrence relationship*) between the three equations, because each right-hand side is the same as the previous one, with the addition of an extra * n term. We can show the recurrence relationship explicitly for equations *(2)* and *(3)* by writing equation *(3)* in the following form:

```
--- power ( n , 4 ) <= power ( n , 3 ) * n ;
```

We can satisfy ourselves that this form of the equation is equivalent to the original by rewriting the term power (n , 3) using equation *(2)* as a rewrite rule (this is left as an exercise to the reader). We can write equations of the same form for other values of the exponent:

```
--- power ( n , 5 ) <= power ( n , 4 ) * n ;
```

The important feature of these new equations is that their right-hand sides all have *two* terms irrespective of the exponent value. Furthermore, the exponent value is always one less on the right-hand side than on the left. We can use the second observation to abstract the exponent value as well and write a *general* equation to define power:

```
--- power ( n , e ) <= power ( n , e - 1 ) * n ;
```

At first sight there appears to be something rather suspicious about this definition, because it is *circular*. Indeed, as the following example illustrates, we cannot use it as a rewrite rule for applications of power (the reductions of subtraction operations have been omitted for conciseness):

$$
\begin{array}{c}
\text{power (10 , 2)} \\
\downarrow \\
\text{power (10 , 1) * 10} \\
\downarrow \\
\text{(power (10 , 0) * 10) * 10} \\
\downarrow \\
\text{((power (10 , -1) * 10) * 10) * 10}
\end{array}
$$

The reduction steps have now begun to generate negative exponents, even though we decided at the outset to consider only non-negative values. The sequence of reductions will never terminate and will eventually fail when the capacity of the Hope Machine to handle the growing expression is exhausted.

In fact the problem does not lie in the circular definition, but in our assumption that all powers must be expressed as a series of multiplications. This is certainly true for exponents greater than zero, but *no* multiplications are needed to evaluate the application `power ( n , 0 )`, which always has the value 1, irrespective of the value of n. The expression which defines `power` must cover this case separately:

```
--- power ( n , e )
    <= if e = 0
         then 1
         else power ( n , e - 1 ) * n ;
```

We can use rewriting to demonstrate that an application of the new version of `power` is equivalent to an expression containing the correct number of multiplications:

$$power (10 , 2)$$
$$\downarrow$$
$$\text{if } 2 = 0$$
$$\text{then } 1$$
$$\text{else } power (10 , 1) * 10$$
$$\downarrow$$
$$power (10 , 1) * 10$$
$$\downarrow$$
$$(\text{if } 1 = 0$$
$$\text{then } 1$$
$$\text{else } power (10 , 0) * 10) * 10$$
$$\downarrow$$
$$(power (10 , 0) * 10) * 10$$
$$\downarrow$$
$$((\text{if } 0 = 0$$
$$\text{then } 1$$
$$\text{else } power (10 , -1) * 10) * 10) * 10$$
$$\downarrow$$
$$((1) * 10) * 10$$

We can now see why the choice operation in a conditional expression is reduced before either the consequent or alternative expressions. If the alternative were to be reduced before the choice, an infinite reduction sequence would occur. Evaluating the choice first enables us to write expressions which are protected against this possibility. It should be noted that although the conditional prevents a negative exponent from being generated when an application of `power` is reduced, there is nothing to prevent us from writing a top-level application such as:

```
power ( 10 , 0 - 1 )
```

which will generate an infinite reduction sequence. A safer definition of `power` might be constructed by changing the conditional to cover this possibility:

```
--- power ( n , e )
    <= if e < 1
       then 1
       else power ( n , e - 1 ) * n ;
```

Functions like `power` which are defined by expressions containing applications of themselves are said to be *recursive*. All recursive definitions must have one special case (called the *base case*) to break the circularity of their definition like that for zero exponents in the example above. Also, each reduction must lead to an expression which is "closer" to the base case in some sense. In this example the non-negative integer exponent is decremented by one with every reduction step and will eventually become equal to the base case value.

2.16 Computational cost

In §2.13 we saw how normal-order reduction can lead to an exponential increase in the size of an an expression and in the total number of steps needed to reduce it to normal form. The size of intermediate expressions is important because the Hope Machine has only a finite amount of storage space for holding them. The number of reduction steps is important because it determines the time taken to reduce the expression to normal form. Taken together, the space and time requirements represent a measure of the *computational cost* of reducing an expression.

When we use Hope as a practical tool for writing programs, we shall often be concerned with the computational cost of one or more functions in the program, since careful design can make the difference between a practical function and one which is too costly to compute. Normal-order reduction is not the only factor which can cause a function to have unexpectedly costly behaviour. The following example shows that for some functions even applicative-order reduction may have the same effect:

```
dec kill : num -> num ;
--- kill n
    <= if n = 0
       then 1
       else 1 + kill ( n - 1 ) * kill ( n - 1 ) ;
```

An application of `kill` will be reduced as follows (the reduction of conditionals is omitted for conciseness):

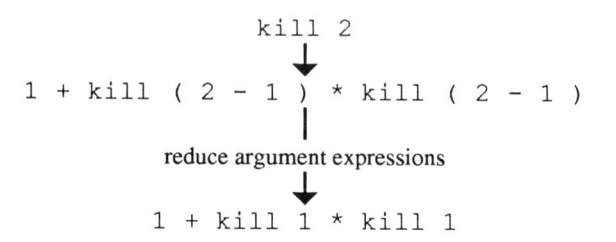

$$\text{kill } 2$$
$$\downarrow$$
$$1 + \text{kill } (2 - 1) * \text{kill } (2 - 1)$$
$$\downarrow$$
$$\text{reduce argument expressions}$$
$$\downarrow$$
$$1 + \text{kill } 1 * \text{kill } 1$$

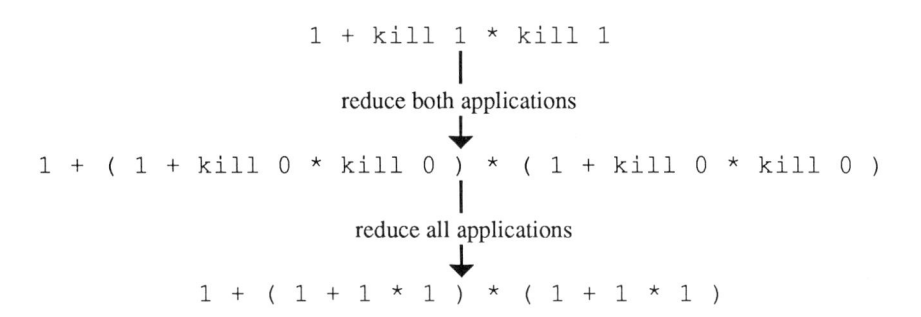

$$1 + \text{kill } 1 * \text{kill } 1$$
$$\downarrow \text{reduce both applications}$$
$$1 + (1 + \text{kill } 0 * \text{kill } 0) * (1 + \text{kill } 0 * \text{kill } 0)$$
$$\downarrow \text{reduce all applications}$$
$$1 + (1 + 1 * 1) * (1 + 1 * 1)$$

If we examine this reduction sequence, we can see that the number of terms in the expression *doubles* each time we perform the reduction steps corresponding to one level of recursion. The application `kill n` requires $2^{n+1}-1$ self-applications for complete reduction. We say that the cost of the function is *order-two-to-the-n*, usually abbreviated to $O(2^n)$; doubling n quadruples the cost of reducing an application. This may not seem a great deal until we realise that increasing n by a factor of 10 increases the time by a factor of more than 1000. The fastest existing computers can execute around 10^8 operations per second. If we assume (very optimistically) that function applications can also be reduced at this rate, it would take about a second to evaluate `kill 27`, an hour to evaluate `kill 41` and over a year to evaluate `kill 54`! $O(2^n)$ functions are effectively *incomputable* for even moderately large values of n.

The $O(2^n)$ behaviour of `kill` could easily have been predicted from its definition, since the expression `kill ( n - 1 )` appears twice on the right-hand side of the defining equation. This is not due to carelessness, but because Hope does not provide a primitive exponentiation operation, so we cannot express `( kill ( n - 1 ) )`^{2} any other way. However, if the `square` function of §2.6 had already been defined, it would be quite natural to write the definition of `kill` like this:

```
--- kill n
    <= if n = 0
       then 1
       else 1 + square ( kill ( n - 1 ) ) ;
```

We can demonstrate that this new definition is equivalent to the original by reducing an application in *normal* order (omitting the reductions of conditionals):

$$\text{kill } n$$
$$\downarrow$$
$$1 + \text{square } (\text{kill } (n - 1))$$
$$\downarrow$$
$$1 + \text{kill } (n - 1) * \text{kill } (n - 1)$$

Notice that we have not instantiated n in this reduction sequence, demonstrating the equivalence for *all* non-zero values of n. The difference in cost between the two definitions of `kill` becomes clear if we reduce an application of the second version in applicative order. In this reduction sequence we omit the reduction of actual parameter expressions and conditionals:

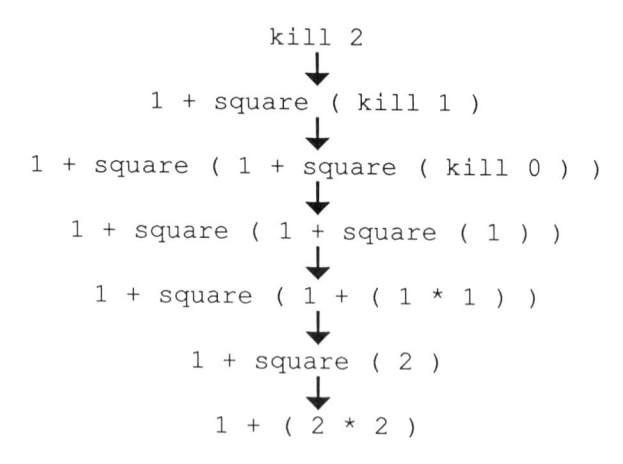

$$\begin{array}{c}
\text{kill } 2 \\
\downarrow \\
1 + \text{square } (\text{ kill } 1) \\
\downarrow \\
1 + \text{square } (1 + \text{square } (\text{ kill } 0)) \\
\downarrow \\
1 + \text{square } (1 + \text{square } (1)) \\
\downarrow \\
1 + \text{square } (1 + (1 * 1)) \\
\downarrow \\
1 + \text{square } (2) \\
\downarrow \\
1 + (2 * 2)
\end{array}$$

An application of `kill n` now generates n applications of `square` and n+1 self-applications of `kill`. We say that the new definition is *order-n* or $O(n)$ in time; doubling n doubles the time taken to reduce an application. The contrast with the behaviour of the original $O(2^n)$ definition is quite startling: `kill 54` can now be reduced in half a microsecond on a 10^8-operation-per-second machine. We shall return to the question of computational cost periodically.

2.17 Qualified expressions

Duplicated terms make expressions hard to understand and cause redundant reduction steps, although this does not always have the same dramatic effect on cost that it did in the case of `kill` in §2.16. The problem was solved by introducing the *auxiliary function* `square`, which improves the definition of `kill` in two ways. The cost is reduced because the recursive application `kill ( n - 1 )` is reduced only once at each level. The value can be used twice in `square` because it is named by the formal parameter n. Also, the definition is clearer because the recursive application is only written once. Naming its value n in `square` makes it clear that it is used twice.

We can always eliminate a duplicated subexpression by introducing an appropriate auxiliary function, but dividing a calculation between two separate functions may actually make simple programs harder to understand. Fortunately, it is not necessary, because Hope provides a construction for abstracting subexpressions from any expression and defining their values separately. It has the general form:

e_1 where n == e_2

Here e_1 and e_2 represent arbitrary expressions; e_1 is called the *qualified* expression and e_2 the *qualifying* expression. The symbol == is read as "is defined as ..." and n represents any name chosen by the programmer. It may be used within e_1 where it is regarded as equivalent to an occurrence of e_2. The entire expression is reduced in applicative order in three steps. First e_2 is reduced to normal form; this value is then used to instantiate n within e_1 and finally e_1 is reduced. For example:

```
          e * ( e + 1 ) div 2
              where e == square 21
                         ↓
          e * ( e + 1 ) div 2
              where e == 441
                         ↓
          441 * ( 441 + 1 ) div 2
```

Qualified expressions may be used as terms in larger expressions with the usual Hope generality. Effectively, where behaves like a low-priority operation. For example:

```
( x * x + 1 where x == 2 ) * 3 ;
15 : num
```

Without the parentheses the expression will be interpreted as:

```
( x * x + 1 ) where x == ( 2 * 3 )
```

and will evaluate to 37. The priority of where is lower than that of any other Hope operation except pairing, so that it effectively qualifies everything to the left up to a comma or open parenthesis. This is particularly important when qualifying a conditional expression which is used in the definition of a recursive function. Here is an attempt to write an O(n) version of the kill function from §2.16 without using an auxiliary function:

```
--- kill n <= if n = 0
              then 1
              else 1 + m * m
                  m == kill ( n - 1 ) ;
```

The intention is to qualify the alternative expression $1 + m * m$. However, because if ... then ... else ... has a higher priority than where, the right-hand side expression is interpreted like this:

```
--- kill n <= ( if n = 0
                then 1
                else 1 + m * m )
              where m == kill ( n - 1 ) ;
```

and the *entire conditional* is qualified. When the expression is reduced in applicative order, the qualifying expression is reduced *before* the conditional, resulting in an infinite reduction sequence. The definition should have been written as follows:

```
--- kill n <= if n = 0
               then 1
               else ( 1 + m * m
                      where m == kill ( n - 1 ) ) ;
```

2.18 Another kind of qualified expression

The use of where corresponds to the commonly used mathematical convention for simplifying expressions by introducing an auxiliary variable and defining its meaning later. Sometimes it may be clearer to define the value of an auxiliary variable *before* using it in an expression. Hope provides a second kind of qualified expression for this purpose; it has the following general form:

```
let  n  ==  e₂  in  e₁
```

Once again e_2 is the qualifying expression which defines the meaning of n and e_1 is the qualified expression, which contains occurrences of n. The applicative-order reduction rule for the expression is to reduce e_2, then instantiate n in e_1, and finally to reduce e_1. Using let, the second example of §2.17 will be written like this:

```
( let x == 2 in x * x + 1 ) * 3
```

Since the qualifying expression is delimited by in, no parentheses are needed when a let-qualified expression is used as a term in a larger expression. However, let has the same low priority as where, and qualifies everything to the right up to a comma or closing parenthesis, so the qualified expression itself may still need to be parenthesised. Without parentheses, the expression above will be interpreted as:

```
let x == 2 in ( x * x + 1 * 3 )
```

and will evaluate to 7 (rather than 15). No parentheses are needed when using let to qualify one branch of a conditional; the $O(n)$ version of kill can be written like this:

```
--- kill n <= if n = 0
               then 1
               else let m == kill ( n - 1 )
                    in 1 + m * m ;
```

Here, only the expression following the in symbol is qualified. When an application is reduced, the conditional will be reduced before the qualified expression, as intended.

2.19 Multiple qualification

Just as conditional expressions may contain embedded conditionals (*cf.* §1.12), so qualified expressions may themselves be qualified, for example:

$$e_0 \text{ where } v_1 == e_1 \text{ where } v_2 == e_2$$

Each where qualifies everything to the left, so the expression is interpreted as:

$$(e_0 \text{ where } v_1 == e_1) \text{ where } v_2 == e_2$$

The auxiliary variable v_1 can be used in e_0 whilst v_2 may be used in both e_0 and e_1. We may nest expressions qualified with let in a similar way:

$$\text{let } v_2 == e_2 \text{ in let } v_1 == e_1 \text{ in } e_0$$

Each let qualifies everything to the right, so this expression is interpreted as:

$$\text{let } v_2 == e_2 \text{ in (let } v_1 == e_1 \text{ in } e_0 \text{)}$$

Once again, the auxiliary variable v_1 can be used in e_0 whilst v_2 may be used in both e_0 and e_1. Multiple qualification can be used to write an expression which requires several auxiliary variables, for example:

$$(x + y) \text{ div } (x - y) \text{ where } x == e_1 \text{ where } y == e_2$$

However, we shall rarely write this construction directly, because Hope allows us to use a single where operation to name more than one value. The values are made into a *pair* on the right-hand side of the == symbol and the corresponding names into a pair on the left-hand side, using the , operation in both cases:

$$(x + y) \text{ div } (x - y) \text{ where } (x , y) == (e_1 , e_2)$$

This defines the name x to have the value e_1 and y to have the value e_2. A similar abbreviation can be used in expressions qualified with let:

$$\text{let } (x , y) == (e_1 , e_2) \text{ in } (x + y) \text{ div } (x - y)$$

In §3.5 we shall see how these abbreviated forms of let and where allow us to name values which cannot be named in any other way.

2.20 More about name scope

The auxiliary variable introduced by a qualifying operation can only be used within the qualified expression, and has no meaning anywhere else. Consider this expression:

```
x + 1 , x * x where x == 3
```

The programmer's intention was probably to define the pair 4 , 9, but , has a lower priority than where, resulting in the following interpretation:

```
x + 1 , ( x * x where x == 4 )
```

Only the second element x * x of the pair is qualified, and the auxiliary variable x may not be used in the first element x + 1. The x in this term is *undefined*, and if we enter the expression into the Hope machine, we shall get an error message:

```
x + 1 , x * x where x == 3 ;
ERROR-99: Undefined name: x
```

In this example, the scope of x may be extended to include the first element of the pair (and hence define the required value 4 , 9) by adding parentheses:

```
( x + 1 , x * x ) where x == 3
```

An important consequence of the limited scope of auxiliary variables is that the same variable can be used to represent *different* values at separate points in an expression, for example:

```
x + 1 where x == 2 , x * x where x == 3
```

There are two distinct auxiliary variables named x in this expression. The scope of the first x is the term x + 1 and that of the second, the term x * x; hence the expression defines the pair 3 , 9.

Qualified expressions which use the same auxiliary variable to represent different values arise naturally when applications of recursive functions are reduced. Here we reduce an application of the intended version of kill from §2.17 (omitting the reduction of conditionals and arithmetic operations):

```
                    kill 2
                      ↓
            1 + m * m where m == kill 1
                      ↓
    1 + m * m where m == ( 1 + m * m where m == kill 0 )
                      ↓
    1 + m * m where m == ( 1 + m * m where m == 1 )
```

This expression contains two different auxiliary variables named m. This can be seen clearly when the expression is reduced further. It contains a single redex, which is the rightmost qualified expression. The remaining reduction steps are as follows:

```
1 + m * m  where  m  ==  ( 1 + m * m  where  m  ==  1 )
             ↓
         1 + m * m  where  m  ==  ( 1 + 1 * 1 )
                     ↓
                 1 + m * m  where  m  ==  2
                             ↓
                         1 + 2 * 2
```

As well as having multiple auxiliary variables with the same name, it is also possible to introduce auxiliary variables with the same names as formal parameters in recursion equations. Consider the following slight variation on the earlier examples:

```
---  f x <= x + 1 , x * x  where  x  ==  3 ;
```

The right-hand side expression contains two variables named x. The first is the formal parameter, and is the one referred to in the first element of the pair; the second is the auxiliary variable, and is the one referred to in the second element. An application such as f 10 thus defines the pair 11 , 9.

An important distinction between this example and the earlier ones is that the definition of the auxiliary variable actually *overrides* that of the formal parameter in the second term, since the scope of the formal parameter would normally be the whole of the right-hand side expression. Effectively, the definition of the auxiliary variable has created a "hole" in the scope of the formal parameter. This is illustrated more clearly in the following example:

```
---  f x <= x * ( x + 2  where  x  ==  x + 1 ) ;
```

Once again the right-hand side contains two variables named x. The one used in the term x + 2 is the auxiliary variable; all others are the formal parameter, *including* the one used in the qualifying expression x + 1. The scope of x is best illustrated diagrammatically:

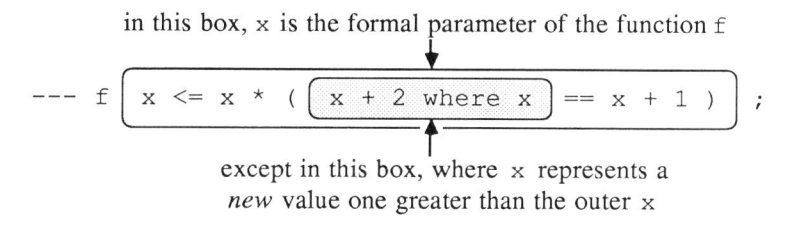

```
         in this box, x is the formal parameter of the function f
                                      ↓
---  f [ x <= x * ( [ x + 2  where  x ] == x + 1 ) ] ;
                                      ↑
              except in this box, where x represents a
              *new* value one greater than the outer x
```

The distinction between the two values can be seen clearly by examining the way in which a typical application of f is reduced:

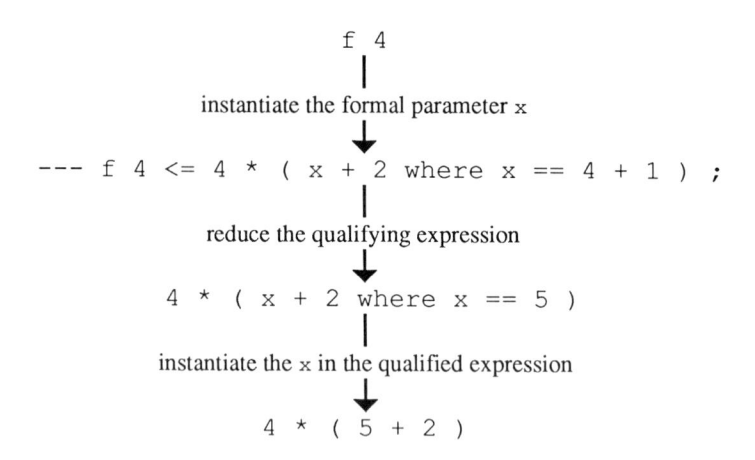

```
                              f 4
                               |
                 instantiate the formal parameter x
                               ↓
      ---  f 4 <= 4 * ( x + 2 where x == 4 + 1 ) ;
                               |
                 reduce the qualifying expression
                               ↓
                 4 * ( x + 2 where x == 5 )
                               |
              instantiate the x in the qualified expression
                               ↓
                         4 * ( 5 + 2 )
```

It is not possible to introduce an auxiliary variable with the same name as a primitive or user-defined function, because all function names have global scope (*cf.* §2.8).

2.21 A word about programming style

Hope imposes no restrictions on the way in which operations may be combined together into an expression provided that the objects in it have the correct types for the context. One consequence of this is that we have complete freedom to write correct expressions whose meanings are unambiguous to the Hope Machine, but which are obscure to the human reader. For example there is nothing to stop us writing an expression which is qualified by both `let` and `where`:

```
   let x == 3 in x * 2 where x == 2
```

Although this is (unfortunately) legal, the two qualifying expressions cannot logically *both* define the value of x in the expression x * 2. How should we (and the Hope Machine) interpret it? Since `let` and `where` have equal priority, the left-association rule for equal-priority operations is used to interpret the expression as:

```
   ( let x == 3 in x * 2 ) where x == 2
```

and evaluate it to 6 (rather than 4). When writing Hope programs, it is good practice to avoid this kind of construction and to write only expressions whose meanings are clear to the human reader. As a general rule, `let` and `where` should never be mixed in the same expression.

The name scope rules for qualified expressions represent a rich source of potential misunderstandings in programs. The best practice is to avoid multiple qualification unless absolutely necessary and to avoid redefining existing names at all costs. The dangers of doing this are illustrated by the following example:

Sec. 2.22] REVIEW 45

```
--- fun x <= x * y where y == ( x where x == 10 ) ;
```

The right-hand side expression uses the formal parameter x and also introduces an auxiliary variable x whose scope is restricted to the qualifying expression. A subtle possibility for error now exists. Suppose that we accidentally forget the parentheses and write the equation as:

```
--- fun x <= x * y where y == x where x == 10 ;
```

Now there is only *one* x on the right-hand side of the equation, which is that defined in the rightmost qualifying expression; fun now ignores its argument and always evaluates to 100, when the intended effect (heavily obscured) was to multiply its argument by 10. This kind of error will be avoided if we use multiple qualification only to introduce *new* names.

2.22 Review
Here is a summary of the main points introduced in this chapter:

- Abstract expressions are constructed by replacing specific values in expressions by formal parameter names.

- New operations and functions are defined by declaring their types and specifying a recursion equation containing an abstract expression.

- Rewrite rules have been given for function application, and applicative-order reduction introduced.

- Functions may be combined together by functional composition to form the building blocks of large programs.

- Functions may have more than one argument. Multiple arguments are bound together into single objects called pairs. Dyadic functions may also be applied as infix operations.

- Recursive functions are defined by applications of themselves and a base case which does not involve self-application. Applications lead to expressions of indeterminate size when reduced.

- Qualified expressions allow abstraction without the need to define auxiliary functions.

2.23 Exercises

1. Write a function `add` of two arguments which will add a single-digit integer onto the right-hand end of an arbitrary-size integer. For example, `add ( 123 , 4 )` should evaluate to `1234`. Ignore the possibility of integer overflow.

2. Write a function `cat` which has the same effect as `add` but which can be applied as an infix operation, *e.g.* `123 cat 4`.

3. The *factorial* of a non-negative integer *n* is denoted as *n!* and defined as:

   $n \times (n-1) \times (n-2) \times (n-3) \ldots \times 2 \times 1$

   0! is defined to be 1. Write a function `fact` which defines the factorial of a *non-negative* integer. Ignore the possibility of integer overflow.

4. Write a function `remainder` which defines the remainder after integer division using only subtraction. Ignore the possibility of division by zero.

5. Write a function `quotient` which defines integer division using only addition and subtraction. Ignore division by zero.

6. Euclid's method for finding the greatest common divisor of two integers is the earliest known example of an *algorithm* (a step-by-step method of performing some calculation). It is given by Donald E. Knuth in *The Art of Computer Programming* as follows: given two positive integers *m* and *n*,

   E1. (Find remainder) divide *m* by *n* and let *r* be the remainder. We will have $0 \leq r < n$

   E2. (Is it zero?) if $r = 0$ the algorithm terminates; *n* is the answer.

   E3. (Interchange) set $m \leftarrow n$, $n \leftarrow r$ and go back to step E1.

   Write a function `gcd` which defines the greatest common divisor of two numbers using Euclid's algorithm.

7. A decimal number may be converted to *binary representation* by the following algorithm:

   (a) If the number is zero, its binary representation is zero.

   (b) Otherwise, divide the number by 2. The *remainder* gives the last digit of the binary representation.

(c) The preceding digits of the binary representation are given by the binary representation of the *quotient* from step *(b)*.

Write a function BinaryOf which takes an integer and converts it to its binary representation. This will be a decimal number consisting only of the digits 0 and 1. You may find it useful to use add or cat for this. Ignore integer overflow.

8. Write a function ChangeBase of two arguments which converts a number to its representation in some specified base ≤ 10. The value produced will be a decimal number containing only the digits which are valid in the new base.

9. Write a function base which has the same effect as ChangeBase but which can be applied as an infix operator.

10. The number of arrangements (permutations) of *r* objects selected from a larger set of *n* objects is denoted as ^nP_r and defined as:

$$n \times (n-1) \times (n-2) \ldots \times (n-r+1) \quad \text{or} \quad \frac{n!}{(n-r)!}$$

Define an infix operation P such that n P r evaluates ^nP_r. The priority should be such that 1 + 5 P 3 evaluates to 61 rather than 120.

11. The number of selections (combinations) of *r* objects from a larger set of *n* objects irrespective of arrangement is denoted as ^nC_r and defined as:

$$\frac{n \times (n-1) \times (n-2) \ldots \times (n-r+1)}{r \times (r-1) \times (r-2) \ldots \times 2 \times 1} \quad \text{or} \quad \frac{n!}{r! \times (n-r)!}$$

Define an infix operation C such that n C r evaluates ^nC_r. What do you expect 4 P 3 C 2 to evaluate to when the priority of C is *(a)* less than *(b)* equal to and *(c)* greater than that of P?

Chapter 3

Data Structures

3.1 Different types of pair

In §2.12 we saw how the dyadic operation , could be used to combine two numbers together into an object called a *pair* which could then be used as the actual parameter of a function of two arguments. Pairs are examples of objects composed of several simpler objects grouped together called *data structures*, which we shall examine in more detail in this chapter. Like the comparison operations, the pairing operation can be applied to objects of arbitrary type, allowing us to define pairs like these:

```
'a' , 'b'           of type   char # char
true , true         of type   truval # truval
```

However, pairing is even more general than comparison, because it can not only combine any two objects of the *same* type, but also objects of *different* types. The following objects are also valid pairs:

```
3 , true            of type   num # truval
'y' , 3             of type   char # num
false , 'z'         of type   truval # char
```

Pairs like this can be used as actual parameters of dyadic functions with two different argument types. For example, the following function "encodes" a lower-case character using the schoolchildren's trick of replacing it by the character occurring a specified number of places later in the alphabet:

```
dec encode : char # num -> char ;
--- encode ( c , n )
    <= chr ( ( ord c - a + n ) mod 26 + a )
        where a == ord 'a' ;
```

Modular arithmetic causes the addition to "wrap around", ensuring that the encoded character is always a lower-case letter. The argument will be a pair containing the letter to be encoded and the number representing the required displacement:

```
encode ( 'y' , 3 ) ;
'b' : char
```

3.2 Tuples

In §2.12 we introduced the function greatest to find the largest of three numbers and applied it like this:

```
greatest ( 2 , 3 , 4 )
```

without further comment. However, the expression defining the actual parameter of the application is worth closer inspection. At first sight it appears to consist of two applications of the pairing operation, but it does not behave quite as we would expect, because the two applications do not associate to the left like other equal-priority infix operations. The expression does *not* construct the following object:

(2 , 3) , 4   *of type*   (num # num) # num

which is a pair whose first component is itself a pair, but the object:

2 , 3 , 4   *of type*   num # num # num

which is called a *triplet*. This object is "flat" with the component values at the same level; the expression 2 , 3 , 4 does not contain two applications of , but a single application of ... , ... , ... which is a *triadic distfix* operation like conditional. In the case of conditional only two of its operands are evaluated and only one value appears in the final result, but in the case of the tripling operation, all three operands are evaluated and all three values appear in the final result. It is possible to construct pairs which contain further pairs like the first example by adding explicit parentheses:

(2 , 3) , 4   *of type*   (num # num) # num
2 , (3 , 4)   *of type*   num # (num # num)

Each of these expressions consists of two applications of the , operation. The resulting objects are both pairs of different types and neither is the same type as the triplet. As with pairing, the tripling operation may be applied to any combination of object types, for example:

```
'a' , 3 , true       of type   char # num # truval
2 , ( 1 , 2 ) , 2    of type   num # ( num # num ) # num
```

Notice that in this example that the triplet ultimately has *four* components, but the second and third have been bound together into a pair, in the same way that we constructed pairs containing further pairs. As we might expect, a flat object with four components can be constructed with three commas:

```
false , 3 , true , 'z'
```

Hope allows us to bind together any number of objects of arbitrary types in this way to form objects called *tuples*. The expression above constructs a 4-tuple; pairs and triplets are also known as 2-tuples and 3-tuples respectively. In general, *n*-tuples of any size can be constructed using an expression with *n* operands separated by *n*-1 commas. We may imagine that Hope has an indefinite number of *distinct* tupling operations called ... , ..., ... , ... , ..., ... , ... , ... , ..., and so on.

The components of a tuple may be defined by any valid Hope expressions, for example:

```
1 = 1 , 1 - 1 , chr ( ord '1' - 1 )
```

defines the tuple `true , 0 , '0'` of type `truval # num # char`. We have already used this generality to write function applications with expressions as actual parameters (*e.g.* `greater` in the definition of `greatest` in §2.12).

Tupling has a lower priority than any other Hope operation including conditional and qualification (*cf.* §2.20), which effectively means that tuples must always be enclosed in parentheses when they are terms in larger expressions. The different tupling operations all have the same priority. This is only of academic interest, because we can never write an expression which contains more than one tupling operation. As we saw above, an expression which contains two applications of , will always be treated as a single application of ... , ... , ... unless parentheses are added to show the required priority explicitly.

3.3 Operations on tuples

Hope provides two primitive operations on tuples. Two tuples of the same type may be tested for equality using the = and /= comparison operations. For example:

```
( 3 , chr ( ord 'a' + 1 ) ) = ( 2 + 1 , 'b' )
```

evaluates to `true`. The type of = in this expression is:

MORE GENERAL FUNCTIONS

```
( num # char ) # ( num # char ) -> truval
```

The low priority of tupling means that the tuples must be parenthesised to prevent the expression from being interpreted as:

```
3 , ( chr ( ord 'a' + 1 ) = 2 + 1 ) , 'b'
```

This expression will be rejected by the type-checking mechanism of the Hope Machine because the operands of = are of different types (a char and a num).

3.4 More general functions

So far we have seen functions which define a single object of any type. However there is no restriction on what the type of the object may be; and in particular it may be a tuple, which effectively gives us a way of writing functions which define more than one object. As an example we shall consider the problem of converting times in seconds into hours, minutes and seconds. On the face of it this might not seem to be a very frequent requirement, but it turns out that many computers are equipped with time-of-day clocks which work by counting the number of seconds which have elapsed since some fixed time.

Let us suppose that we can obtain the time in seconds since midnight and wish to convert it into a form more suitable for human beings. The style of the calculation will be familiar to anyone who attended primary school in the United Kingdom before 1971 and was taught "The Reduction of Pounds, Shillings and Pence". The number of complete hours which have elapsed since midnight is obtained by dividing the number of seconds by 3600 and ignoring the remainder. The remainder will represent the number of seconds which have elapsed since this hour. Dividing the remainder by 60 and ignoring the remainder again gives the number of complete minutes which have elapsed since this hour. The remainder from the second division represents the number of seconds which have elapsed since this minute. Thus we have:

```
s                        seconds since midnight.
s div 3600               complete hours since midnight.
s mod 3600               remaining seconds since this hour.
s mod 3600 div 60        complete minutes since this hour.
s mod 3600 mod 60        remaining seconds since this minute.
```

The second, fourth and fifth expressions define the components of the answer we require, and may be combined into a triplet like this:

```
s div 3600 , s mod 3600 div 60 , s mod 3600 mod 60
```

The low priority of tupling compared to the arithmetic operations means that the latter will be reduced before the triplet is constructed; we also recollect from §1.9 that div and mod are of equal priority and will be reduced in left-to-right order, so no parentheses are required in the expression. Two of the expressions contain the term `s mod 3600` and we might simplify the tuple by abstracting this into a qualifying expression. The higher priority of qualification over tupling means that parentheses will be needed:

```
( s div 3600 , r div 60 , r mod 60 )
   where r == s mod 3600
```

or:

```
let r == s mod 3600
   in ( s div 3600 , r div 60 , r mod 60 )
```

One of these two abstract forms of the result triplet will appear as the right-hand side of the recursion equation which defines the required function. We shall call it `time` and its type will be:

```
num -> num # num # num
```

that is, a function which takes a single number as its argument and which produces three numbers (strictly, a triplet of numbers) as its result. The function declaration will look like this:

```
dec time : num -> num # num # num ;
```

and the the recursion equation will be either:

```
--- time s <= ( s div 3600 , r div 60 , r mod 60 )
                 where r == s mod 3600 ;
```

or:

```
--- time s
       <= let r == s mod 3600
             in ( s div 3600 , r div 60 , r mod 60 ) ;
```

If we enter an application of `time` at the terminal, the result triplet and its type will be displayed on the screen in the usual way:

```
time 45756 ;
12 , 42 , 36 : num # num # num
```

3.5 Defining tuples recursively

The `time` example illustrates how a function may define more than one value by constructing a tuple, but it is not a very typical example because no repetitive calculations are involved, so the function is not recursive. When a tuple is defined by a recursive function, a slight complication arises because we shall need to refer in the recursion equation to the results of another application of the same function. As an example we shall define a recursive function to find both the quotient and remainder after integer division. We shall call it QuotRem and its declaration will be as follows:

```
dec QuotRem : num # num -> num # num ;
```

that is, a function which takes two numbers (the dividend and divisor) and which defines two numbers (the quotient and remainder). Of course, there is a simple non-recursive definition for QuotRem which is just:

```
--- QuotRem ( x , y ) <= x div y , x mod y ;
```

but for the purposes of the example we shall assume that `div` and `mod` are not available. Both these operations may be defined using repeated subtraction; here is the recursive function to perform integer division, as written for exercise 5 of chapter 2:

```
dec quotient : num # num -> num ;
--- quotient ( x , y )
    <= if x < y
       then 0
       else 1 + quotient ( x - y , y ) ;
```

A typical application of `quotient` will be reduced as follows (omitting the reduction of the conditional and subtraction operations):

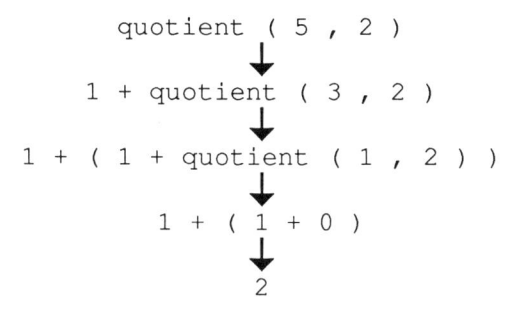

$$
\begin{array}{c}
\text{quotient} (5 , 2) \\
\downarrow \\
1 + \text{quotient} (3 , 2) \\
\downarrow \\
1 + (1 + \text{quotient} (1 , 2)) \\
\downarrow \\
1 + (1 + 0) \\
\downarrow \\
2
\end{array}
$$

Here is the function which defines the remainder after integer division, as written for exercise 4 of chapter 2:

```
    dec remainder : num # num -> num ;
    --- remainder ( x , y )
       <= if x < y
            then x
            else remainder ( x - y , y ) ;
```

It is left as an exercise to the reader to check the correctness of this definition by completely rewriting a typical application. Of course, if we have defined quotient and remainder, we can write a simple non-recursive definition of QuotRem:

```
    --- QuotRem ( x , y )
       <= quotient ( x , y ) , remainder ( x , y ) ;
```

Although this definition is clear, it requires the reader to understand two auxiliary functions as well as QuotRem itself. It is also slightly inelegant, because the repeated subtraction of y from x is performed in both auxiliary functions, leading to duplicated reductions. However, we can write a recursive version of QuotRem which performs the subtractions only once and uses no auxiliary functions. The definition is analogous to the recurrence relationships for quotient and remainder:

$$\text{quotient (x , y)} \equiv 1 + \text{quotient (x - y , y)}$$

$$\begin{array}{l}\textit{The quotient part of}\\ \text{QuotRem (x , y)}\end{array} \equiv 1 + \begin{array}{l}\textit{The quotient part of}\\ \text{QuotRem (x - y , y)}\end{array}$$

$$\text{remainder (x , y)} \equiv \text{remainder (x - y , y)}$$

$$\begin{array}{l}\textit{The remainder part of}\\ \text{QuotRem (x , y)}\end{array} \equiv \begin{array}{l}\textit{The remainder part of}\\ \text{QuotRem (x - y , y)}\end{array}$$

The only remaining problem is to name the quotient and remainder parts of the pair defined by QuotRem (x - y , y). We recollect from §2.19 that the components of a pair may be named in qualified expressions. The examples used explicit pairs on the right-hand side of the == symbol, but there is no reason why the right-hand side pair may not be defined by a function application. The equation for QuotRem may be written as follows:

```
    --- QuotRem ( x , y )
       <= ( 1 + q , r )
            where ( q , r ) == QuotRem ( x - y , y ) ;
```

This expresses the recurrence relationship, but does not specify how the recursion will terminate. If we examine the definitions of quotient and remainder we shall see that the termination condition is x < y in both cases. On termination, the value

DEFINING TUPLES RECURSIVELY

of the quotient is 0 and the value of the remainder is x. The full equation for QuotRem will incorporate this information:

```
--- QuotRem ( x , y )
    <= if x < y
       then ( 0 , x )
       else ( ( 1 + q , r )
              where ( q , r ) ==
                  QuotRem ( x - y , y ) ) ;
```

Notice the extra parentheses so that the qualifying expression applies only to the alternative expression. A typical application will be reduced as follows (once again the reduction of the conditional and subtraction operations are omitted):

```
              QuotRem ( 5 , 2 )
                     ↓
           ( 1 + q , r )
              where ( q , r ) ==
                  QuotRem ( 3 , 2 )
                     ↓
        ( 1 + q , r )
           where ( q , r ) ==
               ( ( 1 + q , r )
                  where ( q , r ) ==
                      QuotRem ( 1 , 2 ) )
                     ↓
     ( 1 + q , r )
        where ( q , r ) ==
            ( ( 1 + q , r )
                where ( q , r ) == ( 0 , 1 ) )
                     |
            reduce the innermost qualified expression
                     ↓
     ( 1 + q , r )
        where ( q , r ) == ( 1 + 0 , 1 )
                     ↓
        ( 1 + q , r )
           where ( q , r ) == ( 1 , 1 )
                     ↓
               ( 1 + 1 , 1 )
                     ↓
                  ( 2 , 1 )
```

3.6 Programming style again

The result of the function time from §3.4 was defined by the triplet:

```
s div 3600 , s mod 3600 div 60 , s mod 3600 mod 60
```

The first element is defined by the expression s div 3600 and the expression defining the second element contains the term s mod 3600. The two terms represent the quotient and remainder respectively after integer division of s by 3600, and both values could have been defined by an application of QuotRem if it had been available when we wrote time:

```
QuotRem ( s , 3600 )
```

The two values in the pair can be named using a qualified expression and used in the triplet expression (which must now be parenthesised):

```
( h , s1 div 60 , s1 mod 60 )
    where ( h , s1 ) == QuotRem ( s , 3600 )
```

We can now see that the two terms s1 div 60 and s1 mod 60 could also be defined by an application of QuotRem in exactly the same way:

```
QuotRem ( s1 , 60 )
```

This expression uses s1 from the first qualifying expression, and must appear within its scope. The triplet expression uses both elements of this pair and also h from the first qualifying expression, so it must appear within the scope of both:

```
( h , m , s2 )
    where ( m , s2 ) == QuotRem ( s1 , 60 )
        where ( h , s1 ) == QuotRem ( s , 3600 )
```

Nested where qualifications are read from *right to left*, hence the introduction of the name s2 must textually *precede* that of s1. In §2.21 it was suggested that multiple let or where operations should be avoided, but occasionally (as in this example), it may be the only way to achieve the desired effect.

Since no expression uses more than one of the three values, we might perfectly well write the equation like this:

```
--- time s
    <= ( h , m , s )
        where ( m , s ) == QuotRem ( s , 60 )
            where ( h , s ) == QuotRem ( s , 3600 ) ;
```

There are three *different* objects named s in this version. The one appearing in the rightmost qualifying expression is the formal parameter s. Working inwards, each new s is defined in terms of the next outermost.

It is debatable whether the final version of time is a better example of good programming style than the previous one. Whilst the difficulty of understanding a program increases with the number of different names used in it, reusing a name for different purposes is a potent source of confusion. It is also reasonable to ask whether either of the versions of time which use QuotRem are better than the original. This is concise and clear because the operations div and mod are available directly in Hope, but if they were not, we would need to define them. If we used recursive definitions, the cost of the original version (with our own div and mod operations) would be greater than that of the version using QuotRem by a factor of about 2.3.

Clarity of expression is an important issue, because it is much easier to satisfy ourselves that a clear program is *correct*, and cost must always be secondary to correctness. In the case of time the higher cost of the clear version probably does not outweigh the extra difficulty of understanding the more efficient one, but this will not always be the case.

3.7 Lists

Tuples are very powerful, but their fixed size is too restrictive in many cases. A tuple of type num # num for example must always contain exactly two numbers because the size of the tuple is part of its type. However, many programs manipulate collections of values where the number of values is not known at the time the program is written. To cater for this requirement Hope provides a second kind of data structure where the number of components may vary. Any number of objects of the *same* type may be grouped together into an object called a *list*. For example, here is a list containing two numbers:

    [3 , 4]

The two numbers have been combined together by an application of the distfix operator [... , ...] to construct an object of type list num. A list may contain *any number* of objects, including none or one. As with the tupling operations there are an indefinite number of list-constructing operations, called [ ], [...], [... , ...], [... , ... , ...], [... , ... , ... , ...] and so on. [...] is a rare example of a monadic distfix operation. It has one argument and defines a list containing one object, known as a *singleton* list. [ ] is an example of something even rarer: a *nulladic* distfix operation. It has no arguments and defines a list containing *no* objects at all, known as the *empty* list. The list-constructing operations can be used to define lists which contain any kind of object, such as:

    [true , false , false , true]

which is of type list truval. Since all the components of a list must have the same type, expressions such as:

    [true , 3 , false]

will be rejected by the type-checking mechanism of the Hope Machine. The expressions above are already in normal form and are considered as the representations of the lists. Lists of characters are reduced to a more concise normal form. The two following expressions are equivalent:

    ['c' , 'a' , 't']   and   "cat"

The objects in a list may be defined by any Hope expressions, provided that they all define the same type of object. The priority of the list-constructing operations is lower than that of any other Hope operation so that expressions within list constructors will not usually need to be parenthesised, for example:

    [if 2 = 2 then 3 else 4 , Square 2 , 6 - 1] ;
    [3 , 4 , 5] : list num

The only exception is when the components of the list are tuples. In this case parentheses must be added to prevent the tuple constructor from being interpreted as part of the list constructor. For example, the expression:

    [(1 , 2) , (3 , 4)]

consists of one application of the 2-list constructor and two applications of the pairing operation and defines an object of type list (num # num). As this example suggests, the components of a list are not restricted to simple objects like numbers or truth values, but may be any kind of object. Here is a list whose components are lists of characters:

    ["where" , "there's" , "life" , "there's" , "Hope"]

Its type is list (list char). When a list contains other lists, the component lists must all have the same type, *i.e.* they must all be composed of the same type of object. The following list of lists would be rejected by the type checker:

    [[1 , 2 , 3] , "4 , 5 , 6"]

since the first sublist is a list of numbers and the second a list of characters. Just as lists may contain tuples, so tuples may contain lists. Because the components of a tuple may have different types, lists containing different types of object may appear in the same tuple, for instance:

```
    true , [ 3 , 4 , 5 ] , "false"
```

which is of type `truval # list num # list char`. We are accustomed by now to the way that Hope expressions are quite general, so that any expression may be used as a term in any other provided it has the correct type. Further, any type of object may appear in a data structure. We may even construct a list of *functions*, provided they all have the same type:

```
    [ Celsius , square , kill ]
```

Here the individual functions have the type num -> num (*cf.* §2.2, §2.6 and §2.16), so we have constructed a `list ( num -> num )`. We shall have to wait until §7.13 to see a use for such a list.

3.8 Operations defining lists

The list-constructing operations introduced in §3.7 do not allow us to define lists containing an unknown number of objects because we must write every component explicitly in the defining expression. Lists of undefined length are constructed using two primitive functions. The first of these is the infix operation `: :` (read as *cons*) with priority 4. It defines a list in terms of a single object and a list of the same type of object. The new list will contain one more object than the original list operand, for instance:

```
    10 :: [ 20 , 30 , 40 ] ;
    [ 10 , 20 , 30 , 40 ] : list num
```

This example illustrates the effect of `: :` but is slightly unrealistic. We would not normally apply it to a list written in normal form since the result list could equally well be written directly. In most cases the list operand will be a named object or will be defined by a function application, as shown in the next section. It is important to observe that the operands of `: :` have *different* types. In the expression above, the operation has the type:

```
    num # list num -> list num
```

This means that we may *not* write an expression like:

```
    [ 20 , 30 , 40 ] :: 10
```

Like tupling, the type of `: :` is actually quite general; for instance, in:

```
    true :: [ false , true ]
```

its type is:

```
truval # list truval -> list truval
```

The type of `::` is less general than that of tupling in one important respect. We can use it to construct lists containing any type of object, but for any given type of component (say α) its type is considered to be:

```
α # list α -> list α
```

It is this property that requires all the objects in a list to have the same type. An expression such as:

```
true :: [ 1 , 2 , 3 ]
```

will be rejected by the type-checking mechanism because the first operand is not the same type as the components of the second (list) operand.

The other primitive operation for constructing lists is the nulladic function `nil`, which defines an *empty* list containing no elements. Every list can be represented by an expression containing only applications of `::` and `nil`. Thus the expression:

```
( 1 :: ( 2 :: ( 3 :: nil ) ) )
```

defines the same list as:

```
[ 1 , 2 , 3 ]
```

Notice that the applications of `::` are enclosed in parentheses. Without them the applications would associate to the left, causing the expression to be interpreted as:

```
( ( 1 :: 2 ) :: 3 ) :: nil
```

This will be rejected by the type-checking mechanism because the second operand in the first two applications of `::` is not a `list num`. The type of list constructed by `nil` is determined by the context. In the expression:

```
3 :: nil
```

the first operand of `::` is a number, hence its second operand must be a `list num` and we can deduce that `nil` constructs an empty list of numbers. In the expression:

```
true :: nil
```

we can similarly deduce that it constructs an empty list of truth values. The Hope Machine uses what is essentially a mechanised version of this form of reasoning to check the types of expressions.

3.9 Other operations on lists

Hope provides three other primitive operations on lists. The infix operation <> (read as *append*) with priority 4 concatenates two lists (joins them end to end) to form a single list. For example:

```
[ 1 , 2 , 3 ] <> [ 4 , 5 , 6 ] ;
[ 1 , 2 , 3 , 4 , 5 , 6 ] : list num
```

Like other primitive operations we have seen so far, the type of <> is more general than the example suggests. For an arbitrary type (say α), its type is:

```
list α # list α -> list α
```

for any consistent interpretation of α. This means that we can apply <> to any two lists of the same type (*i.e.* containing the same type of object) to form another list of the same type. For example, we may write:

```
"Pope" <> "yes" ;
"Popeyes" : list char
```

In this case α is taken to be a char. If the operands contain embedded lists, <> will only concatenate them at the top level. For example:

```
[ "fee" , "fie" ] <> [ "fo" , "fum" ]
```

Here, the operands are of type list (list char), hence α represents a list char. Since the type definition requires the result to be a list (list char) as well, the result of this application will be:

```
[ "fee" , "fie" , "fo" , "fum" ]
```

Finally, two lists may be tested for equality using the = and /= comparison operations. These behave differently from <>, since lists containing embedded data structures (either lists or tuples) will be checked for equality *at all levels*; thus:

```
[ "one" , "two" ] = [ "one" , "two" ]
```

evaluates to true. In this expression, the type of the = operation is:

```
list ( list char ) # list ( list char ) -> truval
```

3.10 Functions which define lists

Functions may be written which define lists, analogous to the tuple-defining functions of §3.4 and §3.5. Such functions will almost always be recursive, because practical programs need lists whose lengths are not known until the program is evaluated, and which cannot therefore be written directly. As an example, suppose that we need a list containing the first *n* natural numbers. This can be defined by a function with a parameter to specify the required number of elements. We shall call the function nats, and its declaration will be:

```
dec nats : num -> list num ;
```

To write the function, we shall try to discover a recurrence relationship for different parameter values, rather as we did with power in §2.15. First we write the results of some typical applications in the form of equalities:

```
nats 1   ≡   [ 1 ]
nats 2   ≡   [ 2 , 1 ]
nats 3   ≡   [ 3 , 2 , 1 ]
```

For reasons which will become clear shortly, the numbers in the lists have been arranged in descending order of magnitude. To make the relationship more explicit, here are the equalities again with the lists defined by expressions involving :: and nil instead of being written in normal form:

```
nats 1   ≡   1 :: nil
nats 2   ≡   2 :: ( 1 :: nil )
nats 3   ≡   3 :: ( 2 :: ( 1 :: nil ) )
```

We can see that each right-hand side is just the previous right-hand side with an extra term at the beginning which is the value of n, hence the recurrence relationship is:

```
nats n   ≡   n :: nats ( n - 1 )
```

To use this as the basis of a recursive definition for nats we must also discover what the base case is. To make the recurrence relationship apply to the first equation, it must be expressed as follows:

```
nats 1   ≡   1 :: nats 0
```

and since this is equivalent to:

```
nats 1   ≡   1 :: nil
```

we can deduce that:

Sec. 3.10]   FUNCTIONS WHICH DEFINE LISTS   63

```
    nats 0   ≡   nil
```

We now have enough information to write down the equation defining nats:

```
--- nats n <= if n = 0
                 then nil
                 else n :: nats ( n - 1 ) ;
```

An application will be reduced as follows (omitting the reduction of conditionals and applications of ::):

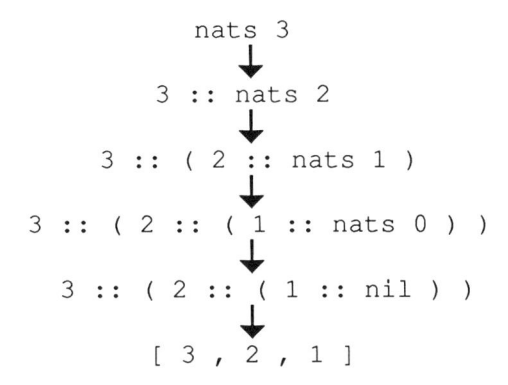

```
                    nats 3
                      ↓
                3 :: nats 2
                      ↓
              3 :: ( 2 :: nats 1 )
                      ↓
            3 :: ( 2 :: ( 1 :: nats 0 ) )
                      ↓
            3 :: ( 2 :: ( 1 :: nil ) )
                      ↓
                  [ 3 , 2 , 1 ]
```

It is reasonable to ask why we defined the list of numbers in descending magnitude, since our natural inclination would probably be to write a list of consecutive numbers in ascending magnitude. The recursive definition means that each application of nats will contribute only the current value of n to the final list. If we use :: to add this value to the list, we obtain a right-hand side expression which incorporates the previous right-hand side *unchanged* as one term of a larger expression, giving a simple recurrence relationship. However, :: is defined to add an element to the *left-hand* end of a list, so the final result is a list in which the values increase as we move towards the left-hand end. The crucial expression which determines the ordering of the list is:

```
    n :: nats ( n - 1 )
```

To define a list whose components are in ascending order, we must add n to the *right-hand* end of the recursively defined sublist. We cannot use :: for this, because its second operand must be a list, and its first operand a list component. The only operation available to add an object to the right-hand end of a list is <> but this requires *both* its operands to be lists. Fortunately, it is very easy to convert n into a (singleton) list. Here are two equivalent ways to do it:

```
    n :: nil          or         [ n ]
```

and here is a function (called `stan` to emphasise its relationship to `nats`) which uses `<>` to define a list of the first n natural numbers in ascending magnitude:

```
dec stan : num -> list num ;
--- stan n <= if n = 0
              then nil
              else stan ( n - 1 ) <> [ n ] ;
```

There is an important similarity between the definitions of `stan` and `nats`. In both cases the result is defined in terms of a single element and a sublist defined by a recursive application. These characteristics are found in all recursive functions which define lists element by element. In general, the recursive application must be closer to the base case to ensure termination, and will define a shorter list. The base-case result must be a fixed-length list (usually `nil`) and the single element will usually (though not necessarily) be derived from the argument value. These observations enable us to to write down the definitions of many such functions directly. Here is a function which defines a list of the squares of the natural numbers in descending order of magnitude:

```
dec squares : num -> list num ;
--- squares n
    <= if n = 0
       then nil
       else n * n :: squares ( n - 1 ) ;
```

Each application uses `*` to contribute the *square* of its argument value to the list. It is left as an exercise to the reader to write a function which defines the list of squares in ascending order of magnitude.

3.11 Functions over lists

In the previous section we saw how to write functions which define lists, but before we are fully equipped to write programs which use lists, we must know how to write functions which operate on their individual elements. These functions will have lists as their actual parameters. As a first example we shall consider a function to find the length of a list of numbers. Here is a suitable declaration:

```
dec length : list num -> num ;
```

When we wanted to find the recurrence relationship for a function over numbers, we wrote out sample applications for different values of the parameter. For a function over lists, we shall write out applications for different values of the list parameter. In this context, different values means lists of *different lengths*, and not lists containing different values:

```
length [ ]              ≡  0
length [ a ]            ≡  1
length [ a , b ]        ≡  2
length [ a , b , c ]    ≡  3
```

The recurrence relationship and the base case can be seen more clearly by rewriting each right-hand side as a series of additions:

```
length [ ]              ≡  0
length [ a ]            ≡  0 + 1
length [ a , b ]        ≡  0 + 1 + 1
length [ a , b , c ]    ≡  0 + 1 + 1 + 1
```

They are:

```
length  an empty list       ≡  0
length  a nonempty list     ≡  length  a list with one item less  + 1
```

One difference between `length` and functions we have seen so far is that we cannot simply name the list parameter, because this does not give us any way of referring to its *components*. We recollect from §3.8 that every non-empty list can be defined by an expression of the form:

an object : : *a list of the same kind of object*

When the actual parameter is a list, we are allowed to write an expression like this on the *left-hand* side of a recursion equation:

```
---   length ( h :: t ) <= ...
```

This equation introduces *two* formal parameters h and t which name *individual parts* of an actual parameter which is a list. The formal parameter h names the first component (known as the *head*) of the list and t names the remaining list (known as the *tail*). The recurrence relationship is expressed by the recursion equation:

```
---   length ( h :: t ) <= length t + 1 ;
```

since t is a list containing one less item than the list which was supplied as the actual parameter. In an application of `length` like:

```
length [ 1 , 2 , 3 ]
```

we may imagine that the actual parameter expression is first rewritten to give:

```
length ( 1 :: [ 2 , 3 ] )
```

the expression `1 :: [ 2 , 3 ]` is compared with the expression `h :: t` on the left-hand side of the recursion equation, and causes `h` to be instantiated to the number 1 and `t` to the list `[ 2 , 3 ]`. The sequence of reductions will be as follows:

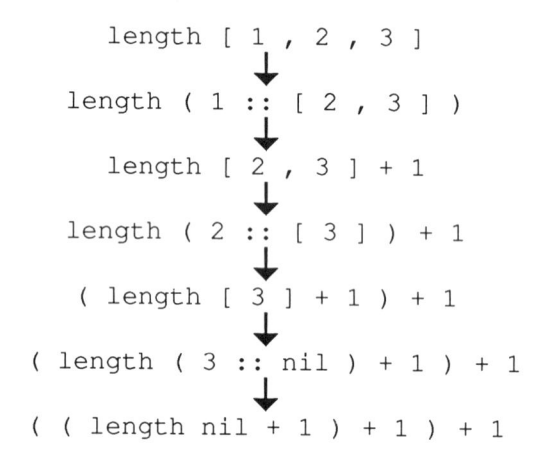

```
           length [ 1 , 2 , 3 ]
                    ↓
         length ( 1 :: [ 2 , 3 ] )
                    ↓
           length [ 2 , 3 ] + 1
                    ↓
         length ( 2 :: [ 3 ] ) + 1
                    ↓
         ( length [ 3 ] + 1 ) + 1
                    ↓
       ( length ( 3 :: nil ) + 1 ) + 1
                    ↓
       ( ( length nil + 1 ) + 1 ) + 1
```

At this point a difficulty appears, because `nil` is the normal form of the empty list and cannot be rewritten to the form `h :: t`. In order to cover the base case, we must add a *second* recursion equation to provide a complete definition of `length`. It will look like this:

```
--- length nil <= 0 ;
```

Each time `length` is applied, the actual parameter expression (rewritten as above if necessary) is examined to discover what the outermost constructor is. If it is `::`, the first equation is used as the rewrite rule, as shown above. However, if it is `nil`, the second equation will be used. Hence the remaining steps of the sequence will be:

```
       ( ( length nil + 1 ) + 1 ) + 1
                    ↓
           ( ( 0 + 1 ) + 1 ) + 1
                    ↓
                    3
```

When we use more than one recursion equation to define a function, we may enter them into the Hope Machine in any order. An attempt to apply a function before all the equations have been entered will cause a run-time error. For instance, if we try to apply `length` before entering the equation for the base case, we would see the following on the screen:

```
length [ 1 , 2 , 3 ] ;
Run time error : no match case found for:
length nil
```

The application of length (and the rest of the program) is rewritten to ***error***.

3.12 More functions over lists

All functions which use every component of a list will have essentially the same form as length, but will usually apply some operation to each component of the input list, instead of just counting it. A more typical example of a function over lists is the following, which adds up all the elements of a list of numbers:

```
dec sum : list num -> num ;
--- sum nil            <= 0 ;
--- sum ( h :: t )     <= h + sum t ;
```

This is the usual form of a function over lists: in the second equation a value derived from the input list is combined with a value defined by a recursive application of the function. In sum the two values are numbers, and are combined together with + to form a single number. However, we can use a list-constructing operation like :: to write a function over lists whose result is also a list. The following function uses cube from §2.15 to define a list whose elements are the cubes of the corresponding parameter list elements:

```
dec cubes : list num -> list num ;
--- cubes nil            <= nil ;
--- cubes ( h :: t )     <= cube h :: cubes t ;
```

If we do not need to refer to individual components of a list parameter on the right-hand side of the recursion equation, we may name the whole list using a single formal parameter in the usual way. As an example, here is a function to concatenate two lists of numbers like the primitive <> operation:

```
dec join : list num # list num -> list num ;
--- join ( nil , l )        <= l ;
--- join ( h :: t , l )     <= h :: join ( t , l ) ;
```

The expression h :: t in the second equation identifies the first list parameter and allows its head and tail to be referred to separately on the right-hand side of the recursion equation. The first equation covers the base case, which is when the first list is empty. In both cases l names the second list parameter whether empty or not.

If formal parameter names are used in more than one equation, each name is considered to be local to the equation in which it appears. In the case of join, the base-case equation could equally well have been written as:

```
    --- join ( nil , h ) <= h ;
```

thus naming the second list parameter h. This meaning of h is local to the first recursion equation; in the second equation h still refers to the head of the first list parameter. Although this is unambiguous to the Hope machine, it may mislead the human reader. From the point of view of programming style it is better to use consistent names for formal parameters which refer to the same object.

3.13 Constructors

In §3.8 we saw that every list may be constructed using an expression containing only applications of the primitive operations : : and nil. These are not simply useful operations on lists, but have a more fundamental significance. Together, : : and nil actually constitute the *definition* of the list data type. The two operations are called *constructor functions*. Every property of lists may be inferred from the properties of : : and nil and all other operations on lists (including <> and the [...] operations) may be written in terms of them.

Every data type in Hope is defined by a set of constructor functions like : : and nil. For instance, pairs are defined by the dyadic ... , ... operation, triplets by the triadic ... , ... , ... and so on. The truth values true and false are actually *nulladic* constructor functions, as are the characters 'a', 'b', *etc*. Even the numbers are defined by two constructor functions. These are the nulladic function 0 which defines the value zero and the monadic function succ. This is of type num -> num and defines the number which is one greater than its argument. In the same way that every list may be written in terms of : : and nil, so every number may be written in terms of 0 and succ. The expression:

```
    succ ( succ ( succ ( succ 0 ) ) )
```

defines the fourth natural number, usually abbreviated to 4. The conventional notation for numbers is provided as a convenient shorthand for large numbers just as the bracketed notation is a shorthand for large lists. In §3.15 we shall see how the strict notation using succ and 0 can be useful.

3.14 Patterns

An expression involving : : and nil describing a formal parameter on the left-hand side of a recursion equation is called a *pattern*. The process of rewriting the actual parameter and selecting the correct recursion equation to name its components is known as *pattern matching*. There are strict limitations on what we may write in a pattern. For instance, we are not allowed to write a left-hand side like:

```
    --- function ( h <> t ) <= ...
```

because there will usually be more than one way of rewriting the actual parameter so that it is in the form h <> t. Thus in the application:

```
function [ 1 , 2 ]
```

the actual parameter [1 , 2] may be rewritten to any of the following expressions, each of which matches the formal parameter pattern:

```
[ 1 , 2 ] <> nil
    [ 1 ] <> [ 2 ]
      nil <> [ 1 , 2 ]
```

Because we cannot deduce which expression was used by examining the result, the pattern is *ambiguous*, and we cannot assign unique values to h and t. A function like <> is called a *many-to-one mapping* because there are many expressions using it which define the same value. The operation + over numbers is also a many-to-one mapping, and allows a number such as 4 to be expressed as 0+4, 1+3, 2+2 *etc.*; it is also forbidden in patterns. Constructor functions do not present this problem, because they are guaranteed to be *one-to-one* mappings. This means that there is only one way to represent a data value using constructors and hence a unique way of rewriting an actual parameter to match a pattern. Thus there is only one way of using : : to define the list "cat", which is the expression 'c' : : "at". For this reason, the only expressions allowed in patterns are constructor function applications.

3.15 Patterns matching other data types

Patterns are not restricted to matching list parameters, but may be used to match any kind of data object by writing expressions containing the constructors of that type. As an example, consider the following function over numbers. The *factorial* of a non-negative integer *n* is denoted as *n*! and defined as:

$$n \times (n-1) \times (n-2) \times (n-3) \ldots \times 2 \times 1$$

The value of 0! is defined to be 1. Exercise 3 of chapter 2 required us to write a factorial function. We probably wrote something like this:

```
dec fact : num -> num ;
--- fact n
    <= if n = 0
       then 1
       else n * fact ( n - 1 ) ;
```

The conditional expression on the right-hand side of the recursion equation is used to decide whether the actual parameter of an application is zero. Since 0 is actually a constructor function, we may use it in a pattern. The following recursion equation will cover the case of a zero argument:

```
--- fact 0 <= 1 ;
```

and will be selected whenever an actual parameter value of zero is supplied in an application. To handle non-zero arguments, we require a second equation. Non-zero numbers are formed by applications of the constructor function succ, so a pattern to match one will look like this:

>   --- fact (succ n) <= ...

but what value does the formal parameter n name? There is exactly one expression involving succ which defines a number *n*, and this is succ (*n* - 1). In the pattern above, n will name the value which is *one less* than the value of the actual parameter. The full equation for the non-zero case will be:

>   --- fact (succ n) <= succ n * fact n ;

If we compare the right-hand side of this equation with the alternative expression in the first version of fact, we see that it no longer contains a subtraction operation; instead, the pattern-matching mechanism generates a value for n which is one less than the actual parameter value supplied in the application. When we wish to refer to the supplied value, we can write the expression succ n. An application of the new version of fact is reduced as follows:

$$\begin{array}{c}
\text{fact 3} \\
\downarrow \\
\text{fact (succ 2)} \\
\downarrow \\
\text{succ 2 * fact 2} \\
\downarrow \\
\text{succ 2 * fact (succ 1)} \\
\downarrow \\
\text{succ 2 * (succ 1 * fact 1)} \\
\downarrow \\
\text{succ 2 * (succ 1 * fact (succ 0))} \\
\downarrow \\
\text{succ 2 * (succ 1 * (succ 0 * fact 0))} \\
\downarrow \\
\text{succ 2 * (succ 1 * (succ 0 * 1))}
\end{array}$$

Pattern matching may even be performed on tuples, and in fact we have already used this feature of Hope unwittingly. When we defined the function greater in §2.9 using a recursion equation with the left-hand side:

>   --- greater (x , y) <= ...

what we actually wrote was a *pattern* involving the pair constructor ,. When we wrote the application greater (2 , 3), the pattern-matching mechanism caused the formal parameters x and y to be instantiated with the corresponding components of the tuple 2 , 3.

3.16 Ambiguity and completeness

When we use patterns to distinguish between zero and non-zero arguments we must be careful to write an equation which uses *each* of the constructors 0 and succ. We must not write the non-zero case equation of fact as:

```
--- fact n <= n * fact ( n - 1 ) ;
```

because the pattern does not contain the application of any constructor function and the formal parameter n can match *any* argument value. The Hope Machine matches arguments against the patterns in the equations in an *undefined order*, and even if there is a separate equation for the zero case, we cannot assume that it will be checked first.

Ambiguity may also occur when a function is defined by more than one equation containing constructors. In the following function:

```
dec ambiguous : num -> num ;
--- ambiguous 0                     <= ... ;
--- ambiguous ( succ x )            <= ... ;
--- ambiguous ( succ ( succ x ) )   <= ... ;
```

no difficulty arises when the argument is 0 or 1, but when it is greater than 1, both the second and third equations can match. For instance, 2 may be rewritten as either succ 1 or succ (succ 0). This set of recursion equations is said to have *overlapping left-hand sides*. We must be careful to avoid writing overlapping patterns, because the Hope Machine checks the equations in an undefined order, so we cannot predict which of the two matching equations will actually be selected.

As a general rule, we must write one (and only one) equation for each constructor defining the data type to ensure that the definition of a function is complete and unambiguous; however, simplification may be possible. As an example, consider the definition of a function merge which takes two ordered lists of numbers and *merges* them to produce an ordered result list. For example, the application:

```
merge ( [ 2 , 6 ] , [ 1 , 3 , 5 , 7 , 9 ] )
```

will define the following list:

```
[ 1 , 2 , 3 , 5 , 6 , 7 , 9 ]
```

The declaration of merge will be as follows:

```
dec merge : list num # list num -> list num ;
```

Each list parameter is defined by two constructors, so for completeness we must write *four* equations to cover the empty and non-empty case of each argument:

```
--- merge ( nil , nil )        <= nil ;
--- merge ( h1 :: t1 , nil )   <= h1 :: t1 ;
--- merge ( nil , h2 :: t2 )   <= h2 :: t2 ;
--- merge ( h1 :: t1 , h2 :: t2 )
    <= if h1 < h2
       then h1 :: merge ( t1 , h2 :: t2 )
       else h2 :: merge ( h1 :: t1 , t2 ) ;
```

When we have written out all the cases in this way, we can see that a number of simplifications are possible. In the second and third equations, there is no reference to the components of the non-empty list parameters on the right-hand sides, and the equations may be written more concisely as:

```
--- merge ( l1 , nil ) <= l1 ;
--- merge ( nil , l2 ) <= l2 ;
```

These patterns do not contain constructors, and the formal parameters `l1` and `l2` can therefore match empty input lists. Either of these equations can match the argument `nil , nil`, so the first equation is redundant and may be omitted. When designing functions, it is good practice to write out a complete set of equations first and then simplify it, as this reduces the possibility of overlooking a case by making an incorrect assumption about the parameters.

3.17 More specific patterns

Any specific actual parameter value may be matched by a pattern containing only constructor applications without formal parameter names. In the case of lists and numbers, these may be written in their concise forms. As an example, consider a function to evaluate the following sequence of numbers:

$$0, 1, 1, 2, 3, 5, 8, 13, 21, 34, \ldots$$

Each number is obtained by adding together the two preceding ones. This sequence was first described in 1202 by Leonardo Fibonacci of Pisa, and the numbers are known as *Fibonacci numbers*. They are more formally defined by the relationships:

$$F_0 = 0, \qquad F_1 = 1, \qquad F_{n+2} = F_{n+1} + F_n \quad \text{for all } n \geq 0$$

The following (somewhat costly) function defines the *n*th. Fibonacci number:

```
dec Fib : num -> num ;
--- Fib 0 <= 0 ;
--- Fib 1 <= 1 ;
--- Fib ( succ ( succ n ) ) <= Fib ( succ n ) + Fib n ;
```

The constant 1 in the pattern of the second equation is the shorthand form of the expression succ 0. The pattern in the third equation contains *two* occurrences of succ and matches only numbers whose value is at least 2. We can write patterns containing the concise form of other data objects in the same way, thus:

```
--- fun [ a , b ] <= ... ;
```

will match only a two-element list and name its elements a and b respectively. The following pattern:

```
--- fun ( 3 :: t ) <= ... ;
```

matches any list of numbers whose first element is 3 and names the remainder of the list t. We may be even more specific than this; the pattern:

```
--- fun [ 3 , b ] <= ... ;
```

will match only a two-element list whose first element is 3 (naming the second element b), whilst:

```
--- another "Hope" <= ... ;
```

matches only the list of four characters "Hope".

3.18 Patterns in qualified expressions

In §2.19 a form of the qualified expression was introduced which allowed more than one name to be introduced in a single qualifying expression. This was done by forming the values on the right-hand side of the == symbol into a tuple and writing the corresponding names in an abstract tuple on the left-hand side. In reality this construction is a pattern match, and the names are instantiated with the components of the right-hand side tuple in exactly the same way that the formal parameters of a two-argument function are instantiated with the values of the corresponding argument tuple. With the usual Hope generality, we are allowed to write any kind of pattern in this context, but care is required. The following function illustrates legal Hope, but unsafe programming practice:

```
--- funny x <= h * sum t
                where h :: t == nats x ;
```

The qualified expression allows the head and tail of the list of numbers defined by the application nats x to be referred to separately in the qualified expression. However, when x has the value 0, the qualifying expression defines an empty list (*cf.* the definition of nats in §3.10). Under these circumstances, the pattern match will *fail*, and the program will terminate with an error.

When patterns are used in qualified expressions, there is no way of matching right-hand side values which may be defined by more than one constructor. For safety, we must always write expressions whose values are guaranteed to be matched by the left-hand side pattern. In this case, we must ensure that nats always returns a non-empty list by never applying it to 0, perhaps by defining funny as:

```
--- funny 0 <= 0 ;
--- funny ( succ x )
       <= h * sum t
           where h :: t == nats ( succ x ) ;
```

However, it is always safe to use a pattern match in a qualified expression when the right-hand side object may only be defined by a single constructor. In particular, it is always safe to match a tuple of any size.

3.19 Pattern synonyms

Patterns are often written to match an actual parameter of specific construction, rather than to decompose the object into its components. When referring to the object in a right-hand side expression, the entire pattern must be repeated, which may obscure the intention of the expression if the pattern is complex, or if several references are made to the object. To avoid this, Hope allows *synonyms* to be defined for objects matched by patterns. This is done using an expression of the form:

name & *pattern*

where *name* is formed according to the usual rules; it identifies the object matched by *pattern* and must be different from any name used in it. It may be used in a right-hand side expression instead of repeating the pattern. For example, the second equation for funny in §3.18 might be written like this using a synonym:

```
--- funny ( w & succ x )
       <= h * sum t
           where h :: t == nats w ;
```

When using synonyms, we can still refer to subparts of the object named in the pattern in the usual way. The general-case equation for fact (from §3.15) might be written like this:

```
    --- fact ( m & succ n ) <= m * fact n ;
```

We may only use & at the top level to name an entire pattern, and it may not be used within a pattern to name a subpart of it.

3.20 Review
Here is a summary of the main points introduced in this chapter:

- Tuples are fixed-size data structures consisting of two or more values of any type. Primitive functions are provided to compare tuples for equality.

- Lists are arbitrarily large data structures containing zero or more values of the same type. Primitive functions are provided to concatenate lists and to compare them element by element.

- Recursive functions may be written to define lists. Functions may also be written to define tuples. If these are recursive, qualified expressions are used to name the separate components of the result.

- Every data type is defined by a set of primitive operations called constructors. The constructors for tuples, lists, truth values, characters and numbers are introduced.

- Patterns are expressions on the left-hand sides of recursion equations composed of formal parameter names and applications of constructors. They serve to associate formal parameter names with subparts of actual parameters.

- Functions may be defined by multiple recursion equations, avoiding explicit conditional expressions on the right-hand sides of recursion equations. Sets of equations must be complete and non-overlapping.

- Pattern matching may be used in qualified expressions to name subparts of abstracted values.

- Synonyms may be defined for objects matched in patterns to avoid repeating the patterns in right-hand side expressions.

3.21 Exercises

1. Write a function sum which will add two numbers using applications of succ only. Use multiple recursion equations and do not use conditional expressions. Remember that there are two parameters, each with two constructors, so a strict definition will require four equations. Can the number of equations be reduced?

2. Write a function `larger` to determine the larger of two positive integers. Use multiple recursion equations and do not use conditional expressions. *Hint:* write down the left-hand sides of the four recursion equations first.

3. Write a recursive function `chop` which takes an *n*-digit number and which uses only subtraction to define a pair of numbers which are the first *n*-1 digits and the last digit respectively. Do not use `div` or `mod` (but you may use conditionals).

4. Write a function `concat` which concatenates the digits of two *non-zero* integers. `concat ( 123 , 456 )` evaluates to `123456` but `concat ( 123 , 0 )` evaluates to `123`. You can use `chop` from exercise 3 and `add` or `cat` from problems 1 and 2 of chapter 2. Estimate the cost of your `concat` function in terms of the number of multiplications it performs.

5. Write a function `product` which will form the product of all the elements of a list of numbers. `product nil` may be considered to evaluate to `1`.

6. Write a function `shout` which converts a word (a list of upper and lower-case letters) into upper-case. `shout "Hope"` should evaluate to `"HOPE"`.

7. Write a function `precedes` which takes two words and which evaluates to `true` if the first is lexically (alphabetically) less than the second.

8. Write a function `before` which has the same effect as `precedes`, but which can be applied as an infix operation. Now modify your function so that it is insensitive to the case of the words which are being compared.

9. Write a function `at` which yields the character at a specified position in a list. Assume that the characters are numbered from 0, and that the specified position will always be found (*i.e.* the list is never too short). `at ( 2 , "Hope" )` evaluates to `'p'`.

10. Write a function `pos` to find the position of a specified character in a list of characters. Assume that the characters are numbered from 0 and that the specified character will always be found). `pos ( 'p' , "Hope" )` evaluates to `2`.

11. Two *anagrams* can be considered to define a *transposition* of the characters of a third string. For instance, `"abcde"` and `"eabcd"` define a transposition in which the last character of a 5-character string is moved to the start. Define a function `transpose` to transpose the characters of a string as specified by two anagrams. `transpose ( "UVWXYZ" , "fedcba" , "ecabdf" )` should evaluate to `"VXZYWU"`. *Hint:* use `pos` and `at`, noting that all three strings are the same length and that each character of the second string is unique and appears exactly once in the third.

12. Write a function `right` which will insert a single character at the right-hand end of a list of characters. `right ( 's', "Hope" )` evaluates to `"Hopes"`.

13. Write a function `reverse` which uses `right` to reverse a list of characters. `reverse "bonk"` evaluates to `"knob"`. Now write an alternative definition which reverses a list directly using `::` and `<>`.

14. Write a function `into` to insert a number into an *ordered* list of numbers, preserving the ordering. `into ( 2 , [ 1 , 3 ] )` evaluates to `[ 1 , 2 , 3 ]`. *Hint*: consider modifying your `right` function from exercise 12.

15. Write a function `order` which uses `into` to sort an *unordered* list of integers. `order [ 3 , 1 , 4 , 2 ]` evaluates to `[ 1 , 2 , 3 , 4 ]`. *Hint*: consider modifying your first `reverse` function from exercise 13.

Chapter 4

New Kinds of Data

4.1 User-defined data types

The primitive data types provided by Hope are adequate for many programs, but are not always exactly what we require. Hope allows the programmer to define new types of data for particular applications, and in this chapter we shall look at various ways to do this.

Suppose that we need a data type which we can use to represent the states of electrical switches. A suitable new data type can be introduced by means of a *data declaration*:

```
data switch == on ++ off ;
```

data is a reserved word and switch is the name of the new type. The symbol == is read as "is defined as ..." and ++ as "or ...". The constructor functions of the new type are named on and off. Constructor names have *global* scope, and must be different from any constructor names introduced by other data declarations, and also from the names of any primitive or user-defined functions. The data declaration is not evaluated by the Hope Machine, but is stored like a function declaration. We can now write functions over switch-valued objects by using the constructor functions on and off in patterns. The following function changes the state of a switch:

```
dec flip : switch -> switch ;
--- flip on  <= off ;
--- flip off <= on  ;
```

The first equation is selected when the actual parameter is constructed using on, and the second when it is constructed using off, for example:

```
flip on ;
off : switch
```

Some justification is needed here. The type switch has two nulladic constructors, and a little examination soon convinces us that it has exactly the same properties as the primitive type truval. If we replace switch by truval, on by true and off by false, then the function flip is no more than the primitive function not under a different name. Why have we gone to the trouble of defining a new type when we could use an existing type with identical properties?

The real reason for introducing the type switch is that it makes a program using it easier to understand. If switch states were represented using truth values, we could equally well represent the *on* state by false and the *off* state by true, but every time we saw a truth value in a program, we would have to pause to remember the convention we were using. Further, if the program used truth values for any other purpose, then we would also have to remember whether a particular truth value represented a switch state or not. Using the switch data type, the *off* state of a switch is represented by the constructor off, and no detective work is needed. A second advantage of defining the type switch is that the type-checking mechanism ensures that we can only manipulate switch-valued objects using functions of the correct type (such as flip), reducing the possibility of mistakes still further.

4.2 Data structures containing user-defined types

A new type introduced by a data declaration behaves in all respects like a primitive type. For example, we can incorporate switch-valued objects into data structures such as tuples or lists. The accumulators of the stored-program computer (*cf.* §1.1) consist of sequences of electronic switches, and we might use a list switch to represent one. We can then write functions over accumulators which effectively simulate the operation of the computer at the underlying electronic level.

An accumulator can be used to perform *binary arithmetic* (arithmetic on numbers expressed to the base 2) by considering the *off* and *on* switch states to represent the binary digits (*bits*) 0 and 1 respectively. The complete accumulator is considered to represent a binary number having its least significant bit at the *left-hand* end (*i.e.* the opposite way round to normal mathematical convention). The function increment below simulates the effect of adding one to the binary representation of a number held in an accumulator:

```
dec increment : list switch -> list switch ;
--- increment nil <= nil ;
--- increment ( off :: t ) <= on :: t ;
--- increment ( on :: t ) <= off :: increment t ;
```

The third equation covers the case when the addition of one causes a carry into the next bit position, as in the following application to a 4-bit accumulator containing a binary representation of the decimal number 5:

```
increment [ on , off , on , off ] ;
[ off , on , on , off ] : list switch
```

The result is a binary representation of the decimal number 6. The base-case equation ensures that there is no carry beyond the rightmost (most significant) bit of the number. If carry were required in this case, the equation would be written:

```
--- increment nil <= [ on ] ;
```

but this would cause the result of the function to contain one more bit than the argument. It was defined in the original way because the physical accumulators of a computer are of *fixed* size, which results in the phenomenon of integer overflow which we saw in §1.9. We can see this in operation by incrementing an accumulator whose switches are all in the *on* state (representing the decimal number 15):

```
increment [ on , on , on , on ] ;
[ off , off , off , off ] : list switch
```

The result is a representation of the decimal number 0, and not 16, which would be the list [off , off , off , off , on] in our right-to-left convention.

Once again some justification is called for. Here is a case where it would seem much simpler and clearer to use lists of numbers directly rather than inventing a new type and having to remember that the constructors actually represent binary digits. In fact there are two good reasons for introducing a new data type. The first is the practical reason that numbers are not restricted to the values 0 and 1, and operations on numbers are not restricted to functions like increment which define lists containing only these values. By defining the type switch, the type-checking mechanism stops us using inappropriate operations (like +) which could generate meaningless switch states. The second reason is more philosophical: it is that the physical accumulators of the computer do not actually contain numbers, but only electronic switches which can take up one of two states. The idea that an accumulator contains a binary number is an interpretation which we place upon it when we want to use it for performing arithmetic (as in §1.1), but it remains nevertheless only an interpretation. If we set out to model the machine at the electronic level, it is actually a source of confusion to assume that the accumulators contain numbers; the use of the type switch is more natural and makes the distinction between numbers and switch states explicit.

4.3 Constructors with parameters

The switch data type has only two nulladic constructors, hence there are only two possible switch values. We can define a data type with a larger range of possible values by allowing its constructor functions to take parameters. In §2.2 we defined a function to convert temperatures from degrees Fahrenheit to degrees Celsius, but we used ordinary numbers to represent temperatures. Here is the declaration of a more appropriate temperature data type :

```
data temp == Celsius num ++ Fahrenheit num ;
```

Celsius and Fahrenheit are the constructors of the new type temp, and each is declared to have a single num parameter. The global scope of constructor names means that we could not use the name Celsius as a constructor if we had already defined the Celsius function of §2.2. An object of type temp can be constructed by applying one of the constructors to a number:

```
Fahrenheit 451 ;
Fahrenheit 451 : temp
```

Effectively the constructors allow us to "disguise" numbers as temperatures. The result is that temperatures are now objects which are distinct from numbers, and which are themselves divided into two subtypes. The number associated with a temperature can be examined by using the constructor in a pattern match. For instance, the definition of a Celsius-to-Fahrenheit conversion function over the new type would be written like this:

```
dec CelsiusOf : temp -> temp ;
--- CelsiusOf ( Fahrenheit f )
    <= Celsius ( ( f - 32 ) * 5 div 9 ) ;
```

Applications of constructor functions have the same (high) priority as those of ordinary functions, so the entire argument expression of Celsius is parenthesised to prevent the right-hand side from being interpreted as:

```
( Celsius ( f - 32 ) ) * 5 div 9
```

which will be rejected by the type-checking mechanism because the first argument of * is not a num. Notice that there is no equation with a pattern which matches the Celsius constructor, because it does not make sense to convert a temperature which is already in degrees Celsius. The new function is much safer than our original Celsius function, which can be applied to any number, whether it represents a temperature or not. CelsiusOf is not only specific to objects of type temp, but specific to Fahrenheit temperatures. The temperature constructors serve as a kind of "label" on the numbers they are applied to. This allows us to write a more intelligent conversion function such as:

```
dec convert : temp -> temp ;
```

```
--- convert ( Fahrenheit f )
    <= Celsius ( ( f - 32 ) * 5 div 9 ) ;
--- convert ( Celsius c )
    <= Fahrenheit ( c * 9 div 5 + 32 ) ;
```

and use it like this:

```
convert ( Celsius 100 ) ;
Fahrenheit 212 : temp

convert ( Fahrenheit 32 ) ;
Celsius 0 : temp
```

4.4 Using constructors to disguise data

The ability of constructors to disguise data objects is useful in many ways. In chapter 3 we saw that all the objects in a list must be the same type, which is often unduly restrictive. Suppose that we wish to write a function which models the operation of a pocket calculator by storing the sequence of calculations as a list and then evaluating them. The items in the list will be a mixture of operands (numbers) and operations (characters), which are different types of object and therefore cannot normally appear in the same list. However, by defining a suitable data type, we can use its constructors to disguise both operands and operators as a single type of object:

```
data item == int num ++ op char ;
```

This declaration introduces int as a constructor which can be applied to a number, and op as a constructor which can be applied to a character. In both cases an object of type item is constructed. Here is the representation of the calculation **3 + 4 * 5** as a list item:

```
[ int 3 , op '+' , int 4 , op '*' , int 5 ]
```

Most calculators treat all operations as having equal priority and evaluate expressions from left to right as they are entered; the calculation above thus evaluates the expression $(3 + 4) \times 5$. A function to evaluate the expression must apply the first operation to the first two numbers and replace all three by the result. This process is repeated until the list is reduced to a single number, which is the required result. Here is the declaration of an evaluation function:

```
dec calc : list item -> num ;
```

The base case is when the list has been reduced to a single numeric item:

```
--- calc [ int x ] <= x ;
```

This equation is specific for a singleton list containing an int-valued item. Its associated number is named by the formal parameter x. The general-case equation will be specific for lists containing at least three items:

```
--- calc ( int x :: ( op '+' :: ( int y :: t ) ) )
    <= calc ( int ( x + y ) :: t ) ;
```

The first and third items must be int-valued, and their associated numbers will be named by the formal parameters x and y. The second item must be op-valued, with the associated character '+'. On the right-hand side the two numbers are added, converted into an item by applying int, and placed on the front of the remaining list, which is then evaluated recursively. Other dyadic operations can be catered for by adding further equations of the same form; for example, multiplication:

```
--- calc ( int x :: ( op '*' :: ( int y :: t ) ) )
    <= calc ( int ( x * y ) :: t ) ;
```

4.5 Constructors with more than one parameter

Constructor functions are not restricted to being monadic, and we may define data types whose constructors take any number of parameters. Hope was not primarily designed for numerical calculations, and one glaring omission in the range of data types provided in the language is any form of non-integral numbers. We shall now look at two ways of defining a suitable data type to remedy this deficiency.

The first method is to represent fractions as *rational numbers* using a pair of numbers to represent the numerator and denominator parts. A possible data declaration might look like this:

```
data rational == rat ( num # num ) ;
```

When a constructor has more than one argument, the type expression defining its argument types must be parenthesised in the same way that the arguments of the function themselves will be parenthesised in applications.

Rational numbers can be manipulated using the familiar rules of elementary arithmetic for handling fractions, for example:

```
dec add : rational # rational -> rational ;
--- add ( rat ( n1 , d1 ) , rat ( n2 , d2 ) )
    <= if d1 = d2
       then rat ( n1 + n2 , d1 ) ;
       else rat ( n1 * d2 + n2 * d1 , d1 * d2 ) ;
```

A typical application of add will be evaluated like this:

```
add ( rat ( 2 , 3 ) , rat ( 3 , 4 ) ) ;
rat ( 17 , 12 ) : rational
```

The example illustrates one problem with rational numbers, which is that their denominators will tend to grow larger with repeated calculations, hence they must be reduced to their lowest terms to avoid integer overflow. One method of doing this (left as an exercise to the reader as usual) is to use the gcd function from exercise 6 of chapter 2. A related problem is that the magnitude of a rational number is limited by the magnitude of its denominator. If the maximum integer which the Hope machine can hold is m, then a rational number with denominator d cannot represent a number greater than m div $d+1$. An alternative representation which overcomes this problem is a triplet whose first element represents the integral part of the number, and whose remaining elements represent the fractional part (which is always less than 1) as numerator and denominator.

4.6 Floating-point numbers

A second method of representing non-integral numbers is based on a notation often used in scientific literature. Using this, the number 3615.962 (for example) is conventionally written as 3.615962×10^3 and can be represented by pair consisting of the significant figures (or *mantissa*) and the power of 10 (or *exponent*). These can both be integers if we use the convention that there is an implied decimal point before the first digit of the mantissa. Using this *floating-point* notation, a very wide range of values can be represented, with some restriction on their accuracy. Floating-point numbers are approximations to the mathematical notion of *real numbers*; the terms are often used interchangeably, but they are not strictly equivalent. A suitable data declaration for floating-point numbers might be:

```
data float == flo ( num # num ) ;
```

Multiplication and division of floating-point numbers are straightforward in principle, and it is only necessary to multiply (or divide) the mantissæ and add (or subtract) the exponents, but there are practical complications. Multiplying two mantissæ may cause integer overflow. It awkward (and expensive) to prevent this by testing their magnitudes before the event, and a more usual technique is to restrict them to values which cannot cause overflow. A typical Hope Machine can hold numbers up to 2^{30} (the decimal number 1073741824), hence the maximum safe value for the mantissa is 2^{15} (the decimal number 32768). For convenience, we shall maintain each number in a standard (or *normalised*) form in which the mantissa is as large as possible (to avoid losing significant digits) without exceeding 32768. Functions over floating-point numbers will assume that their arguments are normalised, and are responsible for renormalising their results. For example, multiplication:

```
infix times : 6 ;
dec times : float # float -> float ;
--- flo ( m1 , e1 ) times flo ( m2 , e2 )
    <= norm ( m1 * m2 , e1 + e2 ) ;
```

Conversely, when dividing floating-point numbers, the dividend should first be extended to the maximum size (typically 9 digits) with zeros to minimise the loss of accuracy caused by integer division. Addition and subtraction are more complex, because the arguments must be scaled so that their exponents are the same. These functions are discussed in the exercises at the end of the chapter. The function norm used to renormalise the result of times is defined as follows:

```
dec norm : num # num -> float ;
--- norm ( 0 , e ) <= flo ( 0 , 0 ) ;
--- norm ( succ m , e )
    <= if a > 32768
       then norm ( succ m div 10 , e + 1 )
       else if a < 3276
            then norm ( succ m * 10 , e - 1 )
            else flo ( succ m , e )
       where a == abs ( succ m ) ;
```

Zero is a special case, as it has no significant digits, and cannot be scaled to the range 3276–32768. The choice of exponent is arbitrary in this case, since 0.0×10^n is zero for all values of n.

Rather than using the flo constructor directly, it is safer and more convenient to use norm to define floating-point numbers. This avoids having to remember the convention for representing them, and also allows us to write them in the most natural form. For instance, the strict (or *canonical*) floating-point representation of the number 999 is 9.99×10^2 and its normalised form is flo (9990 , -1), but we can write it more naturally as norm (999 , 0).

4.7 Constructors with different argument types

The parameters of a polyadic constructor can be of different types. Here is a data type which might be used to hold the names and ages of employees in an organisation:

```
data staff == st ( list char # num ) ;

st ( "Haskell B. Curry" , 43 ) ;
st ( "Haskell B. Curry" , 43 ) : staff
```

The payroll of the organisation might be represented by a list staff. Once again, we have disguised a primitive type (a tuple) as another type by introducing the constructor st. Fixed-size data objects like this are often known as *records*. As before, the justification is that the new type improves the clarity of a program which manipulates it by forcing us to define and use specific functions over staff records. As an example, consider the problem of designing a function to discover the youngest employee in an organisation. The declaration will be as follows:

```
dec youngest : list staff -> staff ;
```

The base case is the singleton list representing a one-employee organisation. The function cannot be defined over an empty list, since even if an organisation could exist without employees, it would certainly not have a youngest one!

```
--- youngest [ e ] <= e ;
```

The general case compares the age of employee at the head of the list with that of youngest employee in the tail of the list. This is found by a recursive application of youngest, so its age component must be identified using a qualified expression:

```
--- youngest ( st ( n , a ) :: t )
    <= if a < y
          then st ( n , a )
          else st ( m , y )
       where st ( m , y ) == youngest t ;
```

It is safe to use a pattern match in the qualified expression because the object being decomposed will always be constructed using st. Here is a sample application of youngest:

```
youngest [ st ( "Ned" , 42 ) , st ( "Pam" , 18 ) ,
           st ( "Sue" , 23 ) , st ( "Tom" , 55 ) ] ;
st ( "Pam" , 18 ) : staff
```

In a practical program which used youngest, the list of staff would be much longer and would almost certainly be generated by the application of another function rather than entered directly from the terminal as in this simple example.

4.8 Types containing user-defined types

We can define data types whose constructors take other user-defined data types as parameters. The mathematical concept of *complex numbers* is a generalisation of the real numbers and involves the representation of numbers in the form $a + ib$ where i is the square root of -1 and a and b are real numbers called the *real part* and *imaginary part* respectively. A data type to represent complex numbers might look like this:

```
data complex == comp ( float # float ) ;
```

Assuming the existence of infix operations plus, minus and times (of priority 5, 5 and 6 respectively) to perform addition, subtraction and multiplication of floating-point numbers, we can write functions over them like the following, which multiplies two complex numbers together:

```
dec multiply : complex # complex -> complex ;
--- multiply ( comp ( r1 , i1 ) , comp ( r2 , i2 ) )
    <= comp ( r1 times r2 minus i1 times i2 ,
              r1 times i2 plus  r2 times i1 ) ;
```

4.9 Constructors as infix operations

Most primitive constructors (*e.g.*, and : :) are applied as infix operations. We are allowed to define our own data types with infix constructors by declaring the priorities of the constructors and using them in infix notation in type expressions. Thus the types rational, float and complex introduced in the previous sections might be more clearly defined as infix operations:

```
infix upon , exp , imag : 1 ;
data rational == num     upon num    ;
data float    == num     exp  num    ;
data complex  == float imag float ;
```

Notice the way in which several infix operations with the same priority have been introduced in the same declaration. It should go without saying that patterns in equations of functions over these objects will now be written with the constructors placed between their arguments. As an example, here is multiply from §4.8:

```
--- multiply ( r1 imag i1 , r2 imag i2 )
    <= r1 times r2 minus i1 times i2 imag
       r1 times i2 plus  r2 times i1 ;
```

Infix constructors in expressions are reduced according to their relative priorities like ordinary infix operations. For example, the right-hand side of the above equation does not require any parentheses, because imag has a lower priority than the arithmetic operations, and the expression is interpreted as:

```
( ( r1 times r2 ) minus ( i1 times i2 ) ) imag
( ( r1 times i2 ) plus  ( r2 times i1 ) )
```

The priorities of infix constructors must also be taken into account when they are used in patterns. Here is a version of times from §4.6 over floating-point numbers constructed with the infix constructor exp:

```
--- ( m1 exp e1 ) times ( m2 exp e2 )
    <= norm ( m1 * m2 , e1 + e2 ) ;
```

Here the *left-hand* side of the equation must be parenthesised because exp has a lower priority than times, and the pattern would otherwise be interpreted as:

```
--- m1 exp ( e1 times m2 ) exp e2 <= ...
```

4.10 Recursive data types
Constructors can have parameters of any user-defined type, including the type which is being defined. We can consider that the primitive type num has already been defined by the (hypothetical) declaration:

```
data num == 0 ++ succ num ;
```

This definition is recursive, so that every non-zero num consists of an application of succ to another num. The nulladic constructor 0 defines a base case, and allows the definition to terminate. By applying succ to an existing num, we can always define a new value, hence in principle, an indefinite number of different num-valued objects can be constructed. The number of different values possible is limited in practice by the capacity of the Hope Machine to represent them, and this limitation is reflected in the phenomenon of integer overflow which we saw in §1.9 and §4.2.

We can define our own recursive data types using the same kind of declaration shown above. As an example of a user-defined recursive data type, we shall define a type to represent arbitrarily large integers. A simple way of doing this would be to represent a number as a list of digits, but this suffers from the drawback that the components of lists must be processed starting from the left-hand end. Since normal operations on numbers start with the least significant digit, we would have to adopt the convention that the least significant digit is at the left-hand end, as we did in §4.2 with machine accumulators representing binary numbers. However, we can represent numbers as sequences of single digits in the conventional order by introducing a suitable data type. For simplicity we shall represent the digits by numbers, although this does not express the important restriction that their values should be within the range zero to nine:

```
data big == dig num ++ extra ( big # num ) ;
```

The declaration expresses the notion that a long number may consist of a single digit (using the dig constructor) or of a long number with an extra digit at the right-hand end (using the extra constructor). Here is the long number representation of the number 456:

```
extra ( extra ( dig 4 , 5 ) , 6 )
```

Unfortunately Hope does not provide a shorthand representation for user-defined data types as it does for lists, so constant long numbers will have to be written out as expressions involving constructors as above. In most cases this will not be a problem because long numbers will be generated by function applications. However, if a program uses many long number constants, or there are large quantities of results to be examined, a less cumbersome representation may be useful. We can make long numbers more concise using a recursive type with an *infix* binary constructor:

```
infix . : 4 ;
data long == ~ num ++ long . num ;
```

Since the constructor names are formed from sign characters, we can even omit the blanks between the constructor names and the digits; the long number representation of 456 (for instance) becomes simply ~4.5.6, We can now write functions over long numbers using the digit-by-digit rules of elementary arithmetic, naming their digits with patterns containing applications of the . and ~ constructors.

We shall give just one example of the use of the new data type: the digit-by-digit addition of two unsigned long numbers. At each step of the addition we must consider the possibility of a carry from the previous digit position, hence the function will require *three* parameters, and we must supply 0 in the top-level application as the initial value of the carry parameter. The declaration of the function will be:

```
dec LongAdd : long # long # num -> long ;
```

The two long numbers are each defined by two constructors, so the function definition will require four equations for completeness. The maximum carry which can result from the addition of two digits is 1; the maximum result of adding two digits and the carry is therefore 19. If this is treated as a two-digit number s, the right-hand digit has the value s mod 10, and the left-hand digit is 1 if s is greater than than 10, and 0 otherwise. The general-case equation is therefore:

```
--- LongAdd ( i1 . d1 , i2 . d2 , c )
    <= if s < 10
       then LongAdd ( i1 , i2 , 0 ) . s
       else LongAdd ( i1 , i2 , 1 ) . s mod 10
       where s == d1 + d2 + c ;
```

The base case is when both long numbers contain a single digit:

```
--- LongAdd ( ~ d1 , ~ d2 , c )
    <= if s < 10
       then ~ s
       else ~ 1 . s mod 10
       where s == d1 + d2 + c ;
```

When the first long number has more digits than the second, we shall have:

```
--- LongAdd ( i1 . d1 , ~ d2 , c )
    <= if s < 10
          then i1 . s
          else LongAdd ( i1 , ~ 0 , 1 ) . s mod 10
          where s == d1 + d2 + c ;
```

A similar equation (not shown) will be required to cover the case when the second argument has more digits than the first.

Although this example has been presented as a digit-by-digit representation, the `LongAdd` function does not depend for its operation on adding numbers which are less than 10, and there is no reason why the individual "digits" of a long number may not be much larger. If our Hope machine can handle nine-digit integers, we can safely use eight-digit numbers as the components of long numbers, since adding two eight-digit numbers can cause a maximum carry of 1 into the ninth (most significant) digit position. The only modifications required to `LongAdd` are to replace occurrences of the constant `10` in the equations by the value `100000000`. If we also wanted to multiply long numbers, the components would have to be limited to four digits to allow for an eight-digit product. The only drawback of using larger numbers is that the leading zeros of intermediate "digits" will not be printed. The problem of printing the results of programs in an æsthetically pleasing form is discussed in chapter 9.

4.11 Indirectly recursive types

In the definitions of the types `big` and `long` in §4.10, each appears as the argument of a constructor on the right-hand side of its own definition, hence the types are directly recursive. We may also define indirectly recursive types. As an example we develop the pocket calculator model of §4.4 to take account of the priority of operations. We can do this by allowing lists representing expressions to contain embedded lists representing higher-priority subexpressions. The definition of `item` must be extended as follows:

```
data item == int num ++ op char ++ term ( list item ) ;
```

The new constructor `term` can be applied to a type which *contains* objects of the type being defined (a `list item`), and allows a complete expression to be treated as a single `item`. To show the priority of operations, the expression $3 + 4 \times 5$ will now be written with the term 4×5 represented by an embedded list as follows:

```
[ int 3 , op '+' , term [ int 4 , op '*' , int 5 ] ]
```

The `calc` function is extended to handle embedded subexpressions by adding an extra equation to match the new constructor. This is straightforward if the subexpression is the first term of the expression to be evaluated:

```
--- calc ( term e :: t )
    <= calc ( int ( calc e ) :: t ) ;
```

The subexpression is evaluated and the result converted to an item and placed on the front of the original list before any other terms at the same level are processed. When the subexpression is not the first term, we shall need an equation of the form:

```
--- calc ( int x :: ( op '+' :: ( term e :: t ) ) )
    <= calc ( int ( x + calc e ) :: t ) ;
```

This leads to a rather unwieldy definition of calc, since we already have a separate equation for each possible operation, so handling the new case for each one will double the number of equations. The possibility of defining a more concise version of calc is discussed in exercise 6 at the end of the chapter.

4.12 Mutually recursive types

A list item (*cf.* §4.4 and §4.11) is a slightly unsatisfactory model of a sequence of calculations, because there is nothing to stop us applying calc to an empty list, which cannot be interpreted as a sequence of calculations. A better model might use a linear data type which is defined to contain at least one component. The declaration of a suitable type might look like this:

```
data series == more ( item # series ) ++ only item ;
```

The declaration of series requires the prior declaration of item, however, we encounter a difficulty if we attempt to define an item:

```
data item == int num ++ op char ++ term series ;
```

because its declaration requires the prior declaration of series. Two types whose declarations refer to each other like this are said to be *mutually recursive*. We did not encounter this problem in §4.11 because the special properties of lists allow the type list item to be used in the declaration of item without being explicitly declared itself. Since Hope requires all user-defined types to be declared before they are used, a special form of declaration is provided for mutually recursive types:

```
data series == more ( item # series ) ++ only item
with item   == int num ++ op char ++ term series ;
```

The second (and any subsequent) declarations are introduced by the reserved word with rather than data. The Hope Machine treats data declarations connected by with as though they had been entered simultaneously. Using this version of the item data type, an expression such as $3 + 4 \times 5$ can be represented by the series:

```
more ( int 3 , more ( op '+' ,
  only ( term ( more ( int 4 , more ( op '*' ,
    only ( int 5 ) ) ) ) ) ) )
```

4.13 New names for old types

User-defined data types allow us to clarify programs by defining types for specific uses (*e.g.* `temp` in §4.3) rather than using more general primitive types (such as `num`) and allow the the Hope Machine to check that only appropriate functions are applied to the new type. The drawback is that programs become more complex because we must provide these functions ourselves. Thus, we cannot use `<>` to concatenate the series of §4.12, but must define a new function specific to series. In many cases we would be happy to use a primitive type, but would like to distinguish between its different uses to make the program easier for the human reader to understand. Hope allows us to achieve this by introducing a *synonym* for an existing type. A type synonym is declared as follows:

```
type word == list char ;
```

Here, `type` is a reserved word and `word` is introduced as an alternative name for the type on the right-hand side of the `==` symbol, in this case the primitive type `list char`. Note that a `type` declaration does *not* introduce a new data type, but only an alternative for an existing type. An object of type `word` is equivalent to a list of characters in all respects.

Type synonyms can be used in the declarations of functions, new data types or further type synonyms. Thus the `reverse` function which we wrote for problem 13 of chapter 3 might be declared as:

```
dec reverse : word -> word ;
```

There are no specific constructors for objects of type `word`, and when we require one in a program, it must be written as a list of characters:

```
reverse "tang" ;
```

The type-checking mechanism of the Hope Machine always replaces type synonyms by their values, so that the result of applying `reverse` will be reported like this:

```
"gnat" : list char
```

Equally, we can apply functions over lists of characters to words:

```
reverse "way" <> reverse "den" ;
"yawned" : list char
```

The right-hand side of a type synonym declaration can be any valid type expression involving primitive or previously defined types. It can also contain type synonyms introduced by earlier `type` declarations, for instance:

```
type fixed     == num ;
type floating  == fixed # fixed ;
type operation == floating # floating -> floating ;
```

The Hope Machine treats the type `operation` as completely equivalent to:

```
( num # num ) # ( num # num ) -> ( num # num )
```

This definition of floating-point numbers should be compared with that introduced in §4.6. There we introduced a new data type whose constructor `flo` could be applied to a pair of numbers to yield an object of type `float`. Here we have only introduced a new *name* for an existing type, so that floating-point numbers and pairs of numbers are objects of identical types.

The type synonym has given us the benefit of making the program more concise and easier to understand without the trouble of inventing new constructors for floating-point numbers. However, there is a hidden drawback, because pairs of numbers and floating-point numbers are no longer *distinct* types, so the type-checking mechanism cannot help us if we mistakenly apply a function over floating-point numbers to a pair of numbers or vice-versa.

4.14 Non-linear data structures

When a recursive data type has constructors with a single argument of the type being defined, each constructor application extends an instance of the type by one item, so its size is proportional to the number of constructors in the expression defining it. It is called a *linear* data structure and is effectively equivalent to (or *isomorphic with*) a list. We shall now examine an important class of recursive data types whose constructors can have more than one argument of the type being defined. Each constructor application extends an instance of the type by two or more items. The size of a data structure defined by n applications of an m-item constructor is proportional to m^n; hence the structure is said to be *non-linear*. Non-linear data structures are often called *trees* because they branch into two or more with each constructor application. The following declaration defines a two-branched (or *binary*) tree which can contain numbers:

```
data binary == end num ++ limb ( binary # binary ) ;
```

The constructor `end` defines a tree in terms of a single number, whilst `limb` defines a tree in terms of two other trees. This expression defines a binary tree of numbers:

```
limb ( limb ( end 1 , limb ( end 2 , end 3 ) ) , end 4 )
```

When we write programs which use trees, it is often convenient to visualise them as two-dimensional structures. We might imagine the tree defined by the expression above to look like this:

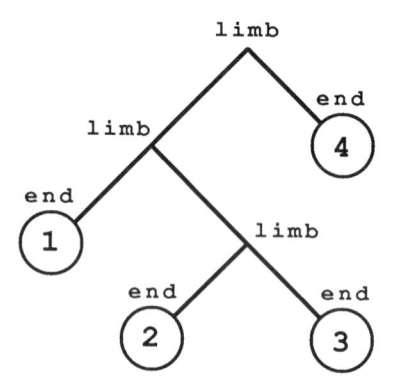

[Tree diagram showing:
- Root: limb
  - Left: limb
    - Left: end 1
    - Right: limb
      - Left: end 2
      - Right: end 3
  - Right: end 4]

The constructor names are shown to emphasise that they can be regarded as labels for the data objects to which they are applied. For obvious reasons, the two arguments of the limb constructor are called the *left* and *right subtrees* respectively. The branch points are usually known as *nodes* and the ends of the branches as *leaves*.

Every function over binary trees will have the same form, in the same way that every function over lists (and other linear data structures) has the same form. We can see this in the following function which adds up all the numbers contained in a binary tree of numbers:

```
dec total : binary -> num ;
--- total ( end n )              <= n ;
--- total ( limb ( l , r ) )     <= total l + total r ;
```

The equation for the recursive case will always contain *two* self-applications, one to process each of the two subtrees. As with other user-defined data types, any required tree must be written as an expression using constructors. The lack of a shorthand notation is not really a drawback, because (like long numbers) most tree values used in programs will be defined by function applications. To add up all the numbers in the example tree above we might write:

```
total ( limb ( limb ( end 1 ,
                      limb ( end 2 ,
                             end 3 ) ) ,
               end 4 ) ) ;
10 : num
```

In the example application, the expression defining the tree has been laid out to suggest its structure. The left of the expression corresponds to the top of the diagram and vice-versa. This means that the expression actually represents the mirror image of the diagram rotated 90° anti-clockwise; however, it is considered to be equivalent to the diagram because the *relative* positions of the components is the same in both.

4.15 Searching binary trees

An important use of binary trees is to speed up the process of searching for a particular data item in a large data structure. Suppose that a company payroll is represented using a list staff (as suggested in §4.7) and that we wish to retrieve an arbitrary record given its position in the list. Exercise 9 of chapter 3 introduced the problem of retrieving the *i*th element from a list. Here is a similar function, adapted for a payroll data structure whose elements are numbered from 0:

```
dec find : list staff # num -> staff ;
--- find ( s :: p , 0 )          <= s ;
--- find ( s :: p , succ e )     <= find ( p , e ) ;
```

The payroll is assumed to contain at least the required number of elements. Finding the *i*th element of a payroll will require *i* self-applications of find in addition to the top-level application. Finding the *i*th element of an *n*-element payroll will require an average of $n/2$ self-applications if values of *i* are distributed randomly between 0 and *n*-1, hence find has O(*n*) cost.

We can obtain much faster access to the items by representing the payroll as a binary tree. The declaration of binary restricts a tree to containing numbers at its leaves, so we must introduce a new data type to hold staff records. Also, end and limb have been used as constructor names for the type binary, so we must choose different constructor names for the new type of tree if both types are to be used in the same program. Here is a suitable declaration:

```
data payroll == record staff ++
                pair ( payroll # payroll ) ;
```

and here is a diagram of an 8-element payroll:

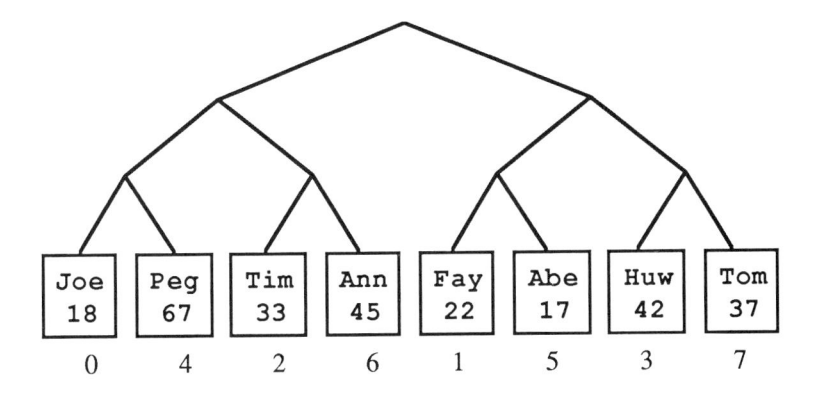

We say that the *depth* of this binary tree is 3 because each data item is incorporated into the tree by 3 applications of the pair constructor. The tree is also said to be *balanced* because it has no short branches and each node contains exactly the same number of data items in its left and right subtrees. As in the list representation of the payroll, the items at the leaves are implicitly numbered from 0 to 7, but they are arranged in the order 0, 4, 2, 6, 1, 5, 3, 7. This arrangement has the property that leaves with increasing numbers appear alternately in the left and right subtrees and that every *subtree* shares this property. We can locate an item in the tree given its index number by checking if the index is odd (using odd from §2.4) and searching the appropriate subtree for the item whose index number is half the original value:

```
dec locate : payroll # num -> staff ;
--- locate ( record e , i ) <= e ;
--- locate ( pair ( l , r ) , i )
    <= if odd i
         then locate ( r , i div 2 )
         else locate ( l , i div 2 ) ;
```

A balanced binary tree of depth n contains 2^n items at its leaves, and any one can be found by n applications of locate. This does not appear much better than find, because we need 3 applications of locate to get a record from an 8-item tree, but only 4 of find (on average) to get one from an 8-item list. However, doubling the size of a balanced binary tree only increases its depth by 1 and getting a record takes one extra application of locate, while doubling the length of a list requires twice as many applications of find. The cost of locate is $O(\log_2 n)$; getting a record from a 1024-item balanced binary tree takes 10 applications of locate, whereas getting an record from a 1024-element list takes an average of 512 applications of find. The cost difference becomes even more dramatic as the amount of data increases.

In practice, the number of records in the payroll we want to search will rarely be an exact power of 2. However, it is still possible to arrange it as a binary tree and search it with locate. For instance, the first 6 elements of the payroll above can be represented by the following tree:

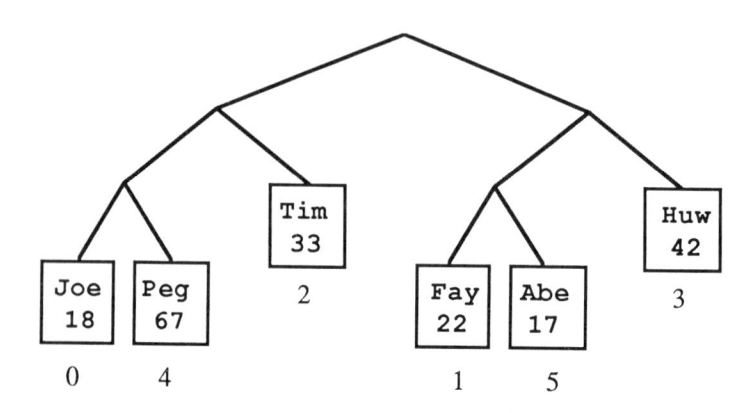

This has the same depth as a tree containing 8 elements (the next higher power of two) and is a similar shape. Leaves corresponding to non-existent records (*i.e.* those with index numbers greater than 6) have been removed and each subtree pruned in this way has been replaced by its remaining leaf. No branch is more than one short of the maximum depth, hence the tree is as nearly balanced as possible.

4.16 Building a balanced binary tree
It is not actually necessary to perform the rearrangement described above, as the tree can be constructed using a general method which does not require the number of elements to be an exact power of two. We shall assume that the items we want in the tree are initially held in a list, and design a function which converts a list into an equivalent tree. Here is a suitable declaration, together with an equation for the base case of a singleton list:

```
dec employ : list staff -> payroll ;
--- employ [ s ] <= record s ;
```

Note that employ is not defined over the empty list, since this has no equivalent binary tree. As we saw in §4.7, every realistic organisation will have at least one employee! The general-case equation will construct its result using pair, supplying two recursively constructed subtrees as arguments. The left subtree will contain all the odd-numbered elements of the initial input list, and the right subtree all the even-numbered ones, so we must divide the input list into two sublists containing alternate elements. Here is a suitable function:

```
dec alternates : list staff ->
                   list staff # list staff ;
--- alternates nil     <= ( nil , nil ) ;
--- alternates [ s ] <= ( [ s ] , nil ) ;
--- alternates ( s :: ( t :: u ) )
    <= ( s :: o , t :: e )
        where ( o , e ) == alternates u ;
```

The equations for empty and singleton lists are base cases only; we must not apply alternates at the top level to lists containing less than two items, to ensure that both final result lists are non-empty. The first sublist will be the same length as the second sublist or one element longer. We can now write down the general-case equation for employ, which covers lists containing at least *two* elements:

```
--- employ ( L & s :: ( t :: u ) )
    <= pair ( employ o , employ e )
        where ( o , e ) == alternates L ;
```

The right-hand side contains one self-application to build each subtree. The arguments are the sublists formed by applying `alternates` to the original list. The pattern synonym L avoids the need to refer to the input list again as (s :: (t :: u)) in the application of `alternates`. A top-level application of `alternates` with an empty or singleton list could generate a pair containing at least one empty sublist, but this possibility will not arise because `employ` applies `alternates` only to lists containing at least two elements. We can test `employ` by constructing the payroll tree shown in §4.15 from the corresponding 6-element list, and retrieving an element:

```
locate ( t , 2 )
  where t ==
    employ [ st ( "Joe" , 18 ) , st ( "Fay" , 22 ) ,
             st ( "Tim" , 33 ) , st ( "Huw" , 42 ) ,
             st ( "Peg" , 67 ) , st ( "Abe" , 17 ) ] ;

st ( "Tim" , 33 ) : staff
```

This might seem unnecessarily complex, but it not actually possible to build the tree any other way. We cannot (for example) add new records one at a time to an existing tree because each addition effectively renumbers the existing components, requiring them to occupy quite different positions in the new tree.

4.17 Flattening a balanced binary tree

Often when we examine the contents of a tree we are not interested in its structure, but only in the order of the values at the leaves (or *fringe*). We can see the order of the fringe values by converting (or *flattening*) the tree into the equivalent list. Here is a suitable function:

```
dec records : payroll -> list staff ;
--- records ( record e ) <= [ e ] ;
--- records ( pair ( l , r ) )
      <= records l <> records r ;
```

Once again the form of the function follows the general plan for functions over binary trees, with the recursive case containing two self-applications, each applied to one of the subtrees. This simple definition of tree flattening may not always give the information we require; the application:

```
records t
  where t ==
    employ [ st ( "Joe" , 18 ) , st ( "Fay" , 22 ) ,
             st ( "Tim" , 33 ) , st ( "Huw" , 42 ) ,
             st ( "Peg" , 67 ) , st ( "Abe" , 17 ) ]
```

yields the list:

```
[ st ( "Joe" , 18 ) , st ( "Peg" , 67 ) , st ( "Tim" , 33 ) ,
  st ( "Fay" , 22 ) , st ( "Abe" , 17 ) , st ( "Huw" , 42 )   ]
```

However, we might want to see the values in a staff tree in "numerical" order, *i.e.* the same order as the list from which it was constructed. In this case, the flattening rules are the inverse of the construction rules: the subtrees are flattened (as with the simple flattening), but instead of appending the resulting lists, they are *interleaved*, since they represent the odd and even elements of the original list:

```
dec numerical : payroll -> list staff ;
--- numerical ( record e ) <= [ e ] ;
--- numerical ( pair ( l , r ) )
       <= interleave ( numerical l , numerical r ) ;
```

The auxiliary function `interleave` which combines the sublists must effectively perform the inverse operation to `alternates`:

```
dec interleave : list staff # list staff ->
                    list staff ;
--- interleave ( nil , nil )  <= nil ;
--- interleave ( o , nil )    <= o ;
--- interleave ( nil , e )    <= e ;
--- interleave ( h :: o , i :: e )
       <= h :: ( i :: interleave ( o , e ) ) ;
```

Four equations are given for completeness (*cf.* §3.16), but the second and third overlap with the first, which can be omitted. We can also omit the third equation, since the first list will never be shorter than the second as a consequence of the way we defined `alternates` in §4.16. The general-case equation selects elements from each list in turn without regard to their values.

4.18 Evaluating expressions using trees

Trees are extremely useful data structures in practical programs. As a further example of their use, we shall construct a more sophisticated program for evaluating arithmetic expressions. Previously (in §4.4, §4.11 and §4.12) we represented expressions as *linear* data structures, corresponding to the way they might be entered into a pocket calculator. Now we shall represent expressions as binary trees, corresponding more closely to the way in which they are evaluated. These trees will be slightly different from those we have seen so far, because they will allow data items to be held both in the leaves and at the *nodes*. Each operation will be held in a node and its operands in the two subtrees. For example, the expression 2 + 3 will be represented by the tree:

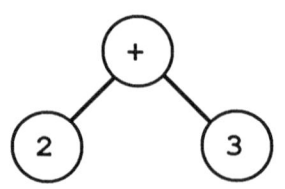

The advantage of the tree representation becomes apparent when we consider expressions containing embedded subexpressions which must be evaluated first. In the linear representation of §4.11, we introduced an extra constructor term to identify subexpressions. In the tree representation, a subexpression is simply represented as a subtree. An expression such as 2 + 3 × 4 will be represented by the tree:

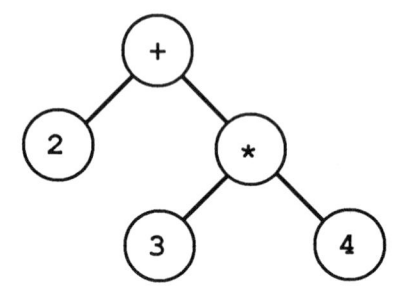

Operations like * which are evaluated earlier appear *lower* in the tree. It will be clear from the examples above that the nodes will always contain operators and the leaves operands. This means we can distinguish between them on the basis of the tree constructors alone, and dispense with the item data type. We are now in a position to write a declaration for a suitable data type:

```
data expression ==
    rand num ++ rator ( char # expression # expression ) ;
```

The trees shown above can now be defined by the expressions:

```
rator ( '+' , rand 2 ,
               rand 3 )
```

and:

```
rator ( '+' , rand 2 ,
        rator ( '*' , rand 3 ,
                      rand 4 ) )
```

As in §4.14, the expressions represent the mirror images of the diagrams rotated 90° anti-clockwise. Here is an evaluation function for expression trees:

```
    dec eval : expression -> num ;
    --- eval ( rand n ) <= n ;
    --- eval ( rator ( '+' , l , r ) ) <= eval l + eval r ;
```

The second equation evaluates only addition operations; other dyadic operations can be handled by further equations of the same form. In the earlier linear solutions, the implicit bracketing in an expression such as 2 + 3 - 4 was imposed by the evaluation function, which processed the elements of the list from left to right. In the tree representation, the bracketing (and hence the evaluation order) is always specified by the structure of the tree itself; the expression 2 + 3 - 4 is represented by the tree:

```
    rator ( '-' , rator ( '+' , rand 2 ,
                                 rand 3 ) ,
                  rand 4 )
```

The lower level nodes of the trees will be evaluated by recursive applications of the evaluation function *before* those at higher levels.

4.19 Choosing the best data structure

For many programs we will have a choice of data types to represent the data which they manipulate. In §4.7 we represented the payroll of an organisation using a linear data structure (a list of staff records) and used the function find to retrieve a record from a specified position with $O(n)$ cost for an n-employee payroll. In §4.15 we saw how a non-linear data structure (an ordered balanced binary tree) allowed faster access. with the function locate retrieving a specified record with $O(\log_2 n)$ cost.

This implies that the tree is "better" representation of a payroll than a list, but the situation is different if we want to add a new staff record at a specified position. We can do this fairly easily with the list representation, perhaps using the following function:

```
    dec inject : staff # num # list staff -> list staff ;
    --- inject ( s , 0 , l ) <= e :: l ;
    --- inject ( s , succ n , h :: t )
            <= h :: inject ( s , n , t ) ;
```

The list elements are implicitly numbered from 0, hence the application:

```
    inject ( st ( "Joe" , 18 ) , 1 , S )
       where S == [ st ( "Peg" , 67 ) , st ( "Tim" , 33 ) ]
```

yields the list:

```
    [ st ( "Peg" , 67 ) , st ( "Joe" , 18 ) , st ( "Tim" , 33 ) ]
```

and the elements following the new insertion are effectively renumbered. Like `find`, `inject` has O(*n*) cost on average.

Adding a new element to the ordered balanced binary tree is less straightforward, because the position of an element in the tree is determined by its (implicit) number, so the renumbering caused by the insertion will change the shape of the tree. A crude but simple way of inserting a new element into a tree is to flatten it into a list (using `numerical` from §4.17), add the new element using `inject` and then reconstruct the tree in its entirety (using `employ` from §4.16). Here we insert an employee e at position n of a payroll p:

```
employ ( inject ( e , n , numerical p ) )
```

The overall cost of evaluating this expression is dominated by the $O(n.\log_2 n)$ cost of `numerical` and `employ`. A further drawback of the tree representation is that it must be flattened (again with $O(n.\log_2 n)$ cost) before we can visualise it, whereas the list can be visualised directly.

It will be clear from this discussion that neither data structure emerges clearly as the best representation of a payroll. The basic operations of construction, search, update and visualisation have different cost behaviour, depending on the chosen representation, so the actual cost of a payroll program will depend on the relative frequencies of the operations. Further, the "big-Oh" concept of cost only tells us how the cost *increases* with the size of the data structure, and says nothing about the *absolute* cost of a program; for small values of *n*, evaluating a program in O(*n*) time may actually be *faster* than evaluating it in $O(\log_2 n)$ time. We may be prepared to tolerate the relative inefficiency of the list payroll when the number of records is small, or when the number of updates is large. Conversely, we might choose the tree organisation if the number of records is large, but then only if the number of updates is small compared to the number of searches.

Finally, there is an aspect of cost which we have not considered so far, which is the cost of the programmer's time. Although this cost is constant for a given program, it is very significant in practice, because computers are cheap (and getting cheaper) whereas programmers' time is expensive (and getting more expensive). Reducing the cost of evaluation has to be balanced against the cost of writing what may be a larger and more complex program. In many cases this extra cost is not justified, perhaps because the amount of data is small, or the program is only used a small number of times. A program which is expensive to write and cheap to evaluate can only be justified if it will be used frequently, or if the equivalent cheap-to-write program is too expensive to evaluate at all.

4.20 Delaying the decision

Often when we begin to develop a program we do not fully understand the problem which we are trying to solve, and have little idea how the program will be used in practice. The discussion in §4.19 suggests that the cost of evaluating a payroll-processing program will be determined by the payroll representation, but also that we cannot predict the best representation. In these circumstances, we would like to delay choosing a representation for as long as possible. A further complication is that programs are often modified after a long period of use to add new facilities, often by someone who is not the original author. However long we delay the decision, our choice may be invalidated by later changes.

The wisest course of action is to try and write our program so that the payroll representation can be changed at *any time* with as little modification as possible. We can do this by minimising the number of functions which depend upon the actual data type chosen. The functions which do will perform a small set of operations which we think of as characteristic of payrolls, such as search, record addition, record deletion, construction and visualisation. The major part of the program must be written so that references to the payroll are only made using these functions, and never using the constructors of the data type chosen for the representation. In this way the payroll program is rendered largely independent of the payroll representation.

The functions which actually manipulate the data structure representing the payroll are called *access functions* and are the only parts of the program which use the constructors of the chosen data type. The payroll is called an *abstract data type* because its properties are defined by the properties of the access functions rather than the constructors of the *concrete data type* used to represent it.

Using this technique, we have the possibility of changing the representation of the abstract data type later, perhaps when we know how the program behaves in practice, or if we discover a better representation. When the properties of an abstract data type are complex, many access functions will be required, and it may be desirable to write two classes of access function. One class will refer directly to the constructors of the representation type, whilst the remainder will always use functions from the first class. This reduces the number of functions which have to be changed if it is decided later to change the representation of the abstract data type.

Abstract data types also offer a convenient and safe way of dividing the work of writing a large program among a team of programmers. The access functions (and hence the properties of the abstract data types themselves) will be defined first. The program and the access procedures can then be written by different programmers with the confidence that design decisions made later by an individual will not affect the work of other team members.

4.21 An abstract data type example

As an example of abstract data types we shall look at one way of implementing a *lookup table* in which words are associated with numeric values. Given a particular word, the corresponding numeric value can be retrieved from the table (or 0 if the word is not present). It should also be possible to update an existing lookup table by adding new entries to it. The table will itself be defined by updating an initially empty lookup table (one containing no words). We shall require three access functions to specify the operations of creating an empty table, adding a word-value pair and finding the value of a given word. Here are suitable declarations:

```
dec empty  : table ;
dec update : entry # table -> table ;
dec lookup : word # table -> num ;
```

Note the nulladic function empty; we have previously seen nulladic *constructor* functions (*e.g.* in §4.1), but this is the first time we have encountered one which is defined by equations. Note also that we have not yet defined the data types table, entry and word. In a real program we would need to declare these before using them in type expressions, but they have been deliberately left until later to emphasise that the properties of the access functions are decided upon *before* choosing a representation for the objects they manipulate. Rather than defining a new data type, we shall choose a simple representation in terms of primitive types:

```
type word  == list char ;
type entry == word # num ;
type table == list entry ;
```

The use of type synonyms serves two purposes. The first is to make it clear when (for instance) lists of characters are being used in the program to represent words rather than for some other purpose. The second is to allow the representation of a data type to be changed later with a minimum of alteration to the program. This is achieved by declaring all functions over abstract types using type synonyms, and performing all operations on data with access functions. The data representation can then be changed by changing only the table declaration and the equations of the three access functions. No changes are required in any other part of the program. Possible definitions of the access functions are given below for completeness:

```
--- empty <= nil ;

--- update ( ( w , n ) , t ) <= ( w , n ) :: t ;

--- lookup ( w , nil ) <= 0 ;
--- lookup ( x , ( w , n ) :: t )
    <= if x = w
       then n
       else lookup ( x , t ) ;
```

Since there are no constructors for type synonyms, all patterns in the access functions use the constructors of the underlying primitive types. In particular, the base-case equation for lookup uses the list constructor nil. We might be tempted to use empty in this context, but this is not allowed, because it is not a constructor.

Lookup tables can now be created by applications of update to an empty table and searched with lookup. For example:

```
lookup ( "B" , t )
  where t == update ( ( "A" , 1 ) ,
          update ( ( "B" , 2 ) , empty ) ) ;
2 : num
```

4.22 Review
Here is a summary of the main points introduced in this chapter:

- New types of data object are introduced by naming their constructor functions in a data declaration. The constructors of user-defined data types can be used in patterns.

- User-defined data objects can be used as the components of primitive data structures such as lists and tuples.

- Constant values are represented by nulladic constructors. Constructors can also have one or more arguments of any primitive or user-defined type. Dyadic constructors can be defined and used as infix operations.

- The constructors of recursive types have objects of the type being defined as parameters. The constructors of a linear data type have one parameter of the type being defined. Those of non-linear data types have two or more.

- The constructors of two or more mutually recursive data types are declared simultaneously using the with construction. The constructors of each type can take objects of the other type as parameters.

- Non-integral numbers can be represented as tuples using the rational or floating-point conventions. Arbitrarily large integers can be represented as linear data structures.

- Alternative names can be introduced for existing types using the type declaration.

- Large collections of data can be accessed efficiently by representing them as balanced binary trees. Methods of constructing and flattening balanced binary trees have been introduced.

- Abstract data types have properties defined by access functions. They allow programs to be independent of the data representation.

4.23 Exercises

1. Define a data type `light` suitable for representing the successive states (red, red-and-amber, green, amber) of a set of traffic lights. Define a function `change` which advances the state of a set of traffic lights.

2. Write functions `both` and `either` to perform logical conjunction (*and*), and disjunction (*or*) on pairs of switches as defined in §4.1.

3. Define infix operations `plus, minus` and `over` to find the sum, difference and quotient respectively of two floating-point numbers as defined in §4.6.

4. Use `plus, minus` and `over` to define a function `root` which finds the square root of a real number. An algorithm familiar from school mathematics is to first *guess* the answer. For a number n, a good first guess is $n/2$. For any value r, a more accurate value is given by the expression $1/2 \, (r + n/r)$. This calculation is then repeated until the difference between two successive values is zero.

5. Write a function `younger` to compare two staff records (as defined in §4.7) and return the record containing the younger of the two employees. Now redefine the `youngest` function of §4.7 using `younger`.

6. The `calc` function of §4.11 requires a large number of equations to cover all possible combinations of operations and operands. A simpler (2-equation) version uses auxiliary functions `operand` of type `item -> num` to evaluate a single operand and `operator` of type `num # char # num -> num` to evaluate an arbitrary operation whose arguments are already evaluated. Write the functions `operand` and `operator` and the new version of `calc` which uses them.

7. Write a function `minor` which uses your `younger` function from exercise 5 to discover the youngest employee in an organisation represented as a `payroll` (as defined in §4.15).

8. Write a function `cut` to divide a list of numbers in two after a specified element, returning the two sublists as a pair. `cut ( 2 , [ 1 , 2 , 3 , 4 , 5 ] )` evaluates to `[ 1 , 2 ] , [ 3 , 4 , 5 ]`.

9. Write a function `build` (like `employ` from §4.16) which will construct a balanced `binary` (as defined in §4.14) from a non-empty list of numbers by using `cut` from exercise 8 to split the input list at each level. Assume that `length` (from §3.11) is available.

10. Write a function `ends` (like `records` from §4.17) which will convert a `binary` to a `list num`, preserving the ordering of the numbers at the fringe.

11. Write a function swap which will interchange the subtrees of a binary at every level. What is the value of ends (swap (build *somelist*)) in general?

12. Write a function improve to convert the linear form of arithmetic expressions from §4.11 to the equivalent objects of type expression from §4.18.

13. Extend the definition of the expression data type and the eval function of §4.18 to handle expressions which contain monadic operations (such as negation, represented by \).

14. A *queue* is a data structure which can contain zero or more elements, ordered by their arrival times. Define an abstract data type to represent queues of customers represented by words containing their names. Provide access functions nobody to create an empty queue, arrive to add a new customer to the rear of an existing queue, first to find the first (least recently arrived) customer in a queue and serve to remove the first customer from the front of a non-empty queue.

Chapter 5

More General Types

5.1 Why lists are powerful

During the course of the previous chapter it will have become apparent that there is something special about lists which is not shared by the kind of linear data structures which we can define ourselves, because every instance of a user-defined linear data structure must contain the same type of component. Thus in §4.10 we defined the type `big` to represent indefinitely long integers as sequences of one or more decimal digits and in §4.12 the type `series` for representing arithmetic expressions as sequences of one or more operands. In each case the data structure was restricted to containing one kind of object (a `num` and a `item` respectively), because the type of the component object was specified in the declaration:

    data big == dig num ++ extra (big # num) ;

    data series == more (item # series) ++ only item ;

Lists are more powerful than user-defined data types because we can create a list containing *any kind* of object, provided of course that all the objects in any particular list have the *same* type. The reason for this generality is that list constructors are *polymorphic* and can be applied *with the same meaning* to any type of argument, for instance:

    3 :: (4 :: (5 :: nil)) ;
    [3 , 4 , 5] : list num

```
true :: ( false :: nil ) ;
[ true , false ] : list truval
```

whilst the constructors of the type `big` (for example) can only be applied to numeric arguments.

5.2 Constructed types

Until now we have presented lists containing various types of object as primitive data types but have been deliberately vague about the meaning of the word `list` itself. In fact `list` is not the name of a type at all, but a *type constructor*. A type constructor is used to introduce a new type by applying it to an existing one within a type expression. An application of a type constructor looks just like a conventional function application, and we have seen many examples already. Here is another:

```
list truval
```

The type constructor `list` is applied to the primitive type `truval`, which is called a *type constant*. Constructed types represent anonymous *type values* and are usually referred to by the expressions which define them (*e.g.* `list truval` in the example above), but they can also be named using a type synonym (*cf.* §4.13), for example:

```
type bits == list truval ;
```

Although type constructor applications *look* like ordinary function applications, they differ in a very important respect. Type constructors are applied by the *type-checking* mechanism of the Hope Machine, and *not* by the reduction mechanism; all the constructed types required in a program exist (and can be checked for consistency) *before* the program is evaluated.

5.3 Universal type declarations

We can imagine that all possible types of list are defined by a (hypothetical) *universal type declaration* which looks like this:

```
data list α == nil ++ α :: list α ;
```

Here α is a *formal type parameter* representing an actual type, and is instantiated when the type constructor is applied. Thus, when `list num` appears in a type expression, we can imagine that every occurrence of α is instantiated to `num` in the universal type declaration, giving a *specific* declaration (also hypothetical) for lists of numbers:

```
data list num == nil ++ num :: list num ;
```

Formal type parameters are instantiated by the type-checking mechanism of the Hope Machine *before* the program is evaluated. The instantiation is performed separately for each type expression containing the `list` type constructor, so that α can represent a different type on each appearance. Note that this is the only way in which specific kinds of list can be introduced. We are *not* allowed to write a data definition in which type constructor is applied to an actual type on the left-hand side like the hypothetical example above.

5.4 User-defined polymorphic data types

Although a list can be used to represent any linear sequence of objects, it is not the best representation for a sequence which must always contain at least one item. This was the reason for defining the data type `series` in §4.12 and the unstated reason for defining `big` in §4.10. We shall now see how to define a *polymorphic* data type suitable for representing non-empty sequences of any type of object. The first step is to introduce a name which can be used as a formal type parameter. We do this with a declaration of the form:

```
typevar alpha ;
```

where `typevar` is a reserved word. The name `alpha` has global scope; it is called a *type variable* and can be used anywhere a formal type parameter is required. The declaration of the data type looks like this:

```
data seq alpha == one alpha ++
                 two ( alpha # seq alpha ) ;
```

and introduces `seq` as a new type constructor, also with global scope. The right-hand side introduces the data constructors in the usual way, except that their parameter types are specified by the formal type parameter. The polymorphic type itself is referred to as a `seq alpha`. Specific instances are created by applying the data constructors to objects of any primitive or user-defined type, for example:

```
two ( false , two ( false , one true ) )

two ( "turtle doves" , one "partridge in a pair tree" )

one ( one 3 )
```

The objects defined by these expressions are a `seq truval`, a `seq ( list char )` and a `seq ( seq num )` respectively. All the objects in an instance of a `seq` must have the same type; the type-checking mechanism of the Hope Machine will reject an expression such as:

```
two ( true , one "day" )
```

As an example of a use of sequences, let us see how we might use one to represent a payroll. In §4.7 we used a `list staff` and noted that the base case of a function which processed it (*e.g.* `youngest`) was not the empty list, but a singleton list representing a one-employee organisation. If we use a sequence to model the payroll we shall have a more natural base case. When we declare a function over a specific type of sequence, the type constructor is applied to an actual type in the type expression (as with functions over lists). Thus the declaration of a function to find the junior employee will be written as:

```
dec junior : seq staff -> staff ;
```

The equations for `junior` will use `seq` constructors in their left-hand side patterns; their right-hand sides will be similar to `youngest` from §4.7:

```
--- junior ( one e ) <= e ;
--- junior ( two ( st ( n , a ) , p ) )
    <= if a < y
       then st ( n , a )
       else st ( j , y )
       where st ( j , y ) == junior p ;
```

We can also use sequences as components of other data structures. For instance, using sequences, the definition of an `item` (*cf.* §4.4 and 4.11) could be written directly as:

```
data item == int num ++ op char ++ term ( seq item ) ;
```

Notice that the use of a polymorphic data type allows us to declare the `seq` and `item` data types separately, and makes it unnecessary to use `with` to declare the two types to be mutually recursive as we did in §4.12.

5.5 Data structures with polymorphic components

In the example above, the `term` constructor was parametrised with a specific type of sequence (a `seq item`) but it is also possible to incorporate a polymorphic type into another data type without instantiating its type parameter. Equally, it is possible for a data type to be only partly polymorphic, and to be parametrised with both constant and polymorphic types. A *vector* is a fixed-size linear data structure whose elements are considered to be numbered sequentially from some starting value called the *lower bound*. Specific vectors can contain different numbers of elements of different types and have different lower bounds. A polymorphic data type suitable for representing vectors of arbitrary objects might be declared as follows:

```
data vector alpha == vec ( num # list alpha ) ;
```

It is assumed that alpha has been previously declared as a type variable. The num represents the lower bound of a specific vector. Individual elements of a vector are selected by *indexing* with a numeric value, which yields the element at that position in the list. The following function will index a vector of numbers:

```
dec index : num # vector num -> num ;
--- index ( n , vec ( m , h :: t ) )
    <= if n = m
          then h
          else index ( n , vec ( m + 1 , t ) ) ;
```

5.6 Spot the deliberate mistake

The definition of index given above assumes that the selected element will be *in range*, or lie within the vector, hence there is no equation to cover the case of an empty vector. This also reflects the idea that vectors are conventionally required to contain at least one item. We might reflect this more explicitly by using a sequence as the data component of a vector, instead of a list:

```
data vector alpha == vec ( num # seq alpha ) ;
```

The index function would now be defined as follows:

```
dec index : num # vector num -> num ;
--- index ( n , vec ( m , two ( h , t ) ) )
    <= if n = m
          then h
          else index ( n , vec ( m + 1 , t ) ) ;
```

However, we must provide a second equation to cover the case of a single-element vector. This introduces the possibility that the index might be *out of range*, or specify a non-existent element:

```
--- index ( n , vec ( m , one h ) )
    <= if n = m
          then h
          else ... ;
```

The problem here is that there is no expression which we can reasonably write to specify the alternative value. Writing the equation as:

```
--- index ( n , vec ( m , one h ) ) <= h ;
```

results in a function which delivers the correct element if the index is within range, but which behaves in a very dangerous fashion if it is not, by simply delivering the last element without warning.

An attempt to select a non-existent element from a vector will always represent some kind of misunderstanding on the part of the programmer, who should be made aware of it. Paradoxically, the list representation of vectors is actually more useful because an out-of-range index will generate a vector containing an empty list, and hence a run-time error, because there is no equation to cover this case.

It is good practice to write functions which check the correctness of their arguments in this way, but it is not always easy to deal with errors which are discovered. The definition of index used the pattern-matching mechanism to detect an evaluation error by omitting the empty list equation, but this was really a piece of serendipity and is not useful as a general technique. In some cases we can force an error by the trick of writing an expression which is guaranteed to be incorrect; for example we might write the one case equation of index as:

```
---  index ( n , vec ( m , one h ) )
     <= if n = m
           then h
           else h div 0 ;
```

If the alternative expression is evaluated, it will cause a division-by-zero error to occur and terminate the program.

Both the zero-division trick and the missing equation trick are unsatisfactory from the point of view of programming style, because it is not obvious from reading the program that the programmer intends deliberate termination. In the case of the zero-division trick, the program does at least contain an explicit expression to cause termination, but in the case of the missing equation trick, termination is caused by something which is not in the program at all! We shall have more to say about error handling in §5.16 and §5.17.

5.7 Less general data structures

Suppose we need a linear data type restricted to contain arbitrary pairs. We do not simply wish to use an instance of a seq alpha, such as:

```
two ( ( 'a' , true ) , one ( 'b' , false ) )
```

because sequences are too general; the definition of the data type does not constrain the elements of the sequence to be pairs. A conventional data declaration which does this is too restrictive, because the types of the pair components must be specified explicitly. For example:

```
data pairs == solo ( char # truval ) ++
              duet ( ( char # truval ) # pairs ) ;
```

A polymorphic data declaration also appears to be too restrictive:

```
data pairs alpha ==
    solo ( alpha # alpha ) ++
    duet ( ( alpha # alpha ) # pairs alpha ) ;
```

because the consistent instantiation rule will require both components of the pair to have the same type. We can obtain the required effect by introducing a polymorphic data type with *two* formal type parameters. The left-hand side of its declaration will consist of the application of a type constructor to a pair of previously declared type variables:

```
data pairs ( alpha , beta ) == ...
```

hence the type is referred to as pairs (alpha , beta). The right-hand side introduces the data constructors as usual; their parameters are explicit pairs, but the types of the pair components are specified by the formal type parameters:

```
...  solo ( alpha # beta ) ++
     duet ( ( alpha # beta ) # pairs ( alpha , beta ) ) ;
```

Each type parameter must be instantiated with the same actual type throughout an instance of the polymorphic type, but the types can now be different, for example:

```
duet ( ( 'a' , true ) , solo ( 'b' , false ) )
```

which has the type pairs (char , truval). The types are are not *required* to be different, and we can write instances in which both components of the pair have the same type, for example:

```
duet ( ( 1 , 2 ) , solo ( 3 , 4 ) )
```

which has the type pairs (num , num). However, the following expression will be rejected by the type-checking mechanism because beta is not consistently instantiated:

```
duet ( ( 1 , "two" ) , solo ( 2 , true ) )
```

whilst the following expression will be rejected because the arguments of the constructors are not pairs:

```
duet ( "Gilbert" , solo "Sullivan" )
```

5.8 Non-linear polymorphic types

Polymorphic types make programs more concise because they require fewer data declarations, and they also make programs easier to understand, because there are fewer constructor names. This is important, because constructor names have global scope, and their meanings must be borne in mind when reading the whole program. In §4.14 we introduced a type `binary` to represent a binary tree of numbers, and in §4.15 a type `payroll` to represent a binary tree of staff records. Not only did we have to write two declarations, but we also had to invent *four* constructor names. Both kinds of tree can be represented using the following polymorphic data type:

```
data bin alpha == tip alpha ++
                  fork ( bin alpha # bin alpha ) ;
```

This assumes that `alpha` has already been declared as a type variable. As usual, it must represent the same type throughout a single instance of a `bin`. For example:

```
tip ( st ( "Methuselah" , 969 ) )

fork ( tip 3 , tip 4 )
```

which are of type `bin staff` and `bin num` respectively.

5.9 Ordered binary trees

In §4.15 we saw how balanced binary trees can be used to organise large quantities of data so that individual items can be located quickly. Starting with a list, the position of each element in the tree was determined by its position in the original list. We can also construct *ordered* binary trees in which the position of each element is determined by some property of the element itself. The ordered `bin num` shown below has the property that every element in the left subtree is less than or equal to any element in the right subtree, and that every subtree has the same property:

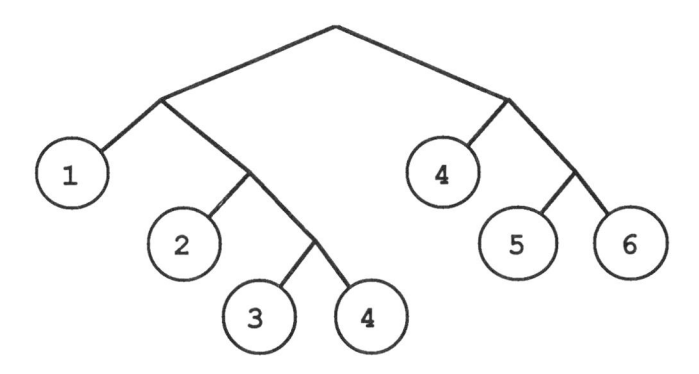

The same set of values can be arranged into a number of different binary trees ordered according to the criterion above, but the order of the values at the fringe will be the same for each. Note that ordered binary trees need not necessarily be balanced and that values which are duplicated (such as **4** above) can appear in widely separated leaves.

We can convert an ordered tree into an ordered list by flattening it in left-to-right order of the items at the fringe. The flattening function will be almost identical to the `records` function which we defined for objects of type `payroll` in §4.17, and is given below without further comment:

```
dec tips : bin num -> list num ;
--- tips ( tip n )              <= [ n ] ;
--- tips ( fork ( l , r ) ) <= tips l <> tips r ;
```

It is straightforward to construct an ordered tree if we already have a list which is ordered using the same criterion as the tree. The function will be almost identical to `build` (from exercise 9 of chapter 4), and is left as a simple exercise for the reader.

Constructing an ordered tree from an *unordered* list is a more interesting exercise, because flattening the resulting tree in left-to-right order of its fringe values effectively orders the original list. The function which constructs the tree (which we shall call `construct`) will also be similar to `build`, and will have the declaration:

```
dec construct : list num -> bin num ;
```

Since trees must contain at least one (leaf) value, the base case is a *singleton* list:

```
--- construct [ h ] <= tip h ;
```

There is no tree corresponding to an empty list. The general-case equation (also analogous to that of `build`) uses an auxiliary function analogous to `alternates` from §4.16 to partition a non-empty list into two sublists which are used to construct the left and right subtrees recursively. The partitioning function (which we shall call `split`) must generate a pair of lists such that every element of the left sublist is less than or equal to every element of the right sublist. Recursive partitioning will eventually generate singleton lists to form the leaves of the tree; thus to construct a node of the tree, the initial argument of `split` must contain at least *two* elements:

```
--- construct ( L & h :: ( i :: t ) )
    <= fork ( construct l , construct r )
       where ( l , r ) == split L ;
```

The auxiliary names `l` and `r` identify the left and right sublists formed by partitioning the initial list L. Since `construct` cannot be defined over the empty list, `split` must always generate a pair of non-empty lists.

We can partition the elements of a list by selecting one element (called the *pivot*) and placing each list element in the left sublist if it is less than or equal to the pivot, and in the right sublist if not. This suggests the following declaration for `split`:

```
        dec split : num # list num -> list num # list num ;
```

where first num parameter represents the pivot value. The application of split in construct must be changed to reflect this definition, and we must therefore choose an initial pivot value. The optimum partition produces two equal-sized sublists, which causes construct to terminate in the fewest possible ($\log_2 n$) steps. This occurs when the pivot is the median of the list (the value having an equal number of values above and below it in magnitude), which is not easy to find. However, since the elements of the list are likely to be randomly ordered, we can simply choose an *arbitrary* element as pivot, because the magnitudes of the remaining values will (on average) be distributed equally above and below it. The first value in the list is the easiest to obtain, so we shall use that as the pivot and change the general-case equation for construct to:

```
    --- construct ( h :: ( i :: t ) )
        <= fork ( construct l , construct r )
            where ( l , r ) == split ( h , i :: t ) ;
```

The general-case equation for split will take the list of remaining elements and recursively partition its tail (using the same pivot value) and finally add the head to the appropriate sublist by comparing it with the pivot:

```
    --- split ( p , h :: t )
        <= if h =< p
            then ( h :: l , r )
            else ( l , h :: r )
            where ( l , r ) == split ( p , t ) ;
```

When considering the base case of split, we must remember that the pivot value p was removed from the original list at the top level, and must eventually appear in one of the result lists. Because both result lists must be non-empty, we need two values with which to construct them. The base case will therefore be the singleton list, itself derived from a two-element list with the pivot removed:

```
    --- split ( p , [ h ] )
        <= if h =< p
            then ( [ h ] , [ p ] )
            else ( [ p ] , [ h ] ) ;
```

Although split places all values less than or equal to the pivot value in the left sublist, the pivot value itself may end up in the right sublist. However, this does not contradict the requirement that every left sublist value is less than or equal to every right sublist value.

By flattening the ordered tree (using `tips`), we obtain an ordered version of the original input list. Here is a complete function for ordering a list of numbers:

```
dec order : list num -> list num ;
--- order nil                   <= nil ;
--- order ( L & h :: t )        <= tips ( construct L ) ;
```

The base-case equation covers the case of the empty list, which cannot be partitioned using `split`, but which can be ordered without constructing a tree.

The program given above is a variant of the algorithm *Quicksort*, first described by C. A. R. Hoare in 1962. Quicksort is one of the most efficient ordering (or *sorting*) algorithms known; we can estimate its cost as follows. Partitioning an n-element list requires n-1 applications of `split`. At the next level, the two result lists are of total length n and generate a total of n-2 applications of `split` and so on, thus the cost of split is $O(n)$ at each level. A randomly ordered input list will (on average) be split in half at each level, giving a balanced tree of depth $\log_2 n$, hence the *average* cost of building an ordered tree using `split` is $O(n.\log_2 n)$.

The cost of `tips` is determined by the cost of `<>`, which is proportional to the length of its first argument list (as in the case of `join` from §3.12). The fringe of an n-element balanced tree will contain n leaves, and will be flattened into n singleton lists. The next higher level performs $n/2$ applications of `<>` each with with cost 1 (since the first argument is a singleton list in each case). The next higher level performs $n/4$ applications of `<>` each with cost 2 (since the first argument in each case is now a two-element list). Each higher level performs half as many applications of `<>`, but since the length of the argument lists doubles each time, the cost remains $n/2$ at each level. The total cost is $n/2.\log_2 n$, which is also $O(n.\log_2 n)$. The cost of `order` is the sum of the costs of `tips` and `split`, hence it is also $O(\log_2 n)$.

5.10 More general trees

In the examples of binary trees which we have seen so far, we have always constructed a complete tree from scratch by recursively partitioning a list using some criterion such as alternation or ordering. The resulting tree was then used without further alterations, either as an efficient lookup mechanism (§4.15) or converted in its entirety to a different data structure (§4.17, §5.9). However, for many applications (such as adding a new employee record to a company payroll) we shall need to construct trees by adding individual items to an existing tree. It is possible to add extra items to the type of tree which we have used so far, but very difficult to preserve a particular ordering. There is no way of deciding where the new item belongs in the tree without examining all the leaf values, and considerable rearrangement of the tree may be required after we have discovered where to place it. The simplest way to insert a new item is to flatten the tree into the equivalent list, add the item to the list and then to reconstruct the entire tree; however, this will be very expensive if we need to make more than a few additions.

The insertion problem can be greatly simplified by using a binary tree like the one used for evaluating expressions in §4.18, which is capable of holding data in its nodes as well as in its leaves. Here is a polymorphic data type suitable for representing trees of this kind:

```
data tree alpha == null ++ leaf alpha ++
                   node ( alpha # tree alpha #
                                  tree alpha ) ;
```

For reasons which will become clear shortly, there is an extra constructor to cover the case of trees containing *no* objects at all.

An ordered tree of this type has the property that every `node` value is greater than any value in its left subtree and less than or equal to every value in its right subtree. Here is a picture of an ordered `tree num`, with `node` values shown in circular boxes and `leaf` values in square boxes:

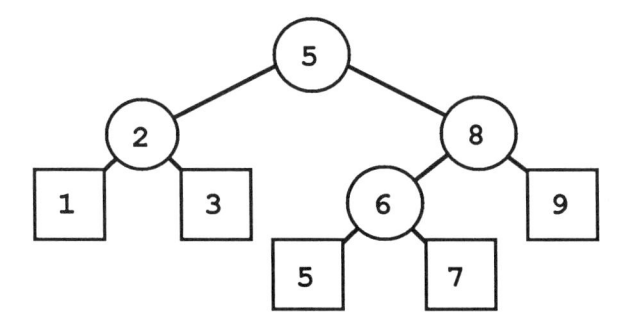

Once again, duplicated values (such as **5** above) may widely separated, and may appear either in a node or a leaf. The useful feature of this kind of binary tree is that it is much easier to add an extra number to an ordered tree, because the node value gives information about the range of values in each of its subtrees and can be used to guide the insertion. Values which are less than the node value must be inserted into the left subtree, otherwise into the right subtree. Here is a function for inserting a new element into an ordered binary tree:

```
dec insert : num # tree num -> tree num ;
--- insert ( n , node ( v , l , r ) )
    <= if n < v
       then node ( v , insert ( n , l ) , r )
       else node ( v , l , insert ( n , r ) ) ;
```

When we come to write the equation for inserting into a `leaf`, we can see the reason for introducing the constructor `null`. In this situation we have only two values with which to construct a three-element tree, hence one of the subtrees cannot contain a value at all:

```
    --- insert ( n , leaf v' )
        <= if n < v
              then node ( v , leaf n , null )
              else node ( v , null , leaf n ) ;
```

Insertion into the empty tree is straightforward:

```
    --- insert ( n , null ) <= leaf n ;
```

We can now see that the `leaf` constructor is superfluous, because leaves can be represented as nodes with *two* empty subtrees. This representation results in slightly larger trees (because every tree will now have a fringe of empty trees, which increases its depth by one). The ordered binary tree of numbers pictured above can also be represented as follows:

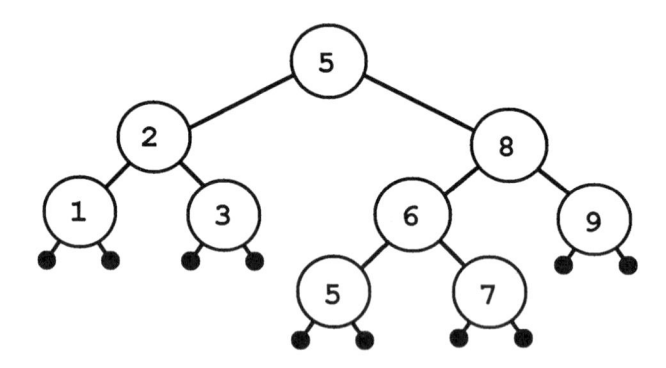

where the small solid circles represent empty subtrees. In spite of the increase in size, the new representation is preferable to that using three-constructor trees because fewer equations are needed in functions over trees. We shall therefore modify the declaration of the `tree` datatype to:

```
    data tree alpha == null ++
                      node ( alpha # tree alpha #
                                     tree alpha ) ;
```

The definition of `insert` must also be modified by removing the `leaf` equation and changing the equation for insertion into an empty tree to:

```
    --- insert ( n , null )
        <= node ( n , null , null ) ;
```

The number of self-applications required to insert a new element depends on the depth of the branch into which the new element is inserted. When the tree is perfectly balanced, all branches have the minimum depth; this is $1+\log_2(n+1)$ for an n-element tree with empty trees at the fringe. The cost of inserting an element into a balanced tree is therefore $O(\log_2 n)$.

Items can be located rapidly in an ordered binary tree by taking advantage of the property used to determine the ordering. The following function checks an ordered tree of numbers to discover whether it holds a specified value:

```
dec holds  : tree num # num -> truval ;
--- holds  ( null , i ) <= false ;
--- holds  ( node ( v , l , r ) , i )
    <= if i < v
          then holds ( l , i )
          else if i > v
                  then holds ( r , i )
                  else true ;
```

`holds` examines only one value at each level in the tree, hence for a perfectly balanced tree its cost is $O(\log_2 n)$. In comparison, locating a specific value in a linear data structure requires $n/2$ items to be examined on average and has $O(n)$ cost.

5.11 More manipulations on trees

The new kind of binary tree can be used for efficiently searching large quantities of data, with the added advantage of being able to add new elements. It can also be used define an efficient sorting method called *insertion sort*. The first step is to construct an ordered binary tree from the data values to be sorted. We can do this by taking the unsorted values one at a time from a linear data structure (such as a list) and inserting them into an initially empty tree. In the following example the objects to be sorted are assumed to be numbers. This function transfers all the elements of a list:

```
dec transfer : tree num # list num -> tree num ;
--- transfer ( T , nil )   <= T ;
--- transfer ( T , h :: t )
    <= insert ( h , transfer ( T , t ) ) ;
```

The top-level application will be:

```
transfer ( null , L ) where L == the list to be sorted ;
```

If the numbers in the list L are randomly ordered, insertions will tend to occur equally in right and left subtrees of T, which will grow in a balanced way and thus have the minimum depth for a given number of elements. The cost of building an *n*-element tree is thus $O(n.\log_2 n)$. A sorted list is obtained by flattening the tree; this is similar to flattening the binary trees of §5.8, except that each node value must be incorporated between its two (flattened) subtrees. We must also add an equation to cover the `null` constructor and remove the equation for the `leaf` constructor:

```
dec flatten : tree num -> list num ;
--- flatten. null <= nil ;
--- flatten ( node ( v , l , r ) )
        <= flatten l <> ( v :: flatten r ) ;
```

Sorting is specified by composing applications of `transfer` and `flatten` together. Unlike Quicksort, the empty list is no longer a special case, so a sorting function will only have one equation. Whilst it is not therefore strictly necessary to define a function, it is still good programming style to "package" the expression into a single-equation function to remind a reader of the program of its intended effect:

```
dec sort : list num -> list num ;
--- sort l <= flatten ( transfer ( null , l ) ) ;
```

The cost of `transfer` is $O(n.\log_2 n)$ for randomly ordered data, and the cost of `flatten` is $O(n.\log_2 n)$ for the balanced trees which would be built from randomly ordered data. The cost of `sort` is the sum of the two costs, hence it is also $O(n.\log_2 n)$ for randomly ordered data.

5.12 More powerful functions

The use of type parameters allows the same declaration and constructor names to be used to define an infinite "family" of data types with analogous structures. However, functions which we have seen so far have been restricted to operating on one specific member of the family. Thus `tips` in §5.9 is of type `bin num -> list num` and cannot be used to flatten a binary tree containing a different type of object, such as a `bin staff`. Primitive functions over polymorphic data types (such as `<>`) do not suffer from this restriction, and can be used regardless of how the type parameter is instantiated, for example:

```
[ 1 , 2 , 3 ] <> [ 4 , 5 , 6 ] ;
[ 1 , 2 , 3 , 4 , 5 , 6 ] : list num

"teal" <> "eaves" ;
"tealeaves" : list char
```

In the first expression, `<>` has the type `list num # list num -> list num` and in the second, `list char # list char -> list char`. We can imagine that the operation is defined by a declaration of the form:

```
dec <> : list α # list α -> list α;
```

and that whenever it is used in an expression, α is instantiated with the type of the list elements to yield a hypothetical declaration such as:

```
dec <> : list num # list num -> list num ;
```

As with polymorphic data declarations, α must be instantiated consistently in any particular application of the operation. In the next section we shall see how to define our own polymorphic functions.

5.13 User-defined polymorphic functions

The length function defined in §3.11 will count the elements of a list of numbers, but it can also be used for lists containing other types of object. To declare a polymorphic version of length, it is only necessary to replace the type constant num in its declaration by a type parameter. If alpha is a previously declared type variable, we can simply change the declaration of length to:

```
dec length : list alpha -> num ;
```

The polymorphic version of length can now be applied to lists containing any type of object. The type of length in any particular expression is determined by the type of the list elements. Thus in the application:

```
length "service"
```

the type of the operand is list char, and we can imagine that alpha is instantiated to char in the declaration of length to yield the notional declaration:

```
dec length : list char -> num ;
```

We are able to make length into a polymorphic function because the equations defining it make no use of the value of any list element, except to check its existence using a pattern match and to count it by adding 1 to the final result of the function:

```
--- length nil         <= 0 ;
--- length ( _ :: t )  <= length t + 1 ;
```

It is also possible to write polymorphic versions of functions over lists which make use of the list elements. The function join (from §3.12) was defined over lists of numbers; here is a polymorphic version:

```
dec join : list alpha # list alpha -> list alpha ;
--- join ( nil , l )       <= l ;
--- join ( h :: t , l )    <= h :: join ( t , l ) ;
```

Although the elements of the first list appear as operands in the right-hand side expression, all operations applied to them are themselves polymorphic; these are the list constructor :: and the recursive application of join. As before, the type of `join` within an expression is determined by the element type of the operand lists, but with the restriction that only types generated by instantiating `alpha` consistently to the *same value* throughout the declaration are valid. Thus the application:

```
join ( "thin" , "king" )
```

is valid because both operands have type `list char`, and `alpha` can be consistently instantiated to `char` to yield the notional declaration:

```
dec join : list char # list char -> list char ;
```

In contrast, the application:

```
join ( "123" , [ 4 , 5 , 6 ] )
```

does not allow a consistent instantiation, and will be rejected by the type-checking mechanism of the Hope Machine. Although type parameters must be instantiated consistently within a particular application, a polymorphic function can have more than one type within a single expression. For example, in the expression:

```
length [ 1 , 2 , 3 ] + length "456"
```

`length` has the type `list num -> num` in the first term and `list char -> num` in the second. The result of both applications is a `num`, so the operands of + have the correct types and the whole expression evaluates to 6.

The essential requirement of a polymorphic function over lists is that the equations defining it must make no assumptions about the type of the list elements. If we examine the function `sum` from §3.12:

```
--- sum ( h :: t ) <= h + sum t ;
```

we see that the operation + is applied to each element of the argument list, which is constrained to be a `list num`, hence `sum` cannot be made polymorphic. This is entirely what we should expect; an expression such as `sum "thing"` would be as meaningless as `'a' + 'b'`.

5.14 More polymorphic functions over lists

Many of the functions which we have seen so far in the book can easily be converted to polymorphic form. As examples we shall examine solutions to exercises 9 and 10 of chapter 3. Exercise 9 required us to write a function `at` to return the character at position *n* in a list of at least *n* characters. Selecting a list element by its position is clearly independent of the type of the elements, so we shall write a polymorphic version of `at` which operates on a list of any type of object and returns a single object of that type; the declaration will be:

```
dec at : num # list alpha -> alpha ;
```

and assumes that `alpha` has previously been declared to be a type variable. The problem assumes that list elements are numbered starting from 0, hence the base-case equation will be:

```
--- at ( 0 , h :: t ) <= h ;
```

The general-case equation must match arguments which are greater than 0, and will use a pattern containing an application of `succ`:

```
--- at ( succ n , h :: t ) <= at ( n , t ) ;
```

It is interesting to compare the style of `at` with the more general `index` over vectors from §5.5 which used conditionals to test for specific argument values. `at` can use pattern matching for this purpose because the subscript is assumed to be within range, so we are only interested in distinguishing zero index values. The assumption also allows the equation for the empty list to be omitted.

Exercise 10 was to write a function `pos` to locate a specified character within a list of characters. At first sight, this does not seem suitable for polymorphic treatment, because we need to examine the value of each list element. However, we recollect from chapters 1 and 3 that equality is defined over any type of object, provided that both operands are the same type. It behaves like a polymorphic operation of type α # α -> `truval` (but see §5.19 however), and can be used to write a polymorphic version of `pos`. The following definition assumes that the target object will be found in the list (as specified in the original exercise) and will fail if it is not:

```
dec pos : alpha # list alpha -> num ;
--- pos ( i , h :: t ) <= if i = h
                          then 0
                          else 1 + pos ( i , t ) ;
```

5.15 More powerful polymorphic functions

Exercise 11 of chapter 3 required us to write a function `transpose` to permute the elements of a string as specified by two anagrams. For instance, `"xyz"` and `"zxy"` specify a permutation in which the last element of a 3-element list is moved to the start, so `transpose ( "ABC" , "xyz" , "zxy" )` evaluates to `"CAB"`. Each character of the result string is found by taking the character at the same position in the third string (using `at`) and finding its position in the second (using `pos`); the character at this position in the first string is the one we require. Thus the character at position 0 in the third string is `'z'`, which is at position 2 in the second string. The character at position 0 in the result string will therefore be that at position 2 in the first string, namely `'C'`. The equations for `transpose` will be as follows:

```
--- transpose ( L , 1 , nil ) <= nil ;
--- transpose ( L , 1 , h :: t )
    <= at ( pos ( h , 1 ) , L ) ::
        transpose ( L , 1 , t ) ;
```

The only function applied to the first list is the polymorphic at. Its elements are never examined, but only rearranged, hence a polymorphic version of transpose is possible. Its type might be:

```
list alpha # list char # list char -> list alpha
```

In the original definition, the required transposition was specified by two lists of characters solely for conciseness. The second list is used only by the function pos and the third matched by the : : constructor, hence it is clear that two lists of any kind can be used, provided that the same values appear in each. A fully polymorphic version of transpose might have the type:

```
list alpha # list alpha # list alpha -> list alpha
```

but this is unduly restrictive, because the consistent instantiation rule will require all three lists to contain the same kind of element. Whilst the second and third lists must have the same type, it should be possible for the first list (and hence the result of the function) to be of a *different* type. We can achieve this effect by defining the type of transpose as:

```
list alpha # list beta # list beta -> list alpha
```

where beta has previously been declared as a type variable. The instantiation rule is similar to that introduced in §5.7 for data structures: a given type parameter is instantiated with the same type throughout a specific function application, but each one can be instantiated differently. However, they are not *required* to be differently instantiated, and we can still write applications of transpose in which all the lists contain the same type of object.

5.16 More deliberate mistakes

It is clear that the operation of indexing a vector (*cf.* §5.6) does not depend on the type of element in the vector, and we might make a polymorphic version of the index function simply by changing its declaration to:

```
dec index : num # vector alpha -> alpha ;
```

This is sufficient if index makes no assumptions about the type alpha. However, the version developed in §5.6 does exactly this, because it uses the trick of dividing a vector element by zero to cause an error when the program is evaluated. We might think of substituting an erroneous expression which does not use a vector element (*e.g.* 1 div 0), but this is not enough, because the expression is still of type num, and may only appear where a num is required. Even an erroneous expression must have the correct type for the context in which it appears! If we are writing a function with a fixed result type, we can usually arrange for the erroneous expression to have the correct type, as in the following examples:

[1 div 0]	*of type*	list num
chr (1 div 0)	*of type*	char
1 div 0 , 'x'	*of type*	num # char
(1 div 0) = 0	*of type*	truval

However, a more serious difficulty arises with polymorphic functions, because we must arrange that the erroneous expression does not have any fixed type at all, and we require a different trick. In §2.21 we saw a qualified expression which did not use the name introduced by the where operation. This possibility actually represents a deficiency in the design of Hope, but we can use it to our advantage as an error-forcing mechanism. Here is a polymorphic version of the base-case equation for index over vectors (from §5.6):

```
--- index ( n , vec ( m , one h ) )
    <= if n = m
       then h
       else ( h where z == 1 div 0 ) ;
```

The qualified expression has the same type as the vector element h, but the type of the qualifying expression is irrelevant because z is not used in the qualified expression.

In this case, it is possible to write the right-hand side expression because the input vector contains a component of the required type (h of type alpha), but this will not always be the case. Suppose we want to modify at over lists (from §5.14) along the lines of index to check for an out-of-range selector (negative, or greater than the length of the list). These cases can both be detected by an equation which matches the empty list:

```
--- at ( n , nil ) <= ... ;
```

Now we do not have an object of type alpha, and we must find a different trick. In §3.18 we saw that qualifying expressions could have an arbitrary pattern on the left-hand side of the == symbol. Pattern matches can fail in qualified expressions if the right-hand side object cannot be matched against the left-hand side pattern. We can exploit this insecurity to write an erroneous expression whose type is *undefined*:

```
--- at ( n , nil ) <= h where ( h :: t ) == nil ;
```

Since `nil` always represents a `list alpha`, the pattern `h :: t` can be used to match it, and `h` has the required type `alpha`. As far as the type-checking mechanism is concerned, the qualified expression has the correct type for the context in which it occurs, but the pattern match will fail when the function is evaluated because the value of the qualifying expression will be constructed by an application of `nil`.

5.17 Not all mistakes are deliberate

It may seem strange to devote so much discussion to ways of forcing programs to fail, when we should really be trying to write programs which *never* fail. Our justification is that many operations used in programs (*e.g.* division, vector indexing) cannot logically be defined over the full range of values represented by a type. If such an operation is applied to an inappropriate value, it means that the program has been wrongly designed, and the careful programmer will wish to be alerted to the fact.

The inventors of Hope appear to have taken the view that programmers will never make design errors, for the language does not contain any mechanism for reporting user-defined errors. The tricks which we have seen in §5.6 and §5.17 represent last-ditch attempts to remedy this deficiency, but they are rather unsatisfactory as aids to program development. The Hope Machine will report zero-division, pattern-matching failure or missing equation, when the programmer really wants to know (for instance) that a vector index is out of range. There will be even more confusion about the true cause of an error if the same trick is used in several user-defined functions, and of course there is always the possibility of a genuinely unexpected error!

Since the chief use of deliberate errors is to help us develop correct programs, we would not expect them to occur once a program is correct and being used for its intended purpose. Unfortunately, there is no technique that can satisfy us once and for all that a program is correct; mathematical correctness proofs are possible, but long and complex proofs can themselves be wrong. We must always try to allow for the possibility of undiscovered design errors because the consequences of not doing so (incorrect results) can be much worse than program failure. This means that other people who use our programs must resign themselves to being baffled by the occasional cryptic error message.

5.18 Polymorphic functions over non-linear data types

In the same way that many of the functions over linear data types which we have seen earlier in the book can be made polymorphic, so also can many of the functions over trees which have been introduced in chapters 4 and 5. We recollect from §5.8 that data types equivalent to `binary` (from §4.14) and `payroll` (from §4.15) can be defined as instances of the polymorphic type `bin alpha`. The function `employ` (from §4.16) converts a list of staff records into a balanced binary tree. However, it does not actually depend on the type of the list (or tree) component, and can be converted to polymorphic form. Here is a suitable version:

```
dec balanced : list alpha -> bin alpha ;
```

Sec. 5.18]   POLYMORPHIC FUNCTIONS OVER NON-LINEAR DATA TYPES   129

```
--- balanced [ h ] <= tip h ;
--- balanced  ( L & h  ::  ( i  ::  t ) )
       <= fork ( balanced o , balanced e )
            where ( o , e ) == alternates L ;
```

The declaration and the equations have been changed to reflect the new function name and the names of the bin constructors, but otherwise they are the same as those of employ. The auxiliary function alternates is exactly the same as that defined in §4.16, except that its type must be changed to:

```
list alpha -> list alpha # list alpha ;
```

Ordered balanced trees can be indexed by integers using a polymorphic version of locate from §4.15. Once again the declaration and equations have been changed to reflect the new function and constructor names:

```
dec pick : bin alpha # num -> alpha ;
--- pick ( tip v , i ) <= v ;
--- pick ( fork ( l , r ) , i )
       <= if i mod 2 = 0
            then pick ( l , i div 2 )
            else pick ( r , i div 2 ) ;
```

The simple flattening function tips from §5.8 can be converted to polymorphic form just by changing its declaration to:

```
dec tips : bin alpha -> list alpha ;
```

and here is the polymorphic equivalent of numerical from §4.17 to flatten an ordered binary tree in index order of its elements:

```
dec numeric : bin alpha -> list alpha ;
--- numeric ( tip v ) <= [ v ] ;
--- numeric ( fork ( l , r ) )
       <= interleave ( numeric l , numeric r ) ;
```

The auxiliary function interleave is identical to that in §4.17, except that its type must be changed to:

```
list alpha # list alpha -> list alpha ;
```

In §5.10 we introduced the type tree alpha which could hold data at the nodes as well as in the leaves. The function flatten introduced in §5.11 to flatten a tree num can also be used polymorphically by just changing its declaration to:

130 MORE GENERAL TYPES [Ch. 5

```
dec flatten : tree alpha -> list alpha ;
```

5.19 Overloading

The observation that the `tree alpha` introduced in §5.10 can be flattened by a polymorphic version of `flatten` from §5.11 suggests that we might be able to write a polymorphic version of `sort` by changing its declaration to:

```
dec sort : list alpha -> list alpha ;
```

The `sort` function uses `transfer`, so the declaration of the latter will also need to be changed to enable it to be used polymorphically:

```
dec transfer : tree alpha # list alpha -> tree alpha ;
```

and since `transfer` uses `insert` (from §5.10), this must be redeclared as:

```
dec insert : alpha # tree alpha -> tree alpha ;
```

At this point a difficulty appears. If we examine the equation which defines `insert` over non-empty trees:

```
--- insert ( n , node ( v , l , r ) )
  <= if n < v
       then node ( v , insert ( n , l ) , r )
       else node ( v , l , insert ( n , r ) ) ;
```

we find that it uses the primitive operation < to compare the value to be inserted with the value at the node of the tree. Although < is defined over numbers (*cf.* §1.10) and characters (*cf.* §1.11), it is *not* defined over any other types of object and is therefore not polymorphic. The operations used in polymorphic functions must make no assumptions about data types, hence we cannot use < to define a polymorphic version of `insert`.

The restriction on the type of < can be understood by imagining it to be truly polymorphic, using it to define polymorphic ordered insertion, and using this in turn to define polymorphic insertion sort. Now suppose that we use this to sort a payroll represented as a `list staff` (*cf.* §4.4). At some stage of the evaluation the parameters n and v in the comparison above will be instantiated by two staff records to yield an expression such as:

```
st ( "Abe" , 65 ) < st ( "Zoe" , 19 )
```

but how should we evaluate this? The answer depends upon how we understand the ordering of staff records. Alphabetical ordering by name would yield `true`, whilst numerical ordering by age would yield `false`. Since < cannot make any assumption about the ordering we require, it cannot be made polymorphic.

Functions like the comparison operations are said to be *overloaded*; although they appear to be defined over several types, in reality each represents a number of *different* operations. The Hope Machine decides which one to apply according to the operand types in each particular application of the overloaded function. For instance, when we use < to compare two characters, it applies a notional character comparison operation which we might imagine to be defined by the abstract expression:

```
ord FirstOperand < ord SecondOperand
```

The comparison operations = and /= are less restrictive, and can be used to compare two values of any type. We might be tempted to regard them as polymorphic, but in fact they are also overloaded, because the Hope Machine must use different equality tests depending on the operand types. For instance, two tuples are equal only if their elements are equal, so a separate test is required for each pair of corresponding elements. Lists must also be compared element by element, but since their lengths are unknown (and can be different), the Hope Machine must use a recursive function and check for empty lists. Non-linear data types must be compared using a multiply recursive function, and so on. Although = and /= are overloaded over most possible data types, they can only be used in polymorphic functions if the type-checking mechanism can decide which comparison operation is required before the function is evaluated. Hope does *not* allow the programmer to define new overloaded functions.

5.20 More powerful abstract data types

In §4.20 we saw how the concept of abstract data types could be used to provide data types whose properties were independent of the actual Hope data structures chosen to represent them. We are now in a position to construct a more powerful abstract data type using a polymorphic data type to represent its objects and polymorphic access functions to perform operations on them. As an example, here is a version of the queue abstract data type from exercise 14 of chapter 4, generalised to allow an arbitrary component type. The declarations of the access functions are as follows:

```
dec nobody : queue ;
dec arrive : customer # queue -> queue ;
dec first  : queue -> customer ;
dec serve  : queue -> queue ;
```

In the usual way we make no statement about the actual representations of the types `queue` and `customer`, but we shall need to do this before we write the definitions of the access functions. The simplest representation is a polymorphic list, requiring the following declarations:

```
typevar alpha ;
```

```
type customer == alpha ;
type queue == list alpha ;
```

Notice that the `type` declaration allows us to define synonyms for type expressions containing *uninstantiated* type variables. The type-checking mechanism replaces type synonyms by the corresponding expressions *before* type variables are instantiated, so the type of `arrive` is first considered to be:

```
alpha # list alpha -> list alpha
```

Possible definitions of the access functions are given below:

```
--- nobody <= nil ;

--- arrive ( c , nil )    <= [ c ] ;
--- arrive ( c , h :: t ) <= h :: arrive ( c , t ) ;

--- first ( h :: t ) <= h ;

--- serve ( h :: t ) <= t ;
```

Ordering by arrival time is enforced by treating the *tail* of the list as the end of the queue, and the *head* of the list as the head of the queue. `arrive` recursively inserts the new customer into the tail of the list, while `first` and `serve` take the oldest customer from the head of the list using a simple pattern match. For an average queue length of n customers, adding a customer has $O(n)$ cost; inspecting and removing the oldest each have constant cost. An alternative ordering convention is to treat the head of the list as the end of the queue and the tail of the list as the head of the queue. This leads to a more costly implementation because we need two recursive access functions with $O(n)$ cost to inspect and remove the oldest customer. We can avoid this by redefining the the abstract data type slightly so that it provides a single access function to deliver both the first customer and the remaining queue:

```
dec leave : queue -> customer # queue ;
```

The introduction of `leave` allows the original access functions `first` and `serve` to be dispensed with. Using the first convention for queue ordering, `leave` can be defined as follows:

```
--- leave ( h :: t ) <= ( h , t ) ;
```

and using the second convention, as:

```
--- leave [ h ] <= ( h , nil ) ;
```

```
--- leave ( h :: ( i :: t ) )
    <= ( c , h :: q )
        where ( c , q ) == leave ( i :: t ) ;
```

Whichever queue ordering convention is adopted, one of the access functions will now have $O(n)$ cost and the others constant cost.

5.21 Review

Here is a summary of the main points introduced in this chapter:

- A polymorphic operation is one which can be applied with the same meaning to any type of object.

- A polymorphic data type is one with polymorphic constructors. It can contain any type of object as a component. A list is an example of a primitive polymorphic data type.

- A polymorphic type name is known as a type constructor. An instance of a polymorphic data type is introduced by applying the type constructor to an existing type constant.

- The type constructor of a new polymorphic type is introduced in a `data` declaration, using one or more type parameters in the left-hand side type expression.

- Vectors are introduced as an example of the use of linear polymorphic data types and some problems of error handling discussed.

- More general trees are introduced as examples of non-linear polymorphic data types. Methods of constructing and flattening them are given and used as the basis of two efficient sorting methods: Quicksort and Insertion Sort.

- Polymorphic functions can be defined over polymorphic data types provided that they make no assumptions about the type of object they operate on.

- Overloaded operations represent families of similar but different operations which can be applied to different data types.

- Polymorphic abstract data types can be implemented using polymorphic data types for representation, together with polymorphic access functions.

5.22 Exercises

1. Write a polymorphic function `elements` which will count the elements of an arbitrary sequence (*i.e.* a `seq alpha` as defined in §5.4).

2. Write a polymorphic version of `reverse` (from exercise 13 of chapter 3) which will reverse the elements of an arbitrary list.

3. Write a polymorphic function `palindrome` which uses `reverse` to form a palindrome from an arbitrary list. For example, `palindrome "madami"` evaluates to `"madamimadam"`.

4. Write a polymorphic function `CatSeq` which will concatenate two sequences to yield another sequence.

5. Write a polymorphic function `RevSeq` which uses `CatSeq` to reverse the elements of a sequence.

6. Write a polymorphic function `SeqToList` to convert a sequence into a list containing the elements of the sequence in the same order.

7. Write a polymorphic function `ListToSeq` which will which will convert an arbitrary *non-empty* list into a sequence containing the list elements in the same order. Why is it impossible to write a completely general function for this purpose? Satisfy yourself that the equalities:

    ListToSeq (SeqToList s) = s

    and

    SeqToList (ListToSeq l) = l

    hold for a variety of values of `s` and `l`.

8. Write a polymorphic function `nodes` which will count the number of non-empty nodes in a general tree (*i.e.* a `tree alpha` as defined in §5.10).

9. Write a polymorphic function `depth` which will find the depth of the longest branch of a general tree.

10. Write a polymorphic function `twist` which will construct the mirror image of a general tree.

Sec. 5.22]
EXERCISES   135

11. Write a polymorphic function `BinToSeq` which uses `CatSeq` to flatten a `bin alpha` (as defined in §5.8) into a sequence which contains the leaf values in left-to-right order. Why is it impossible to write a completely general function to flatten the general trees of §5.10 into sequences?

12. Define a polymorphic data type `NaryTree alpha` to represent generalised (or *n-ary*) trees. Each node of an *n*-ary tree can contain data and can have any number (including zero) of subtrees; empty trees are also permitted. In the following diagram of an *n*-ary tree, the open circles represent data values and the solid circles empty trees:

13. Implement polymorphic vectors (*cf.* §5.5) as an abstract data type. Provide access functions `index` for retrieving the value of a specified element, `update` for replacing a specified element with a given value, `bound` for finding the lower bound, and `size` for finding the number of elements. Assume that all vectors are non-empty and that no error checking is required. How is the cost of `index` and `update` affected by representing vectors as balanced binary trees? What additional access functions might be needed by a program which uses vectors?

Chapter 6

More General Functions

6.1 More about abstraction

Functions are powerful because they capture the essence of calculations without specifying all the values used in them. The `Celsius` function of §2.2 captures the idea of "add 32, multiply by 5 and divide by 9" for every Fahrenheit temperature by abstracting it as the formal parameter `f`. Polymorphism is also an abstraction mechanism, and captures the "shape" of data structures by abstracting the types of their components. Thus lists and sequences capture the idea of indefinitely long linear arrangements of similar objects, whilst binary trees capture that of indefinitely deep branched arrangements. Polymorphic functions abstract both the values of data items (using formal parameters in recursion equations) and the types of formal parameters (using type variables in declarations). The power of abstraction is that it allows us to recognise patterns of data and computation which occur repeatedly in programs, and use a single data type or function to represent or process every instance of that pattern. In this chapter we shall examine another abstraction mechanism which extends the power of Hope still further to deal with common patterns found in programs.

6.2 Common patterns of computation

In chapter 5 we saw how polymorphism could be used to express classes of operations on data structures, provided that no assumptions were made about the types of the objects contained in them. Not all operations on data structures are independent of the values they contain however; for instance, a common requirement is to apply some function to each component. In §3.12 we defined the following function to define a `list num` whose elements are the cubes of a second `list num`:

```
dec cubes : list num -> list num
--- cubes nil            <= nil ;
--- cubes ( h :: t )     <= cube h :: cubes t ;
```

cubes is not polymorphic, because the operation of squaring is defined only over numbers. This example is unremarkable, since we are quite familiar with functions which process every element of list; however, our familiarity arises precisely because processing every list element is a pattern of computation which occurs frequently in Hope programs. We can see it again in the following function which uses the fact function from §3.15 to construct a list of factorials:

```
dec factorials : list num -> list num ;
--- factorials nil            <= nil ;
--- factorials ( h :: t )     <= fact h :: factorials t ;
```

We can see that the two functions have exactly the same "shape"; the difference is only that the second is called factorials instead of cubes and uses fact in its second equation instead of cube. It is easy to see that every function that processes each element of a list will be almost identical to cubes or factorials, but with these two names changed. Let us now see how we can use abstraction to capture the pattern of computation shown in these two examples.

The general scheme of functions which process each element of a list is to form the *head* of the result list by applying a second function (*e.g.* cube or fact) to the head of a non-empty list parameter. The *tail* of the result list is formed by a recursive application of the main function to the tail of the list parameter. We can capture this pattern by abstracting the name of the function which is applied to the head. This is done in a completely familiar way: we simply refer to it using a formal parameter name. The main function (which we shall call each to emphasise that it treats each element of a list of numbers) will now have *two* formal parameters: one representing the list to be processed, and an additional one to represent the function which is applied to the elements of the list. Here is the equation for the case of a non-empty list parameter:

```
--- each ( f , h :: t ) <= f h :: each ( f , t ) ;
```

The first parameter f represents the function to be applied to the elements of the list, which is now the second parameter. The result is a list whose head is formed by applying f to the head of the input list, and whose tail is formed by a recursive application of each to the tail of the input list. Since each is a function of two parameters, the formal function f must appear again as an actual parameter of the recursive application. It should be carefully observed that this construction is *not* functional composition, because f is not applied to an actual parameter. The name is taken to represent the *unevaluated* function, which is supplied to each exactly as if it were a data object.

For empty list parameters the resulting list is always empty, and the formal function will not be applied. The equation for this case is thus:

```
--- each ( f , nil ) <= nil ;
```

Before we can enter the equations for each into the Hope Machine, we must enter its declaration, and hence we must know the types of its parameters. The second parameter is clearly a list num, as in the cases of cubes and factorials. The new parameter represents some actual function such as cube or fact. These are both of type num -> num (*cf.* §2.15 and §3.15 respectively), so the parameter type must also be num -> num. The type of each is therefore:

```
( num -> num ) # list num -> list num
```

Parentheses are required because -> has a *lower* priority than # and also associates to the *right*. Without them, the type expression is interpreted as:

```
num -> ( ( num # list num ) -> list num )
```

In the following example we use each to substitute for cubes by supplying cube as its first actual parameter:

```
each ( cube , [ 2 , 4 , 6 ] ) ;
```

Once again the appearance of a function name (here cube) with no accompanying argument list is taken to represent the unevaluated function. The distinction becomes clear if we examine the first few steps in reducing the application of each:

```
            each ( cube , [ 2 , 4 , 6 ] )
                         |
         rewrite the second parameter to the form h :: t
                         ↓
            each ( cube , 2 :: [ 4 , 6 ] )
                         |
         instantiate f, h and t in the general-case equation
                         ↓
    --- each ( cube , 2 :: [ 4 , 6 ] )
        <= cube 2 :: each ( cube , [ 4 , 6 ] )
```

In the last step, the formal parameter f has been instantiated with the actual parameter expression cube. This looks like normal-order reduction, but is actually applicative order because the actual parameter expression is already in normal form. We can see this by entering it directly into the Hope Machine:

```
cube ;
cube : num -> num ;
```

The expression `cube` cannot be simplified further because it represents the function itself, in exactly the same way that an expression such as 69 cannot be simplified because it represents a number.

The instantiated equation is used as a rewrite rule in the usual way, and the application replaced by its right-hand side:

```
cube 2 :: each ( cube , [ 4 , 6 ] )
```

Within this expression, `cube` appears both in a conventional application (in the first term) and as an actual parameter (in the second). Reducing the first term yields:

```
8 :: each ( cube , [ 4 , 6 ] )
```

The same sequence of operations can now be applied to the second term, giving:

```
8 :: ( 64 :: each ( cube , [ 6 ] ) )
```

and again, giving:

```
8 :: ( 64 :: ( 216 :: each ( cube , nil ) ) )
```

The final application of `each` can now be reduced using the base-case equation:

```
8 :: ( 64 :: ( 216 :: nil ) )
```

which will be rewritten to the normal form for lists and reported as:

```
[ 8 , 16 , 216 ] : list num
```

which is the result we would expect from the application `cubes [ 2 , 4 , 6 ]`.

We can use `each` whenever we wish to apply a monadic arithmetic operation to every element of a list of numbers. Here we use it in a similar fashion to substitute for `factorials`:

```
each ( fact , [ 2 , 4 , 6 ] ) ;
[ 2 , 24 , 720 ] : list num
```

We can also use `each` to substitute for repeated applications of a non-recursive function. Compare the following expression with the way we specified the same calculations in §2.3:

```
    each ( Celsius , [ 40 , 65 , 103 ] ) ;
    [ 4 , 18 , 47 ] : list num
```

Functions like each, which can take other functions as actual parameters are known as *higher-order* functions. Conventional (or *first-order*) functions abstract the values of data items, whilst polymorphic functions abstract their types; higher-order functions go one step further by abstracting the *operations* which are applied to data items.

6.3 More general higher-order functions

The higher-order function each enables us to use a single function to capture the idea of applying a monadic arithmetic operation to each element of a list of numbers, but it does not immediately enable us to capture other program shapes which are almost identical. Consider the function required in exercise 6 of chapter 3, which uses fold from §2.6 to convert every character of a list char to upper-case:

```
dec shout  :  list char -> list char ;
--- shout nil          <= nil ;
--- shout ( h :: t )   <= fold h :: shout t ;

shout "quiet please" ;
"QUIET PLEASE"  :  list char
```

Compare this with the following function, which uses the primitive function not to negate every element of a list truval:

```
dec negate  :  list truval -> list truval ;
--- negate nil          <= nil ;
--- negate ( h :: t )   <= not h :: negate t ;

negate [ true , false , true ] ;
[ false , true , false ]  :  list truval
```

Although both functions have exactly the same shape as each, we cannot use it to substitute for them, because all three functions are defined over lists containing different types of object. To construct a higher-order function which is sufficiently powerful for this purpose, we must employ an additional abstraction mechanism.

If we examine the functions negate, shout and each, we can see not only a common pattern of computation, but also a common pattern in the types of the objects manipulated. In each case the input and result of the function is a list, and in each case the type of object is the same. Furthermore, in each case the formal function operates on a single object of this type and produces a single object of the same type as its result. This suggests that we might abstract the *type* of the list component and write a *polymorphic* version of each. The declaration of the new function (which we shall call every) will be:

```
dec every : ( alpha -> alpha ) # list alpha ->
            list alpha ;
```

This assumes that the formal function is the first argument, the list to be processed second, and that the type variable alpha has been previously declared. The equations will be identical to those of each, except for the new name of the function:

```
--- every ( f , nil    ) <= nil ;
--- every ( f , h :: t ) <= f h :: every t ;
```

every converts a list of any type of object to a list of the same kind of object using a function which produces a single value of that type from another value of the same type. The given function may be user-defined or primitive. We can use every to substitute for negate, shout and its predecessor each, supplying the primitive function not and the user-defined functions fold and Celsius:

```
every ( not , [ true , false , true ] ) ;
[ false , true , false ] : list truval

every ( fold , "quiet please" ) ;
"QUIET PLEASE" : list char

every ( Celsius , [ 40 , 65 , 103 ] ) ;
[ 4 , 18 , 47 ] : list num
```

In these three examples, alpha has been interpreted as a truval, a char and a num respectively.

6.4 Fully general higher-order functions

Consider the following function which uses odd from §2.4 to find the parity of the elements of a list of numbers:

```
dec odds : list num -> list truval ;
--- odds nil           <= nil ;
--- odds ( h :: t ) <= odd h :: odds t ;
```

We cannot immediately use every to substitute for odds, because every expects the range and domain of the formal function to have the same type, whereas in the function odd they are different. However, a simple change to the type of every will make it fully general and allow it to be used in this case:

```
( alpha # beta ) # list alpha -> list beta
```

142   MORE GENERAL FUNCTIONS   [Ch. 6

This assumes as usual that beta has been previously declared as a type variable. We have have now developed a *fully-general* higher-order function, and in this form it is usually known as map. Its equations will of course be identical to those of each and every, except for the change to the function name:

```
dec map : ( alpha # beta ) # list alpha -> list beta ;
--- map ( f , nil )      <= nil ;
--- map ( f , h :: t )   <= f h :: map ( f , t ) ;
```

We have now created a function which converts a list of any type of object to a list of a *different* type of object, using a function which converts a single value of the first type to one of the second. The new function can be used to substitute for odds:

```
map ( odd , [ 1 , 2 , 3 , 4 ] ) ;
[ true , false , true , false ] : list truval
```

In this example, alpha and beta have been consistently instantiated as a num and a truval respectively. If they are instantiated as the same type, map can be used to substitute for the less general function every as well. Higher-order functions (like map) which process every element of a data structure are known as *iterators*.

6.5 Reducing applications of map

It is tempting to imagine that since map traverses the input list from left to right, that it also applies the formal function to the list elements in left-to-right order; however this view is incorrect. To see why, let us look more closely at at the way in which applications of map are reduced. Here we apply an arbitrary function f to a 3-element list:

$$\text{map} (f , [e_1 , e_2 , e_3])$$

rewrite the second parameter to the form h :: t
$$\downarrow$$
$$\text{map} (f , e_1 :: [e_2 , e_3])$$

instantiate f, h and t in the right-hand side of the general-case equation
$$\downarrow$$
$$f\ e_1 :: \text{map} (f , [e_2 , e_3])$$

This expression should be compared with the one we obtained in §6.2 by rewriting an application of each (the precursor of map). On that occasion we rewrote the first term (cube 2, which corresponds to $f\ e_1$ in the current example), conveniently overlooking the fact that the *second* term was also a redex. This time we shall reduce the second term using the reduction sequence above:

$$f\ e_1\ ::\ (\ f\ e_2\ ::\ \text{map}\ (\ f\ ,\ [\ e_3\ ]\ )\ )$$

repeat the previous sequence of steps ↓

$$f\ e_1\ ::\ (\ f\ e_2\ ::\ (\ f\ e_3\ ::\ \text{map}\ (\ f\ ,\ \text{nil}\ )\ )\ )$$

reduce the application of map using the base-case equation ↓

$$f\ e_1\ ::\ (\ f\ e_2\ ::\ (\ f\ e_3\ ::\ \text{nil}\ )\ )$$

rewrite to the normal form for lists ↓

$$[\ f\ e_1\ ,\ f\ e_2\ ,\ f\ e_3\ ]$$

demonstrating that the application of map to a list is equivalent to a list of individual applications of the formal function. In the final expression, all the applications of f are redexes and can be reduced in *any* order.

6.6 Realising the full power of map

The fully polymorphic function map is more general than the examples of §6.4 suggest. As suggested in §6.3, the actual parameter of a higher-order function can be any user-defined or primitive function, and this also includes *constructor* functions. In §4.3 we defined a more sophisticated representation of temperatures by introducing the constructors Celsius and Fahrenheit as "labels" for numbers. A list of Fahrenheit temperatures would be written like this:

    [Fahrenheit 32 , Fahrenheit 98 , Fahrenheit 212]

but using map, it might be written more concisely as:

    map (Fahrenheit , [32 , 98 , 212]) ;

In this expression, alpha is interpreted as a num and beta as a temp. The constructor function Fahrenheit which is used as the actual parameter of map has the required type of num -> temp.

In the examples which we have seen so far, the elements of the input and result lists are scalars, but they can also be arbitrary data structures. Here we apply the function sum from §3.12 to a list whose components are *lists* of numbers:

    map (sum , [[1 , 2 , 3] , [4 , 5] , [ ]]) ;
    [6 , 9 , 0] : list num

In a similar way, the elements of the *result* list can also be data structures. Here we use shout from §6.3 to convert every element of a list of words to upper case:

```
    map ( shout , [ "silence" , "is" , "golden" ] ) ;
    [ "SILENCE" , "IS" , "GOLDEN" ] : list ( list char )
```

In §6.3 we defined shout using two equations, but using map we can simplify it to:

```
    --- shout w <= map ( fold , w ) ;
```

Notice that if we only need applications of shout, we can simply use the right-hand side of this equation, and need not define the single-equation function at all. However, the right-hand-side expression can only substitute for *applications* of the function, and in the map example above we need the definition so that we can supply the function name shout as an actual parameter of map.

The function supplied to map can itself be polymorphic. Here we apply the polymorphic version of length from §5.13 to a list of words:

```
    map ( length , [ "Ware" , "Wye" , "Watford" ] ) ;
    [ 4 , 3 , 7 ] : list num ;
```

In this expression alpha is interpreted as a list char and beta as a num, so the supplied function must be of type list char -> num. In §5.13 we declared length to be of type list alpha -> num, but we recollect that the same type variable can be instantiated differently in separate declarations without confusion. If alpha in the declaration of length represents a char, the function has the correct type to be used as the actual parameter of map.

A particularly interesting case arises if the elements of the list are *tuples*. In this case we must supply as actual parameter a function whose argument is a tuple of the same size. This will be a function which we would normally consider to have *more than one* argument. In the following example the function greater from §2.9 is used to find the largest element of each member of a list of pairs:

```
    map ( greater , [ ( 1 , 2 ) , ( 0 , 5 ) , ( 6 , 3 ) ] ) ;
    [ 2 , 5 , 6 ] : list num
```

A slight difficulty appears if we want to apply a primitive function such as addition or multiplication to a list of tuples in this way, because most binary operations are provided in the form of infix operations. To circumvent this, Hope allows any infix operation to be used in prefix notation by preceding its name with the reserved word nonop. When we do this, its arguments must be bound together into a pair and placed after the name of the operation, as with other prefix operations:

```
    nonop * ( 3 , 4 )
```

An expression of this form can be reduced immediately to the more familiar:

```
( 3 * 4 )
```

and evaluates to `12` as we would expect. Using this mechanism, primitive infix operations can be supplied as the actual parameters of higher-order functions:

```
map ( nonop * , [ ( 1 , 2 ) , ( 0 , 5 ) , ( 6 , 3 ) ] ) ;
[ 2 , 0 , 18 ] : list num
```

6.7 Non-linear higher-order functions

In the same way that we can see a common pattern in functions which process every element of a list and produce a result list which is isomorphic with the original, so we can identify a similar pattern in functions which process the elements of non-linear data structures. As an example, here is a function to invert the values of the elements of a general binary tree (as defined in §5.10) containing truth values:

```
dec invert : tree truval -> tree truval ;
--- invert null <= null ;
--- invert ( node ( v , l , r ) )
    <= node ( not v , invert l , invert r ) ;
```

Once again the resulting data structure is isomorphic with the original, in this case another binary tree. The example of `map` suggests that we might be able to define an analogous higher-order function to replace all functions like `invert`. The declaration of an appropriate higher-order function (which we shall call `MapTree`) will be:

```
dec MapTree : ( alpha -> beta ) # tree alpha ->
              tree beta ;
--- MapTree ( f , null ) <= null ;
--- MapTree ( f , node ( v , l , r ) )
    <= node ( f v , MapTree l , MapTree r ) ;
```

The use of two type variables allows the components of the input and result trees to have different types. The function is *non-linear* because each application generates *two* self-applications, one for each subtree of the original. We can use it to replace applications of functions like `invert` in the same way that we replaced `map` with `negate` in §6.3:

```
MapTree ( not , t )
   where t == some tree truval ;
```

This yields a tree of truth values which is isomorphic to the input tree.

6.8 Another common pattern of recursion

Higher-order functions such as map and MapTree are powerful because they capture a pattern of recursion (iteration over the elements of a data structure) which occurs frequently in Hope programs. Effectively we have abstracted the notion of recursion itself and "packaged" it into a single function. Many recursively defined functions can now be dispensed with and their applications replaced by applications of map or MapTree without *explicit* recursion, making programs even clearer. We did this when we defined a non-recursive version of shout in §6.6. This observation suggests that we might be able to simplify our programs further by discovering other common patterns of recursion and abstracting them into higher-order functions.

A second pattern of recursion which occurs frequently in Hope programs can be seen in the function sum, which adds up all the elements of a list of numbers. This was defined in §3.12 as follows:

```
dec sum : list num -> num ;
--- sum nil          <= 0 ;
--- sum ( n :: l )   <= n + sum l ;
```

However, a function to calculate the product of the elements of a list of numbers will have exactly the same "shape" as sum:

```
dec product : list num -> num ;
--- product nil          <= 1 ;
--- product ( n :: l )   <= n * product l ;
```

The difference between the two functions (apart from their names) is the operation applied to the list elements (+ and * respectively) and value of the base-case result (0 and 1). The underlying pattern of each function is to apply a dyadic function to the head of a non-empty list parameter, together with a value derived from a recursive application of the top-level function to the tail of the list. This defines a *single* value which forms the result of the function.

Let us now see how we can define a single function which can substitute for sum and product. This will be a higher-order function with additional formal parameters to specify those features which differ between them: the dyadic operation and the base-case result. We shall call it combine to reflect its effect on the elements of the input list. A possible declaration will be:

```
dec combine : ( num # num -> num ) # num #
              list num -> num ;
```

Here the first parameter is the formal function, the second the base-case result, and the third the list to be processed. The base-case equation is straightforward: we simply return the base-case result without applying the formal function:

```
--- combine ( f , b , nil ) <= b ;
```

In the general-case equation the formal function is applied to the head of the list, and the second argument of this application is formed by recursively applying `combine` to the tail of the list:

```
--- combine ( f , b , h :: t )
    <= f ( h , combine ( f , b , t ) ) ;
```

We can now use `combine` to substitute for `sum` and `product`:

```
combine ( nonop + , 0 , [ 2 , 4 , 6 ] ) ;
12 : num

combine ( nonop * , 1 , [ 2 , 4 , 6 ] ) ;
48 : num
```

6.9 Making combine fully polymorphic

As in the case of `map`, we can increase the power of `combine` considerably by making it polymorphic. The obvious way to do this is to replace the type constant `num` by a type variable throughout, declaring `combine` as:

```
dec combine : ( alpha # alpha -> alpha ) # alpha #
              list alpha -> alpha ;
```

This allows us to write expressions over other types of list, such as:

```
combine ( or , true , l )
  where l == some list truval ;
```

which yields `true` if any element of `l` is `true`. We can make `combine` even more general by noting that result can have a different type to the list elements. The type of the fully general function is rather complex, and can be deduced as follows. The type of the list elements is taken to be `alpha`. For an arbitrary result type `beta`, the base-case value must also be of type `beta`, since it represents one possible result of `combine`. The first parameter of the formal function application is a list element, and is therefore of type `alpha`. The second parameter of the application is formed by a recursive application of `combine`, and will therefore have type `beta`. The result of this application represents a possible result of `combine`, and therefore has type `beta` as well. The type of the formal function in the most general case will therefore be `alpha # beta -> beta`. The fully general version of `combine` is usually known (somewhat confusingly) as `reduce`. Its complete definition is as follows:

148 MORE GENERAL FUNCTIONS [Ch. 6

```
    dec reduce: ( alpha # beta -> beta ) # beta #
                list alpha -> beta ;
--- reduce ( f , b , nil ) <= b ;
--- reduce ( f , b , h :: t )
        <= f ( h , reduce ( f , b , t ) ) ;
```

We can use `reduce` everywhere that we used `combine`, and also to substitute for functions which iterate over lists to produce a result of a different type to the list elements. In §5.13 we defined a polymorphic version of `length` as follows:

```
    dec length : list alpha -> num ;
--- length nil        <= 0 ;
--- length ( _ :: t ) <= length t + 1 ;
```

A slightly curious feature is that each list element is counted by adding one to the final result, but its *value* is ignored. Nevertheless, `length` exhibits the same pattern of recursion as `sum` and `product` and can be eliminated by using `reduce`. To do this we need a non-strict formal function which ignores the value of its first argument and increments the second. The function `incr` which we saw in §2.14 does exactly this, and can be used provided we make it polymorphic by changing its type to `alpha # num -> num`. We can now find the length of a list containing any kind of object using an expression such as:

```
    reduce ( incr , 0 , "pounds, shillings & pence" ) ;
    25 : num
```

Here `alpha` is interpreted as a `char` and `beta` as a `num`, so that `incr` has the type `char # num -> num` in this context. Higher-order functions like `reduce` which combine the elements of a data structure together into a single value are often referred to as *consolidators*.

6.10 Reducing applications of `reduce`
As in the case of `map`, `reduce` effectively abstracts the notion of recursion, enabling recursive function definitions to be replaced by expressions which are not explicitly recursive. In §6.5 we saw that `map` applies the formal function to the list elements in an undefined order, and we might ask whether this is also true of `reduce`. To answer this question, let us examine the way in which a typical application is reduced:

```
            reduce ( f , b , [ e₁ , e₂ , e₃ ] )
                            |
            rewrite the third argument to the form h :: t
                            ↓
            reduce ( f , b , e₁ :: [ e₂ , e₃ ] )
```

$$\text{reduce (f , b , } e_1 :: [e_2 , e_3])$$

instantiate f, b, h and t on the right-hand side of the *general-case* equation

$$\text{f (} e_1 \text{ , reduce (f , b , } [e_2 , e_3]))$$

This application contains only one redex, the application of reduce. Repeating this sequence of steps for each of the remaining list elements, we obtain:

$$\text{f (} e_1 \text{ , f (} e_2 \text{ , reduce (f , b , nil)))}$$

reduce the application of reduce using the *base-case* equation

$$\text{f (} e_1 \text{ , f (} e_2 \text{ , f (} e_3 \text{ , b)))}$$

The final expression contains three applications of the formal function f, but only the *rightmost* application f (e_3 , b) is a redex; after reducing this, we can reduce the *middle* and finally the *leftmost* application of f. An application of reduce to an *n*-element list is thus equivalent to *n* applications of the formal function composed together and *associating to the right*. The formal function is actually applied to the elements of the input list in *right-to-left* order, a fact which is not intuitively obvious from the examples which we have seen so far. We can see why if we supply nonop * as the formal function, with a base-case value of 1. The resulting expression is:

nonop * (e_1 , nonop * (e_2 , nonop * (e_3 , 1)))

Rewriting the prefix form of the operations to infix form (*cf.* §6.6) gives:

(e_1 * (e_2 * (e_3 * 1)))

in which the elements of the list and the base-case value are multiplied together from right to left. However, operations like * have the special properties of *associativity*, which means that e_1 * (e_2 * e_3) is equivalent to (e_1 * e_2) * e_3, and *commutativity*, which means that e_1 * e_2 is equivalent to e_2 * e_1. These additional equivalences can be regarded as rewrite rules, and allow us to rearrange the final expression to the following form:

(((1 * e_1) * e_2) * e_3)

in which the base-case value and the elements of the list are multiplied together from *left to right* to yield the same result. Many common operations (*e.g.* + and *) are both commutative and associative, and it does not matter which way the expression is bracketed. However, not all operations have these properties (*e.g.* -, div and ::), and we must remember that reduce applies the given function from right to left.

6.11 Realising the full power of `reduce`

Like `map`, `reduce` is much more powerful than it first appears, because the formal function can define any type of object as its result, including data structures. As a simple illustration, we shall supply the primitive operation `::` as the given function, with `nil` as the base-case value:

>   reduce (nonop :: , nil , [e_1 , e_2 , e_3]) ;

As we saw in §6.10, this expression is equivalent to repeated applications of the formal function composed together:

>   nonop :: (e_1 , nonop :: (e_2 , nonop :: (e_3 , nil)))

Rewriting the applications of `::` to infix form gives:

> e_1 :: (e_2 :: (e_3 :: nil))

which can be rewritten to the normal form for lists as:

>   [e_1 , e_2 , e_3]

Reconstructing the original input list might seem a rather pointless exercise except to illustrate the power of `reduce` to build data structures. However, by replacing the base-case value with a non-empty list, we immediately get a much more useful result:

>   reduce (nonop :: , "here" , "now") ;
>   "nowhere" : list char

The two lists have been concatenated without explicit recursion. How has this been achieved? If we examine the result of reducing an application of the list-concatenating function `join` from §3.12, we can see that it is equivalent to replacing the `nil` of its first argument by its second argument. An application of `reduce` is equivalent to replacing every application of `::` in the input list by an application of the given function, and the `nil` at the end by the base-case value. Replacing `::` with itself thus gives the same effect as `join`.

As a further example of the power of `reduce` to build data structures, consider the the following given function:

>   dec SqrCons : num # list num -> list num ;
>   --- SqrCons (n , l) <= square n :: l ;

An application such as:

>   reduce (SqrCons , nil , [2 , 4 , 6]) ;

is equivalent to the expression:

```
SqrCons ( 2 , SqrCons ( 4 , SqrCons ( 6 , nil ) ) )
```

and evaluates to:

```
[ 4 , 16 , 36 ] : list num
```

Here we have applied the function `square` to each element of the input list before assembling the values to form the final list, achieving the effect of an application of `map` with `square` as its actual parameter.

More powerfully still, the given function can assemble the components of the result in a *different order* to the input values from which they are derived. The following function inserts a single character into its correct position in an *ordered* list of characters:

```
dec into : char # list char -> list char ;
--- into ( i , nil ) <= i :: nil ;
--- into ( i , h :: t )
    <= if i < h
        then i :: ( h :: t )
        else h :: into ( i , t ) ;
```

If we apply `reduce` to a list of characters supplying `into` as the given function and `nil` as the base-case value, the input list characters will be successively inserted into the result list. This is initially empty, and each insertion will yield an ordered list; the final result is equivalent to sorting the input list:

```
reduce ( into , nil , "dreads" ) ;
"adders" : list char
```

The sorting method shown here is analogous to the tree insertion sort described in §5.11, except that the elements of the input list are inserted into a *linear* data structure (the result list) instead of a tree. Since it requires $n/2$ comparisons (on average) to insert each element of a randomly-ordered n-element input list into the result, this *list insertion sort* has $O(n^2)$ cost. For this reason, it is not very useful for large lists.

There is no restriction on the type of data structure which can be built using applications of `reduce`, provided that we can supply a suitable function to apply to the list elements. Here, the function `insert` from §5.10 is used to construct an ordered binary tree of numbers:

```
reduce ( insert , null , [ 4 , 2 , 5 , 1 , 3 ] )
```

This expression is equivalent to an application of transfer from §5.11, and the latter might therefore be dispensed with if reduce is available. The reader should determine that this expression constructs the tree:

    node (3 , node (1 , null ,
                            node (2 , null , null))
                 node (5 , node (4 , null , null) ,
                            null))

6.12 Specifying the base case

Although reduce has been introduced as a general mechanism for applying a dyadic function to the elements of a list, difficulties can still arise. For instance, we might try to use reduce with the function greater from §2.9 to find the largest element of a list of numbers:

    reduce (greater , b , l)

The problem is that we cannot specify the base-case value b, because we must choose a value which is guaranteed to be less than than the largest list element. Unless we do this, b will be erroneously returned as the maximum. In order to use greater and similar functions, we must define a consolidator whose base-case result is list element rather than a parameter value. A suitable declaration might be:

    dec compress : (num # num -> num) # list num -> num ;

Notice that there is no parameter to specify the base-case result. The base case can no longer be the empty list because this does not contain a suitable value to return as the result of the function; instead, it will be the *singleton* list:

    --- compress (f , [h]) <= h ;

This implies that compress is not defined over empty lists; however, this is appropriate because it does not make sense to find the largest element of an empty list. The general-case equation covers lists containing at least two elements:

    --- compress (f , h :: (i :: t))
        <= f (h , compress (f , i :: t)) ;

The reader should determine that the application:

    compress (f , [e_1 , e_2 , e_3])

is equivalent to the expression:

SPECIFYING THE BASE CASE

```
f ( e₁ , f ( e₂ , e₃ ) )
```

A new difficulty arises when we try to make compress fully polymorphic by giving f the type alpha # beta -> beta, because the arguments of the rightmost application are both list elements of type alpha. This problem can be solved by introducing a *second* formal function which is applied only in the base case. This will be a monadic function of type alpha -> beta, and a consolidator which uses it will look like this:

```
dec condense :  ( alpha # beta -> beta ) #
                ( alpha -> beta ) # list alpha -> beta ;
--- condense ( f , g , [ a ] ) <= g a ;
--- condense ( f , g , a :: ( b :: t ) )
    <= f ( h , condense ( f , g , b :: t ) ) ;
```

The application condense (f , g , [e₁ , e₂ , e₃]) is equivalent to the following expression:

```
f ( e₁ , f ( e₂ , g e₃ ) )
```

If the value of the final list element is required unchanged in the base case, the second given function can be one which maps objects to themselves. This is known as the *identity* function:

```
dec id : alpha -> alpha ;
--- id a <= a ;

condense ( greater , id , [ 1 , 3 , 5 , 4 , 2 ] ) ;
5 : num
```

This style of consolidator is most useful for data structures whose base case contains a data item (*i.e.* the constructor is parametrised), such as the sequences of §5.4:

```
dec ConSeq :  ( alpha # beta -> beta ) #
              ( alpha -> beta ) # seq alpha -> beta ;
--- ConSeq ( f , g , one p ) <= g p ;
--- ConSeq ( f , g , two ( p , q ) )
    <= f ( p , ConSeq ( f , g , q ) ) ;
```

In the following example we use ConSeq to convert a sequence to a list:

```
ConSeq ( nonop :: , singleton , s )
   where s == two ( 'S' , two ( 'O' , one 'S' ) ) ) ;
"SOS" : list char
```

154 MORE GENERAL FUNCTIONS   [Ch. 6

The function `singleton` which is applied to the final element of the sequence is defined as follows:

```
dec singleton : alpha -> list alpha ;
--- singleton a <= [ a ] ;
```

6.13 Left-associative consolidation

In §6.10 we saw that `reduce` effectively composes together applications of the formal function so that they associate to the right. When the given function is commutative, the resulting expression is equivalent to one in which the applications associate to the left, but when the function is not commutative, the use of `reduce` leads to unexpected or incorrect results:

```
reduce ( nonop - , 0 , [ 1 , 6 , 10 ] ) ;
3 : num
```

When we consider that this application is equivalent to the expression:

```
( 1 - ( 6 - ( 10 - 0 ) ) )
```

the result is less surprising, although probably not what we wanted. The desired effect can be achieved by defining a consolidation function which composes the applications together so that they associate to the left. The equations of such a function will look like this:

```
--- LeftRed ( f , b , nil ) <= b ;
--- LeftRed ( f , b , h :: t )
       <= LeftRed ( f , f ( b , h ) , t ) ;
```

The general-case equation specifies left association by constructing a new base-case value from an application of the formal function with the old base-case value as its *first* parameter. The reader may determine that the application:

```
LeftRed ( f , b , [ e₁ , e₂ , e₃ ] )
```

is equivalent to the expression:

```
f ( f ( f ( b , e₁ ) , e₂ ) , e₃ )
```

However, the use of `LeftRed` can still lead to unexpected results:

```
LeftRed ( nonop - , 0 , [ 10 , 6 , 1 ] ) ;
-17 : num
```

The problem here is that the application is equivalent to the expression:

```
( ( ( 0 - 10 ) - 6 ) - 1 )
```

and we probably wanted to consolidate the list using one of its elements as the base-case value. It is not necessary to define a special function for this purpose as we did with compress and condense, because left association means that the required value will always be the first element of the list, which can simply be removed before making the top-level application of LeftRed:

```
LeftRed ( nonop - , h , t )
   where ( h :: t ) == [ 10 , 6 , 1 ] ;
3 : num
```

The use of :: in the pattern on the left-hand side of the where means that the left-hand side expression must never specify an empty list. This is not a unreasonable restriction, since it makes no sense to consolidate an empty list if we expect the base-case value to be one of its elements.

To write a fully polymorphic version of LeftRed, we must remember that the *second* argument of the formal function will be a list element, whilst the *first* argument will have the same type as the base-case value. The type of the formal function is thus beta # alpha -> beta, and the full declaration is:

```
dec LeftRed : ( beta # alpha -> beta ) # beta #
                 list alpha -> beta ;
```

The equations remain unchanged. In the following example we consolidate a list of numbers using the constructors of the type long, which we defined in §4.10 in such a way that left association naturally leads to correct expressions:

```
LeftRed ( nonop . , ~ h , t )
   where ( h :: t ) == [ 1 , 2 , 3 ] ;
( ( ( ~ 1 ) . 2 ) . 3 ) : long
```

Finally it should be pointed out that the order in which the list elements are combined together will also depend on exactly how how they are handled by the dyadic formal function. Given the following function to perform *inverse* subtraction:

```
dec RevSub : num # num -> num ;
--- RevSub ( x , y ) <= y - x ;
```

the reader should compare the results of evaluating the following expressions:

```
    LeftRed ( nonop - , h , t )
      where ( h :: t ) == [ 10 , 6 , 1 ] ;

    LeftRed ( RevSub , h , t )
      where ( h :: t ) == [ 10 , 6 , 1 ] ;

    condense ( nonop - , id , l )
      where l == [ 10 , 6 , 1 ] ;

    condense ( RevSub , id , t )
      where l == [ 10 , 6 , 1 ] ;
```

6.14 Consolidating non-linear data structures

Although `reduce` can produce a non-linear data structure as its *result*, the input must always be a list. However, by analogy with the non-linear iterator `MapTree` of §6.7, we can also define consolidators for non-linear data structures. As an example we shall define a consolidator (which we shall call `RedTree`) for the binary trees of §5.10. As a first step towards understanding what is required, we shall consider the result of `RedTree` to be a single value, as we did at first in the case of `reduce`.

The base-case equation is straightforward, because the empty tree contains no data value, and the formal function is not applied:

```
    --- RedTree ( f , b , null ) <= b ;
```

The left-hand side of the general-case equation will be:

```
    --- RedTree ( f , b , node ( v , l , r ) ) <= ...
```

In this expression there are *three* values of interest, the node value v, and the left and right subtrees l and r. In the case of `reduce`, there were only two such values, the head and tail of the input list. The tail was consolidated by a recursive application of `reduce`, and this was combined with the head value by applying the formal function. In the case of `RedTree` we must consolidate the left and right subtrees using two separate recursive applications of `RedTree`. This yields *two* values which must be combined with the node value to form the final result, and implies that the formal function must have *three* arguments:

```
    <= f ( v , RedTree ( f , b , l ) ,
               RedTree ( f , b , r ) ) ;
```

When consolidating a tree alpha, a node value will be an alpha and the result of consolidating a subtree will be a beta, hence the formal function must have type alpha # beta # beta -> beta. The full definition of RedTree will thus be:

```
dec RedTree : ( alpha # beta # beta -> beta ) # beta #
               tree alpha -> beta ;
--- RedTree ( f , b , null ) <= b ;
--- RedTree ( f , b , node ( v , l , r ) )
    <= f ( v , RedTree ( f , b , l ) ,
               RedTree ( f , b , r ) ) ;
```

To use RedTree we need a formal function of three arguments. In the following example we use greatest (of type num # num # num -> truval) from §2.12:

```
RedTree ( greatest , 0 , t )
  where t == some tree num ;
```

Although this illustrates the use of RedTree, it is an unsatisfactory method of finding the largest element of a binary tree of numbers because of the implicit assumption that at least one of the elements is greater than 0 (*cf.* §6.12).

As in the case of reduce, we can also use RedTree to generate an arbitrary data structure. For example, a tree alpha can be flattened to a list alpha by supplying the following function as its actual parameter:

```
dec sandwich : alpha # list alpha # list alpha ->
               list alpha ;
--- sandwich ( i , l , r ) <= l <> ( i :: r ) ;
```

Using sandwich as the actual parameter of RedTree, the type of alpha is determined by the component type of the actual tree parameter, and the type of beta will be list alpha. The base-case value is nil, since this is the base case of a list alpha:

```
RedTree ( sandwich , nil , t )
  where t == some tree alpha ;
```

A particularly interesting use of RedTree is to flatten a tree which has been constructed by consolidating a list with insert (as in §6.11):

```
RedTree ( sandwich , nil , t )
  where t == reduce ( insert , null , l )
    where l == [ 4 , 2 , 5 , 1 , 3 ] ) ;
[ 1 , 2 , 3 , 4 , 5 , 6 ] : list num
```

In this example we have used two different consolidation functions to specify a tree insertion sort without explicit recursion. Each of the two consolidation functions contains a "packaged" pattern of recursion appropriate to the "shape" of the data structure over which it is defined.

6.15 Variations on a theme

We can define a version of `RedTree` (analogous to `combine` of §6.12) where the base-case result is generated by applying a second given function to a tree element:

```
dec ConTree : ( alpha # beta # beta -> beta ) #
              ( alpha -> beta ) # tree alpha -> beta ;
```

The base case is a tree containing a single data item (*i.e.* having depth 2):

```
--- ConTree ( f , g , node ( v , null , null ) )
    <= g v ;
```

The general-case equation is a tree whose depth is 3 or more; this is specified with a pattern containing two levels of constructor applications:

```
--- ConTree ( f , g , node ( v , node l , node r ) )
    <= f ( v , ConTree ( f , g , node l ) ,
               ConTree ( f , g , node r ) ) ;
```

Here we use `ConTree` with `greatest` (from §2.12) and `id` (from §6.12) to find the largest element of a non-empty tree of numbers:

```
ConTree ( greatest , id , t )
  where t == some non-empty tree num ;
```

Because `ConTree` is fully polymorphic, we can use it to consolidate the components of a non-empty tree to an arbitrary data structure. Here we flatten a non-empty tree containing any kind of object into a sequence:

```
ConTree ( SeqSand , one , t )
  where t == some non-empty tree alpha ;
```

The auxiliary function `SeqSand` is analogous to `sandwich` over lists from §6.14:

```
dec SeqSand : alpha # seq alpha # seq alpha ->
              seq alpha ;
--- SeqSand ( i , l , r )
    <= CatSeq ( l , two ( i , r ) ) ;
```

`one` and `two` are the constructors of the type `seq alpha` and `CatSeq` is the function to concatenate two sequences from exercise 4 of chapter 5.

This style of consolidator is essential for processing non-linear data structures whose base case is defined by a parametrised constructor, such as the `bin alpha` of §5.8. Here is a suitable function:

```
dec ConBin : ( beta # beta -> beta ) #
              ( alpha -> beta ) # bin alpha -> beta ;
--- ConBin ( f , g , tip v ) <= g v ;
--- ConBin ( f , g , fork ( l , r ) )
    <= f ( ConBin ( f , g , l ) ,
           ConBin ( f , g , r ) ) ;
```

Note that the first formal function has only two arguments, since there is no value at the node, and it need only combine the consolidated subtrees, which are both of type beta. Here we use ConBin to flatten a binary tree to a sequence:

```
ConBin ( CatSeq , one , t )
    where t == some bin alpha ;
```

6.16 Polymorphic sorting revisited

As well as capturing common patterns of recursion, higher-order functions enable us to simplify programs which would otherwise require several functions for essentially the same purpose. In §5.19 we discussed the possibility of writing a polymorphic sorting function and concluded that it was impossible. This was because the relational operations used to determine the ordering of the items were not truly polymorphic, but only *overloaded* over the primitive data types num and char. Thus the sort function ultimately depended on insert, defined in §5.10 by the equations:

```
--- insert ( n , null )
    <= node ( n , null , null ) ;
--- insert ( n , node ( v , l , r ) )
    <= if n < v
       then node ( v , insert ( n , l ) , r )
       else node ( v , l , insert ( n , r ) ) ;
```

The general-case equation is only valid if the operands of the primitive operation < are characters or numbers, for no assumption can be made about the ordering of other data objects such as tuples.

Higher-order functions allow us to get round this problem by abstracting the comparison operation and making it an additional formal parameter of the insertion function. In the following insertion function, the new formal function (referred to as o to represent an arbitrary ordering function) appears as the *first* parameter:

```
--- place ( o , n , node ( v , l , r ) )
    <= if o ( n , v )
       then node ( v , place ( o , n , l ) , r )
       else node ( v , l , place ( o , n , r ) ) ;
```

160   MORE GENERAL FUNCTIONS [Ch. 6

The base case is straightforward, as the ordering function is not applied:

```
---   place ( o , n , null )
      <= node ( n , null , null ) ;
```

The ordering function compares two objects of the same type and yields a truth value, hence its type is `alpha # alpha -> truval`. This means that the declaration of `place` must be:

```
dec place :   ( alpha # alpha -> truval ) # alpha #
              tree alpha -> tree alpha ;
```

The consistent instantiation rule allows the type-checking mechanism to determine that a specific ordering function given in an application of `place` has the correct type for the object being inserted.

The original version of `insert` was applied by `transfer`. This must be modified both to reflect the new name of the insertion function, and to allow for the formal function. A suitable new definition will therefore be:

```
dec convey :  ( alpha # alpha -> truval ) # list alpha #
              tree alpha -> tree alpha ;
---   convey ( o , nil , T ) <= T ;
---   convey ( o , h :: t , T )
      <= convey ( o , t , place ( o , h , T ) ) ;
```

Finally, `sort` must be changed to incorporate the new parameter. We shall call the new version `allsort` to reflect its generality:

```
dec allsort :   ( alpha # alpha -> truval ) #
                list alpha -> list alpha ;
---   allsort ( o , l )
      <= flatten ( convey ( o , l , null ) ) ;
```

`flatten` is the polymorphic version from §5.18. To use `allsort`, we must supply a suitable ordering function as its actual parameter. By supplying the primitive function < we can mimic the original `sort` function of §5.19:

```
allsort ( nonop < , "liquorice" ) ;
"ceiiloqru" : list char
```

Even when sorting lists of characters, the new function is more flexible than our original `sort`, for we can sort the characters into *reverse* lexical order simply by supplying a different ordering function:

Sec. 6.16]   POLYMORPHIC SORTING REVISITED   161

```
allsort ( nonop > , "liquorice" ) ;
"urqoliiec" : list char
```

In sort, the ordering function < appeared explicitly in insert, which would have to be changed if a different ordering were required.

We can also use allsort to sort objects which cannot be compared using the primitive relational operations. For exercise 7 of chapter 3 we wrote a function precedes for ordering two words (lists of characters). We can use allsort together with precedes to sort a list of words:

```
allsort ( precedes , l )
   where l == [ "fie" , "fum" , "fee" , "fo" ] ;
[ "fee" , "fie" , "fo" , "fum" ] : list ( list char )
```

We are finally in a position to solve the problem which gave rise to the discussion of polymorphic sorting in §5.19: sorting a list of staff records. To sort the records into ascending order by age, we can supply the following non-strict ordering function:

```
dec ageless : staff # staff -> truval ;
--- ageless ( st ( _ , a ) , st ( _ , b ) ) <= a < b ;
```

Notice the use of _ to indicate that we are not interested in the name components of the staff records. We can use ageless with allsort like this:

```
let s == [ st ( "Joe" , 18 ) , st ( "Peg" , 67 ) ,
           st ( "Tim" , 33 ) , st ( "Abe" , 17 ) ,
           st ( "Fay" , 22 ) , st ( "Huw" , 42 ) ]

    in allsort ( ageless , s ) ;

[ st ( "Abe" , 17 ) , st ( "Joe" , 18 ) ,
  st ( "Fay" , 22 ) , st ( "Tim" , 33 ) ,
  st ( "Huw" , 42 ) , st ( "Peg" , 67 ) ] : list staff
```

We can use the following ordering function to sort the records into alphabetical order of employee name:

```
dec nameless : staff # staff -> truval ;
--- nameless ( st ( n , _ ) , st ( m , _ ) )
    <= precedes ( n , m ) ;
```

This time we use _ to indicate that the age components are not used to define the result of the function. The records are sorted like this:

```
        let s == [ st ( "Joe" , 18 ) , st ( "Peg" , 67 ) ,
                   st ( "Tim" , 33 ) , st ( "Abe" , 17 ) ,
                   st ( "Fay" , 22 ) , st ( "Huw" , 42 ) ]

        in allsort ( nameless , s ) ;

        [ st ( "Abe" , 17 ) , st ( "Fay" , 22 ) ,
          st ( "Huw" , 42 ) , st ( "Joe" , 18 ) ,
          st ( "Peg" , 67 ) , st ( "Tim" , 33 ) ]  :  list staff
```

6.17 Higher order functions over abstract data types

The idea of processing every element of a data structure is so fundamental that higher-order functions should always be provided among the standard access functions for any abstract data type we implement. To see why, consider the abstract polymorphic vectors from exercise 13 of chapter 5. Its access functions include `index` (of type `num # vector alpha -> alpha`) to obtain the value of a specified element and `update` (of type `num # alpha # vector alpha -> vector alpha`) to replace a specified element with a new value, but do not include any iterators or consolidators. Suppose that we are writing a program which uses vectors and wish to write a `MapVector` function for convenience. The access functions can only locate elements by numeric index, so a function to treat successive elements will need extra variables to count the elements. The following function applies an arbitrary function f to consecutive elements i through j of a vector v:

```
        dec repeat :  ( alpha -> alpha ) # num # num #
                      vector alpha  ->  vector alpha ;
        --- repeat ( f , i , j , v )
             <= if i > j
                then v
                else ( repeat ( f , i + 1 , j , w )
                        where w == update ( i , a , v )
                        where a == f ( index ( i , v ) ) ) ;
```

It is straightforward to write `MapVector` using `repeat`, and the access functions `bound` (of type `vector alpha -> num`) to find the lower bound of a vector and `size` (also of type `vector alpha -> num`) to find the number of elements:

```
        dec MapVector :  ( alpha -> alpha ) # vector alpha ->
                         vector alpha ;
        --- MapVector ( f , v )
             <= repeat ( f , b , b + size v - 1 , v )
                 where b == bound v ;
```

Sec. 6.17] HIGHER ORDER FUNCTIONS OVER ABSTRACT DATA TYPES 163

Although it is not difficult for the user of the abstract data type to write `MapVector`, the result is unsatisfactory for two reasons. The first is that the result vector is restricted to containing the same component type as the input vector because `repeat` uses `update` to replace individual elements. Since all elements of a vector must have the same type, it is logically impossible for `update` to change the type of a single element. The second reason is that `repeat` uses `index` and `update` to obtain and change each element from the input vector, increasing the cost of `repeat` by a factor proportional to the vector size. Its actual cost depends on the total cost of `index` and `update`. If vector elements are held in a linear data structure (such as a list or a sequence) then `index` and `update` have O(n) cost, and `repeat` has O(n^2) cost. If the vector elements are held in a balanced binary tree, `index` and `update` will have O($\log_2 n$) cost, so the cost of `repeat` will be O($n.\log_2 n$).

We can only write a general vector iterator (*i.e.* yielding a `vector beta`) with optimal cost if we have detailed knowledge of the representation type, implying that `MapVector` should be an access function of the abstract type. Suppose that we have chosen the following representation for vectors:

```
data vector alpha == vec ( num # list alpha ) ;
```

then provided that we already have an iterator for lists (such as `map` from §6.4), we can simply write `MapVector` like this:

```
dec MapVector : ( alpha -> beta ) # vector alpha ->
                 vector beta ;
--- MapVector ( f , vec ( n , l ) )
    <= vec ( n , map ( f , l ) ) ;
```

which has O(n) cost because `map` has O(n) cost. Furthermore, since `map` can yield a `list beta`, `MapVector` can yield a `vector beta`. To improve the cost of `index` and `update`, the exercise also suggested an alternative representation of vectors as binary trees, perhaps:

```
data vector alpha == vec ( num # bin alpha ) ;
```

If we have a suitable iterator for objects of type `bin alpha` (say `MapBin`, left as an exercise to the reader), then `MapVector` may be written as follows:

```
--- MapVector ( f , vec ( n , b ) )
    <= vec ( n , MapBin ( f , b ) ) ;
```

Changing the vector representation will not reduce the cost of `MapVector`, because we must (by definition) process every element. However, its O(n) cost is still an improvement on the O($n.\log_2 n$) cost of the version which used `index` and `update` to obtain and change the vector elements.

6.18 Review

Here is a summary of the main points introduced in this chapter:

- Higher-order functions allow the operations in their defining expressions to be abstracted as formal parameters.

- Many common patterns of computation found in programs can be represented using a single higher-order function.

- The higher-order function `map` represents a class of iterators which apply a function to every element of a list to generate an isomorphic list.

- An application of `map` to a given function and list of values is equivalent to a list of applications of the function to the individual list elements.

- Primitive infix operations can be supplied as actual parameters by prefixing them with `nonop`.

- The input and result list of `map` can be arbitrary data types, allowing a polyadic function to be applied to a list of tuples.

- Iterators are introduced which apply a given function to every element of a non-linear data type to generate an isomorphic structure.

- The higher-order function `reduce` represents a class of consolidators which apply a dyadic function to adjacent pairs of list elements and a final base value.

- Applying `reduce` to a list is equivalent to composing together applications of the given function to the list elements and the base value.

- The input list and result of `reduce` can be arbitrary data types, allowing lists to be converted to non-linear structures.

- Consolidators may apply the given function left-associatively and define the base value by a second given function.

- Consolidators may apply a polyadic function to the elements of a non-linear data type. They can be used to convert a non-linear data structure to a linear one.

- Polymorphic sorting functions can be written as higher-order functions which abstract the operation used to order individual pairs of objects to be sorted.

- Higher-order iterators and consolidators for abstract data types should be provided as access functions of the abstract type.

6.19 Exercises

1. The traffic lights in a street are linked and change at the same time. The state of the street is represented by a list light (as in exercise 1 of chapter 4). Use change (from the same exercise) and map (from §6.4) to show the state of the street after each set of lights has changed once.

2. An accumulator in a digital computer is represented by a list switch (as defined in §4.1) and represents numbers in binary notation. A negative binary number is represented in *two's complement* form by flipping every bit of its positive equivalent and adding one to the result. Use map, flip (from §4.1) and increment (from §4.2) to form the two's complement of the binary number represented by an accumulator.

3. Write the following higher-order iterators:

    (a) MapSeq over objects of type seq alpha (as defined in §5.4).

    (b) MapBin over objects of type bin alpha (as defined in §5.8). This is the function which we required in the final example of §6.17.

4. Write a higher-order iterator choose which applies a given *predicate* (a function of type alpha -> truval) to the elements of a list and returns a list of the elements for which the predicate is true. Write expressions which use choose to eliminate all the even numbers from a list of numbers (use odd from §2.4) and to count the number of lower-case letters in a string (use LowerCase from §2.4 and the polymorphic version of length from §5.13).

5. Write a higher-order iterator pairwise, which given a dyadic function and *two* lists, applies the function to corresponding pairs of list elements to yield a list of results. pairwise (nonop - , [9 , 7 , 5] , [8 , 5 , 2]) evaluates to [1 , 2 , 3]. Allow for the possibility that all three lists may contain different types of object. Write expressions which use pairwise with both and either (from exercise 2 of chapter 4) respectively to form the switch-by-switch conjunction and disjunction of two accumulators. Suggest a more robust definition of pairwise which will not fail when the input lists are of different lengths.

6. Write expressions using reduce (from §6.9) which evaluate to on if *any* of the switches of an accumulator are on (using either) and if *all* of the switches are on (using both). Assume that all accumulators hold at least one bit.

7. Write a function RightInsert (of type list alpha # alpha -> list alpha) to insert an object into the *right-hand* end of a list. Write an expression which uses reduce and RightInsert to reverse a list. What is the cost of evaluating this expression?

8. Write a function LeftAdd (of type list alpha # alpha -> list alpha) to add an object to the *left-hand* end of a list. Write an expression which uses LeftRed (from §6.13) and LeftAdd to reverse a list. What is the cost of evaluating this new expression?

9. A *word* is represented as a seq char and a sentence as a seq *word*. Write an expression using MapSeq (from exercise 3 above), elements (from exercise 1 of chapter 5) with ConSeq and id (both from §6.12) to calculate the average word length in a given sentence.

10. Use RedTree (from §6.14) to form the mirror image of a tree alpha as defined in §5.10. *Hint:* first define a suitable given function; this will have three arguments and return a tree.

11. Write a higher-order consolidator SquashTree over the type tree alpha which takes a *dyadic* given function (be careful with the associativity). What is the most general possible type that SquashTree may have?

12. Write an expression using SquashTree which will flatten a tree alpha to a list alpha. What is its cost?

13. Write an expression using SquashTree and insert from §5.10 which will construct an ordered tree of numbers from an unordered tree. What is its cost?

Chapter 7

Creating New Functions

7.1 Anonymous functions

Before using `allsort` in §6.16 we needed to define the functions `ageless` and `nameless` to supply as actual parameters of applications. Both the definitions were trivial, consisting of a single non-recursive equation, and each was used only once. Their definitions may actually confuse a reader of the program because they are never applied using their names; they are effectively renamed when supplied as the actual parameter of a higher-order function and are applied within it using the name of the corresponding formal parameter. In cases like this the auxiliary functions are really being used only to create abstract expressions which will be evaluated later when values are available for their formal parameters.

To avoid the need to define trivial functions for this purpose, Hope provides a form of abstract expression called a *lambda expression* which may be written directly in the program at the point it is required, such as an actual parameter in a higher-order function application. Here is a lambda expression which corresponds to the abstract Celsius-to-Fahrenheit conversion expression of §2.1:

```
lambda f => ( f - 32 ) * 5 div 9
```

The symbol => can be read as "is defined as ...", and is followed by the abstract expression. `lambda` is a reserved word, and `f` is a formal parameter which is used in the expression. The lambda expression may be considered to represent an *anonymous function* with one formal parameter. The => symbol is equivalent to the <= symbol of a conventional recursion equation, whilst the abstract expression corresponds to the

168 CREATING NEW FUNCTIONS [Ch. 7

right-hand side. The abstract expression is known as the *body* of the lambda expression and the complete "equation" is called a *rule*. The formal parameter f is local to the rule.

If we had not already defined the Celsius function in §2.2, we might use this lambda expression directly as the actual parameter of map to find the Celsius equivalents of a series of Fahrenheit temperatures:

```
map ( lambda f => ( f - 32 ) * 5 div 9 , l )
    where l == [ 40 , 65 , 103 ] ;
[ 4 , 18 , 47 ] : list num
```

In this example the second argument of map has been abstracted solely to make the expression more readable.

7.2 More complex bodies

We may use lambda expressions to substitute for many of the named functions used as actual parameters in the examples of chapter 6. For instance, the following lambda expression is equivalent to the function square used in §6.2:

```
lambda n => n * n
```

The formal parameter and the result of the expression may be of any arbitrary type; the following lambda expression yielding a truth value is equivalent to the function odd used in §6.4:

```
lambda n => n mod 2 = 1
```

The body may contain any valid Hope construction, including conditionals and applications of user-defined functions; the following lambda expression is equivalent to the function fold used in §6.3:

```
lambda c => if LowerCase c
            then chr ( ord c + ord 'A' - ord 'a' )
            else c
```

We may abstract more than one formal parameter from the body. Such a lambda expression corresponds to a function of more than one argument. The following lambda expression is equivalent to the dyadic function max used in §6.6:

```
lambda ( x , y ) => if x > y then x else y
```

The expression which introduces the formal parameters is identical to the left-hand side of a recursion equation, and represents a *pattern match* on a pair of values in just the same way. Any valid pattern may appear on the left-hand side of a lambda rule, matching any constructors or using _ to represent formal parameters not used in the body. The following lambda expression is equivalent to the function `ageless` defined in §6.16:

```
lambda ( st ( _ , a1 ) , st ( _ , a2 ) ) => a1 < a2
```

A lambda expression cannot represent a *recursive* function directly because it is anonymous, hence there is no way it can refer to itself within the body. However we have seen that many recursive functions may be written without explicit recursion using map, and these can be represented by lambda expressions. The following lambda expression is equivalent to the non-recursive version of `shout` from §6.6:

```
lambda w => map ( fold , w )
```

7.3 Finding the type of a lambda expression

An important difference between lambda expressions and named functions is that we do not need to declare their types to the Hope Machine. The type of a lambda expression can be deduced from the type of the expression forming the body and the constructors (if any) used on the left-hand side of the rule. For example, the lambda expressions replacing `ageless` and `nameless` have a pair of parameter expressions containing `staff` constructors and form their results by applying `truval`-valued functions (< and `precedes` respectively) in their bodies; they therefore have the type `staff # staff -> truval`.

In the case of the lambda expression representing `shout`, the reasoning is more subtle because there are no constructors on the left-hand side and the body applies a *polymorphic* function. The type of map is (alpha -> beta) # list alpha -> list beta. The first actual parameter in the application of map is `fold`, which has been declared as `char -> char`, hence alpha and beta must both be characters. From this we can deduce that both the formal parameter w and the result of applying map are lists of characters and hence that the type of the lambda expression is `list char -> list char`.

If we are unsure about the type of a lambda expression which we propose to use in a program, we may leave the hard work of deduction to the Hope Machine by entering the expression directly. The declarations of any user-defined types or functions which are referred to in the body of the lambda expression must already have been entered:

```
lambda w => map ( fold , w ) ;
lambda w => map ( fold , w ) : list char -> list char
```

The lambda expression is already in normal form, so the Hope Machine simply displays it as it was entered, together with its type.

7.4 Programming style again

Deciding when to supply a lambda expression as an actual parameter and when to define a named function for the purpose is a matter of judgment similar to deciding when to use a qualified expression. As a general rule of thumb, a subexpression which is used more than once should be named unless it is particularly simple. Even when it is only used once it may still be a good idea to name it, especially when it is a complex term in an otherwise simple or well-understood context. We did just this in §7.1 when we abstracted the list of Fahrenheit temperatures to clarify the application of map.

We can use similar criteria to decide when to use a lambda expression, but we have a choice of two abstraction mechanisms. As well as defining a named function we may abstract and name the lambda expression using a qualifying expression. For example, we might equally well have clarified the example of §7.1 by writing the application of map as:

```
map ( c , [ 40 , 65 , 103 ] )
  where c == lambda f => ( f - 32 ) * 5 div 9
```

Although we can use this mechanism to name a lambda expression, the result is still not equivalent to a named function, because it cannot be recursive. We might try to use a lambda expression like this to find factorials:

```
fact 8
  where fact == lambda x
                => if x = 0
                   then 1
                   else x * fact ( x - 1 ) ;
```

but the Hope Machine will report:

```
ERROR-99: Undefined name: fact
```

The expression is invalid because the qualifying expression introduces a *new* name distinct from those in the qualified expression (*cf.* §2.18). The fact applied in the body of the lambda expression is *different* to that applied in the top-level application, and it is this one which is undefined.

Although program clarity is an important criterion in deciding when to use a lambda expression, it is rather subjective. In §6.11 we saw how to obtain the effect of map by using reduce with the auxiliary function SqrCons. The latter was defined solely for use in this context and we can dispense with it by using a lambda expression:

```
lambda ( n , l ) => square n :: l
```

The lambda expression seems just as clear as the named function, and the program as a whole is more concise, but there is a more subtle clarity issue. By abstracting the function `square` from this example, we can see that in general:

```
map ( f , l )
```

is equivalent to:

```
reduce ( lambda ( n , l ) => f n :: l , nil , l )
```

Notice that there are *two* objects named l in this expression. The first is a formal parameter of the lambda expression (and hence local to it) whilst the second is the actual parameter of the application of `reduce`.

In theory the use of this construction allows us to dispense with the definition of `map` itself, but there are good reasons not to do so. The issue is not the clarity or conciseness of a lambda expression as against a named function, but that of the expression as a whole. It is far from obvious that `reduce` is being used here simply to mimic `map`. Using `map` explicitly alerts the reader of the program to the fact that a well-understood pattern of recursion is being used, whereas the version using `reduce` has more of the quality of an intellectual puzzle than a straightforward statement of intent. This objection also applies to the original example using `SqrCons`, which should be seen as an illustration of the power of `reduce` rather than a serious alternative to using `map`.

Finally, it should be remembered that a named function is often clearer than a lambda expression because its type appears explicitly in its declaration, whereas the type of a lambda expression must be deduced by the reader. A knowledge of object types is essential for reading a program; the discipline of writing type declarations is also essential for writing one because it forces the author to think clearly about the types of objects before writing functions to manipulate them.

7.5 Partial application

Suppose we want to multiply every element of a list of numbers by 2. This is clearly a job for `map`, given a suitable function to supply as its actual parameter. This will be a very simple function, and may easily be represented by a lambda expression:

```
lambda n => n * 2
```

This expression represents the anonymous monadic function which multiplies its argument by 2, and will be used like this:

```
map ( lambda n => n * 2 , [ 1 , 2 , 3 , 4 ] ) ;
[ 2 , 4 , 6 , 8 ] : list num
```

The body of the lambda expression is an application of * with its first operand abstracted. An alternative interpretation is that the body is an application of * with only its second operand instantiated. The function which it represents can be thought of as a *specialised version* of * whose second argument is always 2. Using a lambda expression in this way to fix one or more of the arguments of an existing function and define a new one of fewer arguments is called *partial application*. The value 2 is said to be *bound in* to the application of * in the lambda body.

Partial application is a useful technique. The insertion sorting function sort of §5.11 was later developed in two different ways: in §6.11 we eliminated the auxiliary function transfer by using reduce, whilst in §6.16 we defined a higher-order polymorphic version allsort, parametrised with an ordering function. It is hard to combine these two ideas because the auxiliary function place of §6.16 cannot be used as a parameter of reduce (as into was in §6.11), because it has the wrong type. However, using partial application we can fix the second argument of place to define a specialised ordered insertion function of type alpha # list alpha -> list alpha. There is no restriction on the type of object which may be bound into a lambda expression; here we bind in the primitive operation < to give a lambda expression representing a function with the same type and effect as into:

    lambda (i , t) <= place (i , nonop < , t)

place can be specialised in any number of ways by binding in an appropriate ordering function. By partially applying it to ageless (from §6.16) we obtain a function for inserting staff records into staff record trees ordered by age:

    lambda (i , t) <= place (i , ageless , t)

We can use this with the polymorphic version of flatten and reduce to sort a list of staff records by age; qualified expressions are used for clarity:

    let l == [st ("Joe" , 18) , st ("Peg" , 67) ,
               st ("Tim" , 33) , st ("Abe" , 17) ,
               st ("Fay" , 22) , st ("Huw" , 42)]

      in let f == lambda (i , t)
                  => place (i , ageless , t)

         in flatten (reduce (f , null , l))

7.6 Why lambda expressions are powerful

After reading §7.4, the reader might wonder if it is *ever* preferable to use a lambda expression instead of a named function. In fact there are occasions when we cannot actually achieve the desired effect using a named function. In §7.5 we partially applied

* to 2 and used it with `map` to double every element of a list of numbers. Here we do the same again, but slightly differently:

```
map ( lambda n => n * i , [ 1 , 2 , 3 , 4 ] )
   where i == 2
```

The difference is that the value of the second (fixed) parameter of * is not specified directly in the body of the lambda expression, but *indirectly* using a qualifying expression. When the qualified expression is reduced and `i` has been instantiated, the expression becomes:

```
map ( lambda n => 2 * n , [ 1 , 2 , 3 , 4 ] )
```

which is the identical to the one we wrote in §7.5. This seems unremarkable, but it has an important implication: we do not know what function the lambda expression represents until the qualified expression has been reduced. Effectively, the lambda expression represents an indefinitely large *set* of monadic functions, each of which "scales" its argument by a constant factor (determined by the value of `i`). Within the lambda expression, `i` is called a *free variable*, in contrast to the the formal parameter n, which is called a *bound variable*.

Lambda expressions containing free variables must always appear as terms of larger expressions which define the values of the free variables. In the following example, the lambda expression for scaling numbers appears on the right-hand side of a recursion equation defining a named function:

```
dec scale : list num # num -> list num ;
--- scale ( l , i ) <= map ( lambda n => n * i , l ) ;
```

Notice that although `i` is free in the body of the lambda expression, it is bound in the recursion equation because it is a formal parameter of `scale` and will be instantiated when the latter is applied:

```
            scale ( [ 1 , 2 , 3 , 4 ] , 10 )
                          ↓
map ( lambda n => n * 10 , [ 1 , 2 , 3 , 4 ] )
                          ↓
                 [ 10 , 20 , 30 , 40 ]
```

The ability to use free variables in the bodies of lambda expressions makes them more powerful than named functions because recursion equations may contain only bound variables. The declaration of a named function introduces a *constant* function. A lambda expression does not represent a function directly, but rather *yields* one when it is evaluated; it thus represents a *variable* function.

7.7 Multi-rule lambda expressions

In §7.2 we saw that the pattern on the left-hand side of a lambda expression may be used to match any constructor function. Suppose that we wish to remove the first letter from every word in a sentence. One way of doing this might be to use `map` with a suitable lambda expression:

```
map ( lambda ( _ :: t ) => t , l )
   where l == [ "the" , "mate" , "climbs" ] ;
[ "he" , "ate" , "limbs" ] : list ( list char )
```

This is concise and clear, but it is *unsafe* for the same reason that patterns using list constructors are unsafe in qualified expressions (see §3.18 and §5.17): the pattern match will fail if the lambda expression is applied to an empty list. This implies that any lambda expression over a data type defined by more than one constructor will be unsafe. Fortunately, Hope provides a way out of this difficulty by allowing a lambda expression to contain more than one rule. It is written like this:

```
lambda r₁ | r₂ | ... | rₙ
```

Here, r_1, r_1, etc. are rules of the form *pattern* => *body* where *body* is any valid Hope expression, as described in §7.2. The symbol | separating the rules is a "vertical bar" and should be carefully distinguished from similar symbols such as 1, I and l.

A multi-rule lambda expression is equivalent to a function defined by more than one recursion equation. When it is applied, the correct rule is selected by pattern matching on the constructors used to form the actual parameter. As with named functions, the set of patterns must be complete and non-overlapping for safety. It should go without saying that the expressions forming the bodies must all have the same type, which is also the type of the whole expression. We may decapitate lists safely with a multi-rule lambda expression:

```
lambda ( _ :: t ) => t | nil => nil
```

Because a multi-rule lambda expression is harder to write and understand than a single-rule one, we may wish to satisfy ourselves that it is correct before using it in a program. Since a lambda expression represents a function, we may test it by applying it directly to an actual parameter of the correct type:

```
f nil
   where f == lambda ( _ :: t ) => t | nil => nil ;
nil : list alpha
```

In this example, the qualified expression was used solely for clarity, and we can dispense with it by instantiating f with the entire lambda expression:

```
( lambda ( _ :: t ) => t | nil => nil ) "crest" ;
"rest" : list char
```

When writing a lambda expression in this context, it must be parenthesised because there is no explicit symbol to mark the end of it. Without parentheses, the expression will be interpreted as:

```
lambda ( _ :: t ) => t | nil => ( nil "crest" )
```

which will be rejected by the type-checker because we may not apply `nil` to the actual parameter `"crest"`. When reading lambda expressions, it is useful to think of the symbols `lambda`, `=>` and `|` as being a distfix operation. Like the tupling and list-constructing operations, there are an indefinite number of these "lambda-forming" operations, called `lambda ... => ...`, `lambda ... => ... | ... => ...` and so on. The priority of the lambda-forming operations is less than any other operation except for `,` and a lambda expression must be parenthesised unless a `,` or `;` follows. In particular, the priority of the lambda-forming operations is less than that of `where`, so that:

```
lambda p₁ => e₁ | p₂ => e₂ where v == e₃
```

is interpreted as:

```
lambda p₁ => e₁ | p₂ => ( e₂ where v == e₃ )
```

and the value of v is defined only within the expression e_2. If we want to qualify both bodies, we must parenthesise the whole lambda expression:

```
( lambda p₁ => e₁ | p₂ => e₂ ) where v == e₃
```

For the same reason we could not have simplified the example of §7.1 by writing:

```
map ( c , l )
  where c == lambda f => ( f - 32 ) * 5 div 9
    where l == [ 40 , 65 , 103 ]
```

because the second `where` qualifies only the right-hand side of the lambda expression, and the name `l` in the application of `map` is *undefined*. To get the required effect, we must write:

```
map ( c , l )
  where c == ( lambda f => ( f - 32 ) * 5 div 9 )
    where l == [ 40 , 65 , 103 ]
```

or more subtly:

```
map ( c , l )
  where l == [ 40 , 65 , 103 ]
    where c == lambda f => ( f - 32 ) * 5 div 9
```

With the `let` form of qualified expression, the entire expression following the `in` symbol is qualified, and a lambda expression in this context need not be parenthesised provided a `,` or `;` follows:

```
let v == e₃ in lambda p₁ => e₁ | p₂ => e₂
```

If we want to qualify only e_1, the lambda expression may be written:

```
lambda p₁ => e₁ where v == e₃ | p₂ => e₂
```

or, using the `let` form:

```
lambda p₁ => let v == e₃ in e₁ | p₂ => e₂
```

Since `lambda ... => ... | ... => ...` represents an indivisible distfix operation, we can qualify the whole lambda expression, or an individual expression forming the body of a rule. There is no way of using a single `let` or `where` operation to qualify (for instance) two out of three bodies.

7.8 Functionals

In chapter 6 we saw how functions may be passed as actual parameters to applications of higher-order functions, and in §7.6 how they may be created as the result of evaluating lambda expressions. Hope treats functions as data objects in a completely general manner, and it will come as no surprise to find that they may also be returned as the *results* of function applications. Functions which yield functions as their results are called *functionals*. The function `scale` of §7.6 created a partially applied version of `*` which was then supplied as the actual parameter of an application of `map`. In the following example we create the same new function, but return it directly as the result of the function which creates it:

```
dec multiplier : num -> num -> num ;
--- multiplier i <= lambda n => n * i ;
```

Notice that the type expression is not parenthesised because the `->` symbol associates to the right (*cf.* §6.2), and the expression is interpreted as:

```
num -> ( num -> num )
```

as required. Here we evaluate `multiplier` by entering an application directly into the Hope Machine:

```
multiplier 3 ;
lambda n => n * 3 : num -> num
```

We can see that the actual parameter of the application has been bound into the lambda expression, and that the result is a partially applied version of * which multiplies its argument by 3. The new function may itself be evaluated by applying it directly to an argument in the usual way:

```
multiplier 3 10
```

There are *two* applications here; since they are of equal priority, they associate to the left and the expression is interpreted as:

```
( multiplier 3 ) 10
```

so that `multiplier` is first applied to 3, and the resulting function is then applied to 10, leading to the following sequence of reductions:

$$(\text{multiplier } 3) \ 10$$
$$\downarrow$$
$$(\text{lambda } n => n * 3) \ 10$$
$$\downarrow$$
$$(10 * 3)$$

As we saw in §7.5, there is no restriction on the type of an object which is bound into a lambda expression. The following generalisation of `multiplier` creates a monadic function by partially applying an arbitrary dyadic function to a specific argument value. In general, the type of a dyadic function is `alpha # beta -> gamma`, and we shall fix the second argument with a value of type `beta`. The resulting monadic function will therefore be of type `alpha -> gamma`, and the declaration of a function to create it (which we shall call `monadic`) will be:

```
dec monadic : ( alpha # beta -> gamma ) # beta ->
              ( alpha -> gamma ) ;
```

The result will be defined by a lambda expression containing two bound-in values, one of which is the the given dyadic function, and the other the required value for the second argument:

```
--- monadic ( f , y ) <= lambda x => f ( x , y ) ;
```

The following application of `monadic` creates a specialised version of `power` (from §2.15) which is equivalent to `square` (from §2.6):

178 CREATING NEW FUNCTIONS [Ch. 7]

```
monadic ( power , 2 ) ;
lambda x => power ( x , 2 ) : num -> num
```

7.9 Programming style revisited
As in the case of the function created by applying `multiplier`, we may apply the result of `monadic` directly to an argument:

```
monadic ( power , 2 ) 101 ;
10201 : num
```

but in general we would not do this because it is much simpler to dispense with the definition of `monadic` and to write:

```
lambda x => power ( x , 2 ) 101
```

directly, or more simply still:

```
power ( 101 , 2 )
```

We would normally use a functional such as `monadic` only in situations where the resulting function will not be applied immediately, for instance when it is supplied as the actual parameter of a higher-order function:

```
map ( monadic ( power , 3 ) , nats 8 ) ;
[ 512 , 343 , 216 , 125 , 64 , 27 , 8 , 1 ] : list num
```

Of course we still do not actually need to define the functional, because we can always supply the equivalent lambda expression in this context:

```
map ( lambda x => power ( x , 3 ) , nats 9 ) ;
```

The final criterion is always clarity. The use of a named function will certainly be clearer if it represents a commonly-required abstraction, and is therefore used more than once. Even if it is only used once, it may still be clearer to define a named function, particularly if its name is chosen carefully to reflect the programmer's intention.

7.10 Generalising functions
The function `monadic` introduced in §7.8 can be used to fix the second argument of any dyadic function. A more common requirement is to create a monadic function from a dyadic one by fixing its *first* argument. We can do this using the following functional:

```
dec fix : ( alpha # beta -> gamma ) # alpha ->
          ( beta -> gamma ) ;
--- fix ( f , x ) <= lambda y => f ( x , y ) ;
```

We can use `fix` to create new functions over scalar types in the same way that we used `monadic`. Here we create a function for evaluating powers of 2:

```
fix ( power , 2 ) ;
lambda y => power ( 2 , y ) : num -> num
```

The resulting "powers of two" function may be applied directly to an argument:

```
fix ( power , 2 ) 16 - 1 ;
32767 : num
```

However, `fix` is more powerful than this simple example suggests, because we are not restricted to fixing the arguments of functions over scalar objects. In the following example we use it to create a specialised version of `map` by fixing its first argument as the `square` function:

```
fix ( map , square ) ;
lambda y => map ( square , y ) : list num -> list num
```

The Hope Machine tells us that the function created by the application of `fix` is of type `list num -> list num`. If we apply it to a list of numbers:

```
fix ( map , square ) [ 1 , 2 , 3 , 4 ] ;
[ 1 , 4 , 9 , 16 ] : list num
```

we can see that it is a function for squaring the elements. Fixing the first argument of `map` creates a function over *lists* from a function over *scalar* objects. In this case the function for squaring numbers has been turned into a function for squaring *lists* of numbers. This is a very powerful idea, because the function bound in to `map` is not restricted to scalar objects, and any function of type `alpha -> beta` can be *generalised* to one of type `list alpha -> list beta`. We may even generalise the "list-squaring" function itself:

```
fix ( map , fix ( map , square ) )
```

In this case `alpha` and `beta` are both of type `list num`, so the resulting function will be of type `list ( list num ) -> list ( list num )`, *i.e.* a function for squaring *lists* of lists of numbers:

180 CREATING NEW FUNCTIONS [Ch. 7

```
fix ( map , fix ( map , square ) ) ll
    where ll == [ [ 1 , 2 ] , [ 3 , 4 ] ] ;
[ [ 1 , 4 ] , [ 9 , 16 ] ] : list ( list num )
```

The idea of generalising functions to work on lists is sufficiently powerful that we might define a functional specifically for the purpose:

```
dec listify : ( alpha -> beta ) ->
              ( list alpha -> list beta ) ;
--- listify f <= lambda l => map ( f , l ) ;
```

Using `listify`, the first of the two examples above using `fix` can be written more simply as:

```
listify square [ 1 , 2 , 3 , 4 ]
```

This contains two function applications and is interpreted as:

```
( listify square ) [ 1 , 2 , 3 , 4 ]
```

because the two applications are of equal priority and associate to the left. The expression is reduced like this:

```
           ( listify square ) [ 1 , 2 , 3 , 4 ]
                          ↓
( lambda l => map ( square , l ) ) [ 1 , 2 , 3 , 4 ]
                          ↓
           map ( square , [ 1 , 2 , 3 , 4 ] )
```

The equivalent expression is sufficiently simple that the reader might wonder whether it is worth bothering to define `listify`. Its usefulness is clearer if we consider the second of the two `fix` examples. Using `listify` it will be written like this:

```
listify ( listify square ) ll
    where ll == [ [ 1 , 2 ] , [ 3 , 4 ] ]
```

Notice the parentheses; without them the first two function applications will associate to the left and the expression will be interpreted as:

```
( ( listify listify ) square ) ll ...
```

which will be rejected by the type-checking mechanism of the Hope Machine for reasons which will become clear in §7.11. Once again we can use rewriting to discover the equivalent expression which uses `map`:

```
              listify ( listify square ) ll ...
                            |
                reduce the inner application of listify
                            ↓
   listify ( lambda l => map ( square , l ) ) ll ...
                            |
              reduce the remaining application of listify
                            ↓
      map ( lambda l => map ( square , l ) , ll )
```

The equivalent expression is considerably more obscure than the original version using listify. The unconvinced reader is invited to square a *list of lists of lists* of numbers using map directly. Using listify, this can be specified quite simply:

```
listify ( listify ( listify square ) ) lll
   where lll ==  some list ( list ( list num ) )
```

7.11 Recursive lambda expressions

Alternative definitions of listify are possible, in particular the following, which does not use map at all:

```
dec listify :  ( alpha -> beta ) ->
               ( list alpha -> list beta ) ;
--- listify f
   <= lambda nil      => nil |
             h :: t => f h :: ( listify f ) t ;
```

Like the definition of a named recursive function, the lambda expression contains two rules, one for the base case of an empty input list and one for the general case of a non-empty input list. If we reduce a typical application of the new function, we obtain the following reduction sequence:

```
                 listify fold "shh"
                        |
              reduce the application of listify
                        ↓
   ( lambda nil    => nil |
           h :: t => fold h :: ( listify fold ) t ) "shh"
                        |
     reduce the application of the lambda expression using the general-case rule
                        ↓
            fold 's' :: ( listify fold ) "hh"
```

The resulting expression contains a further application of listify to fold, which will generate another copy of the lambda expression when it is reduced. The lambda expression thus behaves as though it is recursive.

We can see how this effect has been achieved by examining the new definition of listify. Here the term listify f appears both on the left-hand side of the recursion equation and in the body of the lambda expression on the right-hand side. If we consider the equation to be an equality (as we did in §2.5), the left-hand side can be thought of as a *name* for the right-hand side. The term listify f in the right-hand side lambda expression is thus a reference to *the lambda expression itself*. We failed to achieve this effect in the factorial example of §7.4 because of the name scope rules for qualified expressions. We have succeeded now because the name scope rules for recursion equations allow names from the left-hand side to be used throughout the right-hand side with the same meaning.

7.12 Analogues of listify

We may design functionals analogous to listify which will generalise functions over scalars to other types of data structure. Here we define a treeify function to generalise functions over the polymorphic trees of §5.10:

```
dec treeify : ( alpha -> beta ) ->
              ( tree alpha -> tree beta ) ;
--- treeify f
    <= lambda null => null |
              node ( v , l , r )
                 => node ( f v , treeify f l ,
                                 treeify f r ) ;
```

The definition is "from first principles" and uses a recursive lambda expression similar to that introduced in §7.11. Like all functions over non-linear data types, the left-hand side of the general-case lambda rule contains multiple applications of the function being defined, which we can think of as treeify f. We might use the new function like this:

```
let t == node ( 5 , node ( 7 , null , null ) ,
                    node ( 3 , null , null ) )

    in treeify square t ;

node ( 25 , node ( 49 , null , null ) ,
            node ( 9 , null , null ) ) : tree num
```

Simpler definitions of treeify are possible; using the tree iterator MapTree of §6.7, we can define it as:

```
    --- treeify f <= lambda l => MapTree ( f , l ) ;
```

The lambda expression could be eliminated by using `fix` from §7.10:

```
    --- treeify f <= fix ( MapTree , f ) ;
```

7.13 Functions in data structures

The functional `listify` introduced in §7.10 is a general mechanism for creating a function over *lists* from a function over *scalar* objects, and can be applied to any function of type `alpha -> beta`. What if we apply `listify` to a function which is itself a functional? Consider the application:

```
    listify multiplier
```

The type of `multiplier` is `num -> ( num -> num )`, hence `alpha` is a `num` and `beta` is a `num -> num`. The result of the application will therefore be an object of type `list num -> list ( num -> num )`, *i.e.* a function which takes a list of numbers and produces a *list of functions*. It should come as no surprise to us that we can create a data structure containing functions. Functions can be supplied as the actual parameters of other function applications or returned as their results; they are *first-class objects* and can appear anywhere that data items can appear. We saw an example of this in passing in §3.7 with the object:

```
    [ Celsius , square , kill ]
```

of type `list ( num -> num )`. In that example, the components of the list were named or *constant* functions, and it is hard to imagine a realistic use for it. The functional produced by applying `listify` to `multiplier` allows us to construct an arbitrary-length list of *variable* functions:

```
    listify multiplier [ 2 , 3 , 4 ] ;

    [ lambda n => n * 2 ,
      lambda n => n * 3 ,
      lambda n => n * 4 ] : list ( num -> num )
```

The functions have been produced by instantiating the free variable of the lambda expression with different values. This result may be easier to understand when we remember that an application of `listify` is equivalent to an application of `map` (*cf.* §7.11):

```
    map ( multiplier , [ 2 , 3 , 4 ] )
```

and that an application of map is equivalent to a list of applications of the given function (*cf.* §6.5):

```
[ multiplier 2 , multiplier 3 , multiplier 4 ]
```

The question which naturally arises at this point is exactly how we might use the resulting list of functions. We cannot apply it directly to an argument, because it is a list and not a function. Instead, we must write a specific function for the purpose which takes the list of functions and a list of arguments (of the same length):

```
dec listapply : list ( alpha -> alpha ) # list alpha ->
                list alpha ;
--- listapply ( nil , nil ) <= nil ;
--- listapply ( f :: ff , n :: nn )
    <= f n :: listapply ( ff , nn ) ;
```

We will use listapply like this:

```
listapply ( ff , [ 5 , 6 , 7 ] )
   where ff == listify multiplier [ 2 , 3 , 4 ] ;
```

listapply exhibits a familiar pattern of recursion, suggesting that we may be able to write a non-recursive version using a higher-order function. We cannot use map because it applies the *same* given function to each list element, whereas listapply applies successive elements of a list of given functions. Instead, a function is required which will associate the corresponding elements of the two lists together. Exercise 4 of chapter 6 required a function pairwise to apply a given function to pairs of corresponding elements from two given lists. Here is a possible definition:

```
dec pairwise : ( alpha # beta -> gamma ) # list alpha #
               list beta -> list gamma ;
--- pairwise ( f , nil , nil ) <= nil ;
--- pairwise ( f , h1 :: t1 , h2 :: t2 )
    <= f ( h1 , h2 ) :: pairwise ( f , t1 , t2 ) ;
```

pairwise captures the idea of combining the elements of two lists together and applying a dyadic function to each pair. We can certainly use it to combine the elements of a list of functions and a list of arguments together, but what function should we apply to the resulting pairs? The required operation is simply that of *function application itself.* Hope has no explicit operation to specify application, so we must provide a function for the purpose:

```
lambda ( f , a ) => f a
```

If we need to do this kind of thing very often, it may be clearer to define a named function, such as:

```
dec apply : alpha # beta -> gamma ;
--- apply ( f , a ) <= f a ;
```

We can now use `pairwise` with `apply` (or the equivalent lambda expression) to substitute for `listapply` and evaluate our list of functions:

```
pairwise ( apply , ff , [ 5 , 6 , 7 ] )
   where ff == listify multiplier [ 2 , 3 , 4 ] ;
[ 10 , 18 , 28 ] : list num
```

7.14 Using functions in data structures

As a more realistic example of the use of data structures containing functions, we shall now develop a program for evaluating arithmetic expressions which is rather more sophisticated than those of chapter 4. There we represented expressions as data structures containing a mixture of numbers and operations, with the latter represented as characters. Our solution will also use trees, but the operations will be representing as functions of type num # num -> num. The declaration of the type expression must be changed to reflect the type of binary operations:

```
data expression == rand num ++
                   rat ( ( num # num -> num ) #
                         expression # expression ) ;
```

The tree representation of 2 + 3 × 4 (for example) will now be written like this:

```
rat ( nonop + , rand 2 ,
           rat ( nonop * , rand 3 ,
                           rand 4 ) )
```

The real benefit which results from this representation is the simplification of the evaluation function `eval`. The declaration and base-case equations remain the same as in §4.18, but the general-case equation will *apply* the function held at the node:

```
--- eval ( rat ( f , l , r ) )
    <= f ( eval l , eval r ) ;
```

The advantage of the new representation now becomes apparent. Because the required function is held in the tree, we no longer require a separate equation for each possible operation. Also we may incorporate *any* function of type num # num -> num into the expression tree with no change to either the data declaration or the evaluation function. An expression such as $2^3 + 4$ can immediately be represented by a tree containing the power function of §2.15:

```
rat ( nonop + , rat ( power , rand 2 ,
                                rand 3 ) ,
                  rand 4 )
```

and evaluated directly by the new version of eval.

7.15 Programming style yet again

The expression data type defined for §7.14 is specialised for holding operations and operands, conflicting with the desire to keep the number of data types used in a program to a minimum for clarity and generality. The expression evaluation program corresponds to the sort of thing which we might have written in chapter 4 if we had known about higher-order functions. After we had been introduced to polymorphism in chapter 5, the style of our programs began to change, using a few general polymorphic data types rather than many specialised data types. If we had defined the polymorphic type tree alpha of §5.10, we might expect to use it for representing expressions rather than defining a specialised expression type. Since a polymorphic tree must contain the same type of object throughout, we must reintroduce the item data type of §4.4 to "disguise" the operators and operands as a single data type, but suitably modified to allow the operations to be functions:

```
data item == int num ++ op ( num # num -> num ) ;
```

The expression $2^3 + 4$ would now be represented by the following tree item:

```
node ( op nonop + ,
       node ( op power ,
              node ( int 2 , null , null ) ,
              node ( int 3 , null , null ) ) ,
       node ( int 4 , null , null ) )
```

Although we have eliminated the type expression, we have introduced the type item, so there is no overall reduction in program complexity. However, if we already have the polymorphic type tree alpha, it is quite likely that we will also have a suitable consolidator for it. In this case we can also dispense with the eval function. ConTree from §6.15 is suitable for this purpose, since its base case is that of nodes with empty subtrees. We recollect that its type is:

```
( alpha # beta # beta -> beta ) # ( alpha -> beta ) -> beta
```

Since alpha (the tree component type) is an item and beta (the reduced tree) is a num, the first given function must be of type item # num # num -> num and the second of type `item -> num`. The `item` argument of the first given function will be derived from a non-terminal node, and will contain a function to be applied to the two num arguments. The `item` argument of the second function will be derived from a terminal node of the tree and will contain a num to be returned as the result. Here we represent both given functions by lambda expressions:

```
ConTree ( lambda ( op f , l , r ) => f ( l , r ) ,
         lambda ( int n ) => n , T )
  where T == some tree item ;
```

7.16 True functional programming

In §3.10 we squared a list of numbers using `squares` to apply `square` to every element. In chapter 6 we learned about higher-order functions, and used `map` to express repetition, eliminating `squares`. However, even with `map`, squaring the elements of a *list* of lists needed a named "list-squaring" function (which could itself be defined using `map`) to apply to each sublist. In this chapter we have seen how a lambda expression may be used instead of a named list-squaring function. Finally we have seen functionals as a way of generalising existing functions.

As we have learned more about the power of Hope, we have written programs using fewer named functions, and functionals seem to be just one more step along this path. However, the `listify` and `treeify` examples actually represent a radically *different* style of program. Until now, our programs have created a series of new data objects by successively applying functions (using functional composition) to some initial data object to yield a final data object as the result of the program. The `listify` and `treeify` examples take a different approach, creating a series of *new functions* by successively applying *functionals* (using composition again) to an initial function to yield a "final" function. This is then applied to the initial data object to yield the result of the program in a single application. As a further example of this technique, we use both `listify` and `treeify` to generalise the `fold` function from §2.6 in two stages, first to a function over *words* (represented as lists of characters) and then to a function over trees of words:

```
let t == node ( "whisper" ,
                node ( "who"   , null , null ) ,
                node ( "dares" , null , null ) )

   in treeify ( listify fold ) t ;

node ( "WHISPER" ,
       node ( "WHO"   , null , null ) ,
       node ( "DARES" , null , null ) )
 : tree ( list char )
```

This is truly "programming with functions", and in the following sections we shall see further examples of programs written in this style.

7.17 Generalised functional composition

Suppose that we have been given a list of numbers and asked (for reasons which are obscure) to produce a list of their squares in binary representation. The functions `square` (from §2.6) and `BinaryOf` (from exercise 7 of chapter 2) perform the required operations on a single number, and the problem may then be solved easily using two applications of `map` composed together:

```
map ( BinaryOf , map ( square , l ) )
   where l == some list num
```

The solution is clear and correct, but slightly unappealing because we perform two list traversals, once to form a list of squares (which is then discarded) and again to produce the list of binary representations. However, if we had a function to find the binary representation of the square of a number, the problem could be solved with a single traversal and no intermediate list. The required function is easily defined by the following lambda expression:

```
lambda n => BinaryOf ( square n )
```

The body of the lambda expression represents successive applications of the functions to a single number. We can generalise this idea to construct a functional which will compose together a pair of arbitrary monadic functions. We shall call it `compose`, and it will be defined as follows:

```
--- compose ( f , g ) <= lambda x => g ( f x ) ;
```

The right-hand side consists of the lambda expression which we saw above, but with the functions abstracted as the formal parameters `f` and `g`. Note that the names are reversed in the body of the lambda expression, so that `f` is applied first to the formal parameter `x`, and `g` then applied to the result. In general, `f` will be of arbitrary type `alpha -> beta`. The argument of `g` must be then be of type `beta`, but its result can be of arbitrary type (say `gamma`). The type of `compose` is therefore:

```
( alpha -> beta ) # ( beta -> gamma ) -> ( alpha -> gamma )
```

The result is a function which transforms an object of type `alpha` directly to one of type `gamma`. If we use `compose` to construct a "binary square" function:

```
compose ( square , BinaryOf )
```

alpha, beta and gamma are all instantiated to num. In the following example we compose the polymorphic version of length from §5.13 with odd from §2.4:

    compose (length , odd)

length has the type list alpha -> num and odd the type num -> truval, so the result is a function of type list alpha -> truval which determines whether a list has an odd number of elements. In a context such as:

    compose (length , odd) "Oddly enough"

it has the type list char -> truval (and evaluates to false).

7.18 Functions as alternatives to data structures

The idea of successively transforming functions rather than data structures can be used to design programs in which information is implicit in the behaviour of functions rather than explicitly held in a data structure. As an example, we shall consider an alternative implementation of the lookup table abstract data type of §4.21 in which tables are represented by *functions*. We recollect that the properties of the lookup table data type are defined by the following functions:

    dec empty   : table ;
    dec update : (word # num) # table -> table ;
    dec lookup : word # table -> num ;

For the new implementation, the type synonym table will be redefined as follows:

    type table == word -> num ;

Using this representation, the lookup function becomes trivial, because the table *is* the required function. It must still be provided however, because of the need to retain compatibility with programs using it. Its definition is simply:

    --- lookup (w , t) <= t w ;

The update function will change radically. The first implementation created a new data structure containing the original information together with the new entry. Since the type of update remains the same (taking a new entry and an existing lookup table and creating a new table), we must arrange to create a *new function* whose behaviour is the same as the original for existing entries, and which is also defined over the new word. A possible definition is:

    --- update ((w , n) , t)
        <= lambda x => if x = w then n else t x ;

The right-hand side defines a function which checks its argument to see if it is the most recently added entry, otherwise it uses the original table function (identified by the free variable t) to check the argument against the earlier entries.

Finally, the empty function (defining an empty lookup table) must return a non-strict function which will evaluate to 0 for any argument, such as:

```
--- empty <= lambda _ => 0 ;
```

It is instructive to examine the representation of a non-empty table. We can do this by reducing an expression which defines one, such as:

```
update ( ( "A" , 1 ) , update ( ( "B" , 2 ) , empty ) )
```

The first step is to reduce the application of empty (the appearance of a nulladic function name always represents an application, since no parameters are required):

```
update ( ( "A" , 1 ) ,
         update ( ( "B" , 2 ) , lambda _ => 0 ) )
```

This step creates an empty table which will evaluate to 0 if applied later to any actual parameter. The next step is to reduce the inner application of update:

```
update ( ( "A" , 1 ) ,
         lambda x
            => if x = "B"
                 then 2
                 else ( lambda _ => 0 ) x )
```

This step creates a table with one entry. The empty table instantiates the formal parameter t and becomes bound into the lambda expression. It will only be evaluated if the single-entry table function is applied later to an actual parameter which is not "B". The final step is to reduce the outer application of update:

```
lambda x
   => if x = "A"
        then 1
        else ( lambda x
                  => if x = "B"
                       then 2
                       else ( lambda _ => 0 ) x ) x
```

This step creates a table with two entries. The formal parameter t has now been instantiated with the *entire lambda expression* resulting from the inner application of update, and this has become bound into the new lambda expression. It will only be

Sec. 7.18] FUNCTIONS AS ALTERNATIVES TO DATA STRUCTURES 191

evaluated if the two-entry table function is later applied to an actual parameter which is not "A". Notice that there are two *different* formal parameters named x in the final expression; the outermost x is the formal parameter of the two-entry table, and the innermost x is the formal parameter of the embedded single-entry table.

The way in which the table function works is best understood by examining the reduction sequence resulting from a typical application. Here we apply the simple two-entry table which we constructed above to the word "B":

```
( lambda x
    => if x = "A"
         then 1
         else ( lambda x
                  => if x = "B"
                       then 2
                       else ( lambda _ => 0 ) x ) x ) "B"
```
              |
instantiate x to "B" in the body of the *outer* lambda expression
              ↓
```
if "B" = "A"
   then 1
   else ( lambda x
            => if x = "B"
                 then 2
                 else ( lambda _ => 0 ) x ) "B"
```
              |
           reduce the conditional
              ↓
```
( lambda x
    => if x = "B"
         then 2
         else ( lambda _ => 0 ) x ) "B"
```
              |
instantiate x to "B" in the body of the *outer* lambda expression
              ↓
```
if "B" = "B"
   then 2
   else ( lambda _ => 0 ) "B"
```
              |
           reduce the conditional
              ↓
              2

7.19 Review

Here is a summary of the main points introduced in this chapter:

- Lambda expressions represent anonymous functions, and are written directly in the program at the point they are used.

- The type of a function denoted by a lambda expression is deduced by the Hope Machine rather than being given explicitly.

- Lambda expressions cannot directly represent recursive functions.

- Partial application allows one or more of the arguments of an existing function to be fixed, defining a new function of fewer arguments.

- Lambda expressions may contain unbound variables which are not formal parameters of the expression. They represent variable functions.

- Lambda expressions may be defined which have multiple rules which are selected by pattern matching.

- Functionals are higher-order functions which return constant or variable functions as their results.

- Data structures may be defined which contain constant or variable functions among their components.

- The use of functionals leads to a style of programming in which functions themselves are systematically transformed rather than data objects.

- Functions may defined which are equivalent to data structures.

7.20 Exercises

1. Write expressions using `MapSeq` (from exercise 3 of chapter 6) and a lambda expression to:

    (a) double every element of a `seq num`.

    (b) Find the parity of numbers in a `seq num`. The result should be a `seq truval` containing `true` for even numbers and `false` for odd ones.

    (c) As for *(b)* but each element of the output sequence should contain the original number together with the word `"odd"` or `"even"` as appropriate.

2. Write expressions using ConSeq from §6.12 with lambda expressions to:

    (a) Find the smallest element of a seq num.

    (b) Convert a seq alpha into the equivalent list alpha.

3. Write expressions using RedTree from §6.14 with a lambda expression to:

    (a) Form the mirror image of a binary tree.

    (b) Find the depth of (the longest branch of) a binary tree.

    (c) Calculate the average value (as a floating-point number) of the elements of a binary tree of numbers by traversing the tree only once.

4. Write a higher-order iterator MapNary over objects of type NaryTree alpha (as defined for exercise 12 of chapter 5). *Hint:* use map from §6.4.

5. Write a higher-order consolidator RedNary over objects of type NaryTree alpha. *Hint:* use map and consider the type of the given function carefully.

6. Write an expression using RedNary and a lambda expression to flatten an *n*-ary tree into a list. *Hint:* consider using reduce from §6.9.

7. Write non-recursive versions of the following higher-order iterators using the relevant higher-order consolidator together with one or more lambda expressions:

    (a) MapSeq from exercise 3 of chapter 6 using ConSeq from §6.12.

    (b) MapTree from §6.7 using ConTree from §6.15.

    (c) MapBin from exercise 6 of chapter 6 using ConBin from §6.15.

8. Write an expression using choose from exercise 4 of chapter 6 and compose (from §7.17) to select the elements of a list l for which a predicate p is false.

9. Write an expression using compose and fix together with transfer and flatten from §5.11 which creates a function equivalent to sort from §5.11.

10. Use compose to define a functional twice which can be applied to a monadic function f to create a function which applies f *twice* to its argument; for instance twice succ yields a function for adding 2 to a number. What do you expect *(a)* twice twice; *(b)* twice twice succ 0; and *(c)* twice twice twice succ 0 to evaluate to?

Chapter 8

Lazy Evaluation

8.1 How long is a list?

Exercise 4 of chapter 6 required a function `choose` which applied a given predicate to the elements of a list and return a list containing those elements for which the predicate yielded `true`. Here is a possible definition:

```
    dec choose : ( alpha -> truval ) # list alpha ->
                 list alpha ;
--- choose ( p , nil ) <= nil ;
--- choose ( p , h :: t )
    <= if p h
         then h :: choose ( p , t )
         else choose ( p , t ) ;
```

Here we use `choose` to select odd numbers from a list using `odd` from §2.4:

```
    choose ( odd , l )
      where l == some list num ;
```

Many similar problems can be solved using `choose`. Suppose we want to find all the integers less than 100 which are exactly divisible by either 3 or 5. One method is to generate a list of all integers less than 100, and then use `choose` to select those divisible by 3 or 5. For convenience we first define an auxiliary function to discover whether one number is a factor of a second:

```
dec factor : num # num -> truval ;
--- factor ( d , n ) <= n mod d = 0 ;
```

In the following example the predicate to test for divisibility by 3 or 5 is defined by a lambda expression which uses `factor`, and for simplicity the list of integers less than 100 is constructed using `nats` from §3.10:

```
choose ( lambda x => factor ( 3 , x ) or
                     factor ( 5 , x ) ,   nats 99 )
```

In this problem, the list is being used as a *set*, because we are only interested in the values of its elements and not in their order, which is descending magnitude because we used `nats` to generate the list of candidates. We can use `stan` (also from §3.10) if we really need the answers in ascending magnitude.

Many problems can conveniently solved by generating a set of candidate values and using `choose` to pick out suitable ones. When there are several selection criteria, it may be more convenient to do this in separate steps. Here we find all integers less than 100 which are divisible by 7 and also greater than 50, using `fix` from §7.10 to construct appropriate predicate functions from primitive binary relations:

```
choose ( fix ( nonop < , 50 ) , s )
   where s == choose ( fix ( factor , 7 ) , nats 99 )
```

The inner application of `choose` selects multiples of 7, and the outer application then selects those multiples of 7 which are greater than 50.

From the point of view of clarity, this program is slightly unsatisfactory. Of the three criteria for selecting an integer (less than 100, divisible by 7 and greater than 50), two appear explicitly as predicates in applications of `choose`, but the first is only *implicit* in the application of `nats`. It would be more consistent (and thus clearer) if all three selections were made explicitly with `choose`; however, we would still need to specify the size of the initial list produced by `nats`. Specifying a larger list would mislead readers of the program as to its intention, and make it unnecessarily expensive to evaluate, so perhaps we should live with the difficulty. Unfortunately, even if we are prepared to do so, we shall see that this is not always possible.

8.2 Infinite lists

An apparently slight variation of the number-selection problem is to find the *first* 100 numbers which are divisible by either 3 or 5. Now we have a real difficulty because there is nothing in the problem to suggest how large the starting list should be. We might reason that 300 is a good guess, since it will at least contain 100 multiples of 3, but this kind of reasoning is not generally useful, and would not help us guess the size of list guaranteed to contain (for instance) the first 100 prime numbers. We are forced to the conclusion that the only possible candidate is a list which contains *all possible* numbers — a list of *infinite* length.

It is surprisingly easy to write a Hope function to define an infinite list; indeed it is quite likely that the reader has already written one by mistake. Here is a function which defines the list of all integers from a specified starting value:

```
dec ints : num -> list num ;
--- ints n <= n :: ints ( n + 1 ) ;
```

We can see why this definition of `ints` represents a mistake by examining the first few reduction steps resulting from an application:

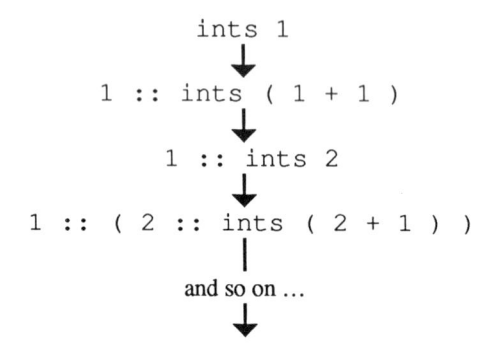

$$\begin{array}{c} \text{ints 1} \\ \downarrow \\ 1 :: \text{ints} (1 + 1) \\ \downarrow \\ 1 :: \text{ints 2} \\ \downarrow \\ 1 :: (2 :: \text{ints} (2 + 1)) \\ | \\ \text{and so on ...} \\ \downarrow \end{array}$$

It is clear that `ints` really does define an infinite list, and equally clear that it is not a useful function because (unsurprisingly) generating an infinite list requires an infinite number of reduction steps.

8.3 Lazy evaluation

Although `ints` is a perfectly good *definition* of an infinite list, we cannot use it in a practical program, because the Hope Machine (which has only a finite capacity) will always try to construct the list which it defines. This is a consequence of the applicative-order evaluation mechanism, which always evaluates the arguments of a function before applying it. In this case the function is :: and it is the evaluation of its second argument which generates the infinite reduction sequence. We first saw this problem in a slightly different form in §2.15 with the recursive definition of the `power` function. On that occasion (and subsequently) we used a conditional operation to terminate the sequence of reduction steps. This works because the conditional operation is not reduced in applicative order; instead, the evaluation of its second and third arguments (the consequent and alternative) is *delayed* until its first argument (the choice) has been evaluated (*cf.* §1.12). If all the arguments were evaluated before the choice were made, an infinite reduction sequence would still occur. Delaying the evaluation of certain arguments until their values are actually required is a form of normal-order evaluation, and is usually called *lazy evaluation*. Evaluating conditional operations lazily prevents the generation of infinitely large expressions.

8.4 Lazy constructors

In addition to the conditional, Hope provides one further operation which is evaluated lazily. This is the constructor function : : : (known as "lazy cons") which has the special property that only its first argument is evaluated. The effect of this can be seen by entering an application of : : : at the terminal:

```
( 1 + 2 ) ::: nats 4 ;
3 ::: nats 4 : list num
```

We can see from this that the first argument (1 + 2) has been reduced, whilst the second (nats 4) has not. The application of : : : is not a redex, because its arguments are not in normal form. The result is not yet an actual list, but an expression which represents one.

An important feature of this expression is that it may be used anywhere that a conventional list of numbers is required. For instance, we can count the elements using length from §3.11 or add up the elements using sum from §3.12:

```
length ( 3 ::: nats 4 ) ;
5 : num

sum ( 3 ::: nats 4 ) ;
13 : num
```

Lists constructed using : : : are known as *lazy lists*. Conventional lists (constructed with : :) are known as *strict lists* when we need to distinguish them from lazy lists.

8.5 Patterns matching lazy constructors

In the previous section we saw that it is possible to apply conventional functions such as length and sum to lazy lists. We can do this because the normal list constructor : : used in patterns on the left-hand sides of function definitions will also match the : : : constructor. However, there is an important difference between the behaviour of the two constructors in pattern matches, which can be seen by reducing an application of (for instance) sum. We recollect from §3.12 that the function is defined by the two equations:

```
--- sum nil          <= 0 ;
--- sum ( h :: t )   <= h + sum t ;
```

In an application of sum to a conventional list such as:

```
sum [ 3 , 2 , 1 ]
```

an initial reduction is performed to "expose" the first constructor of the list by rewriting it to the form h :: t:

```
sum ( 3 :: [ 2 , 1 ] )
```

This expression can now be matched against the pattern in the second recursion equation, instantiating h to 3 and t to [2 , 1]. If we apply sum to a lazy list such as that from §8.4, the first constructor is already exposed, and the instantiation step can be performed directly:

```
             sum ( 3 ::: nats 2 )
                     ↓
--- sum ( 3 :: nats 2 ) <= 3 + sum ( nats 2 )
```

Here the entire expression forming the second argument of :: is used to instantiate t, so that the reduction is effectively performed in *normal order*. The instantiated recursion equation can be used as a rewrite rule in the usual way, replacing the original application with the right-hand side of the equation:

```
3 + sum ( nats 2 )
```

This expression does not contain any further applications of ::: and can be reduced conventionally, first reducing the application of nats to a list in normal form:

```
3 + sum [ 2 , 1 ]
```

followed by reducing the recursive application of sum.

8.6 Practically infinite lists

The lazy constructor ::: enables us to define lists which behave as though they were infinite for practical purposes. As an example, consider the following slight (but significant) variation of ints from §8.2:

```
--- ints n <= n ::: ints ( n + 1 ) ;
```

Although the change involves only replacing :: by ::: the new version of ints behaves very differently from the original. If we enter an application at the terminal:

```
ints 1 ;
1 ::: ints ( 1 + 1 ) : list num
```

we can see that the lazy list is only evaluated up to the first ::: operation. The second argument remains completely unevaluated, including the argument expression of the recursive application; it effectively represents the infinite list of all remaining integers. The result list is a *finite* object however, and can be used in practical programs. Infinite lazy lists are sometimes known as *streams*. Of course we can never evaluate the whole of a stream, but for many problems we shall only need to

Sec. 8.6] PRACTICALLY INFINITE LISTS 199

use part of it. As a simple example, consider the following function, which selects a specified number of elements from the start of an arbitrary list:

```
dec first : num # list alpha -> list alpha ;
--- first ( succ n , h :: t )   <= h :: first ( n , t ) ;
--- first ( succ n , nil )      <= nil ;
--- first ( 0 , l )             <= nil ;
```

The second equation ensures safe behaviour if first is mistakenly applied to a list containing too few elements; the entire list is returned in this case. For example:

```
first ( 3 , "hugely" ) <> first ( 2 , "s" ) ;
"hugs" : list char
```

More interestingly, we can use first to select a finite number of elements from the start of an *infinite* list:

```
first ( 2 , ints 99 ) ;
[ 99 , 100 ] : list num
```

There is no danger here of the input list containing too few elements! To understand how this effect has been achieved, let us look at the way the application is reduced:

first (2 , ints 99)
|
rewrite the first argument to the form succ n and reduce the application of ints
↓
first (succ 1 , 99 ::: ints (99 + 1))
|
reduce the application of first using the first equation
↓
99 :: first (1 , ints (99 + 1))
|
rewrite the argument of ints
↓
99 :: first (1 , ints 100)
|
rewrite the first argument of first and reduce the application of ints
↓
99 :: first (succ 0 , 100 ::: ints (100 + 1))
|
reduce the application of first using the first equation
↓
99 :: (100 :: first (0 , ints (100 + 1)))

```
                99 :: ( 100 :: first ( 0 , ints ( 100 + 1 ) ) )
                                       |
                    rewrite the argument of ints and reduce its application (2 steps)
                                       ↓
        99 :: ( 100 :: first ( 0 , 101 ::: ints ( 101 + 1 ) ) )
                                       |
                    reduce the application of first using the third equation
                                       ↓
                        99 :: ( 100 :: nil )
```

The important feature of this sequence is that applications of ints are reduced only to the point where the lazy list constructor becomes visible. The two elements of the resulting lazy list then instantiate the equations for first in *normal order*. In the final reduction of first, the unevaluated infinite list is eliminated, leaving an expression which contains only applications of the normal list constructor and which represents a finite 2-element list. Instead of attempting to evaluate the list of all integers before applying first, reductions of ints *alternate* with those of first and elements are evaluated only as required. The removal of ::: by pattern matching allows the unevaluated argument to be reduced; the lazy constructor is said to be *forced* by pattern matching.

8.7 Solving problems with infinite lists

We can use infinite lists to solve selection problems where we cannot predict the size of the starting list. As before, we shall select elements using choose; however this requires a slight modification first. The reason can be seen in the following example which uses the version shown in §8.1 to select the odd integers from the list of all integers. The first few reduction steps are as follows:

```
                        choose ( odd , ints 1 )
                                    |
                        reduce the application of ints
                                    ↓
                    choose ( odd , 1 ::: ints ( 1 + 1 ) )
                                    |
                reduce the application of choose using the general-case equation
                                    ↓
            if odd 1
                then 1 :: choose ( odd , ints ( 1 + 1 ) )
                else choose ( odd , ints ( 1 + 1 ) )
                                    |
                            reduce the conditional
                                    ↓
                    1 :: choose ( odd , ints ( 1 + 1 ) )
```

The application of choose in this expression will be reduced in the same way as the top-level application, *i.e.* using the general-case equation. Since the list generated by ints will never be empty, the base-case equation will never be used and an infinite reduction sequence will result as successive applications of choose cause ints to be evaluated to completion. We can avoid this problem by modifying the second equation of choose so that it constructs its result list *lazily*:

```
--- choose ( p , h :: t )
    <= if p h
        then h ::: choose ( p , t )
        else choose ( p , t ) ;
```

The reduction sequence will be exactly the same as that shown above, except that the final expression will now be:

```
1 ::: choose ( odd , ints ( 1 + 1 ) )
```

and neither the recursive application of choose nor the application of ints which forms the second argument of ::: will be reduced. This modification to choose allows it to produce an infinite list as its result as well as consuming one. With more forethought we could have predicted the need for this, since the required list of odd integers is also infinite.

In order to evaluate the elements of a lazy list, it must form the argument of some function which actually requires them. The function first from §8.6 is one possibility. Here we evaluate the first 10 odd integers:

```
first ( 10 , choose ( odd , ints 1 ) )
```

and here the first 100 integers which are divisible by either 3 or 5 as required by the problem proposed in §8.2:

```
first ( 100 , choose ( divisible , ints 1 ) )
   where divisible == lambda x => factor ( 3 , x ) or
                                   factor ( 5 , x )
```

A small incidental benefit of using ints is that the results are in ascending order (rather than descending as with nats). Producing them in descending order is now more difficult, since it is not logically possible to generate an infinite list of integers starting with the largest! Instead, the final (finite) list must be explicitly reversed, perhaps using reverse from exercise 2 of chapter 5.

8.8 Using infinite lists safely

Because conventional list patterns may match the lazy list constructor, programs need few changes to enable them to use lazy lists. However, certain precautions must be taken if a program is to use *infinite* lists safely.

As a general rule, a function over lists whose only base case is the empty list must not be applied to an infinite list, or an infinite reduction sequence will result. Whilst functions such as sum and length can be applied without modification to *finite* lazy lists (refer to §8.4), it is clearly a mistake to write an expression like:

```
length ( ints 1 )
```

For safety, a recursive function which is applied to an infinite list must use some other method to control the recursion. One possibility is illustrated by first, which uses the value of its (finite) numeric parameter. Since infinite lists will never contain too few elements, we might be tempted to remove the second equation from its definition. This is unwise, because we may still wish to apply first to a finite list, and safe behaviour should be retained in this case.

A second possibility is to use some property of the list elements themselves to control the recursion. The following function uses a given predicate to select list elements until a value is found for which the predicate yields true:

```
dec until : ( alpha -> truval ) # list alpha ->
            list alpha ;
--- until ( p , nil ) <= nil ;
--- until ( p , h :: t )
    <= if p h
          then nil
          else h :: until ( p , t ) ;
```

The base-case equation protects us against applying until to a finite list containing no element which satisfies the predicate; as with first, the whole list is returned in this case. However, if we apply until to an infinite list, we must be sure that the list will contain at least one element which satisfies the predicate. Not all mistakes will be as obvious as this one:

```
until ( lambda x => x < 10 , ints 20 )
```

The two techniques shown above for controlling recursion apply to all functions over lists, irrespective of their result type. A third technique is specific to functions which produce lists, with the recursive application defining the tail of the result list. If the result list is constructed lazily, the recursive application will be delayed until the an element of the list which it defines is actually required. We used this technique in §8.7 to prevent choose attempting to evaluate the infinite list of integers. We can also use it to improve the definition of until, changing its second equation to:

```
--- until ( p , h :: t )
    <= if p h
       then nil
       else h ::: until ( p , t ) ;
```

Once again the base-case equation is redundant for infinite input lists, but should be retained for safe behaviour with finite lists. Using this definition of `until`, the "deliberate mistake" example above will now be reduced as follows:

$$\text{until (lambda x => x < 10 , ints 20)}$$
$$\downarrow \text{reduce the application of } \texttt{ints}$$
$$\text{until (lambda x => x < 10 , 20 ::: ints (20 + 1))}$$
$$\downarrow \text{reduce the application of } \texttt{until} \text{ using the general-case equation}$$
$$\begin{array}{l}\text{if (lambda x => x < 10) 20} \\ \text{then nil} \\ \text{else 20 ::: until (lambda x => x < 10 , ints (20 + 1))}\end{array}$$
$$\downarrow \text{reduce the conditional}$$
$$\text{20 ::: until (lambda x => x < 10 , ints (20 + 1))}$$

Once the `:::` constructor is exposed, no further reductions are performed. Recursive applications which are delayed using this mechanism will be evaluated when the application of `:::` is removed from the top-level expression, *i.e.* when the elements of the lazy list are actually required. We saw an example of this in §8.7 when we constructed a list of the first 10 odd integers using elements from the head of a lazy list of all odd integers. It is left as an instructive exercise to the reader to examine the resulting reduction sequence.

8.9 Infinite lists and non-strict functions

It is always safe to supply an infinite list to a function which is not strict in the corresponding argument. Here we apply the polymorphic version of `incr` from §6.9 to the infinite list of all integers:

```
incr ( ints 1 , 10 ) ;
11 : num
```

This is unsurprising, since `incr` ignores its first argument (*cf.* §2.14). Hope's applicative-order evaluation mechanism makes non-strict functions less useful than they might be, because any unused arguments are always evaluated. At best this leads to redundant computation; at worst an error in evaluating an unused argument will cause the entire program to fail, as shown in §2.14. The lazy list constructor provides a restricted form of normal-order evaluation, and increases the usefulness of non-strict functions.

A function does not need to ignore an argument to be non-strict; it is sufficient that it does not require the argument to be fully evaluated. For example, consider the join function which we defined in §5.13 as follows:

```
dec join : list alpha # list alpha -> list alpha ;
--- join ( nil , l )      <= l ;
--- join ( h :: t , l ) <= h :: join ( t , l ) ;
```

The second argument appears as a term in the expression defining the result, however, it is never decomposed by pattern matching, and its construction and value are irrelevant to the behaviour of join. This means that we may safely supply an infinite list as the second argument. For example:

$$join ([1 , 2] , ints\ 3)$$

rewrite the first argument to the form h :: t and reduce the application of ints

$$join (1 :: [2] , 3 ::: ints (3 + 1))$$

reduce the application of join using the general-case equation

$$1 :: join ([2] , 3 ::: ints (3 + 1))$$

rewrite the first argument of join to the form h :: t

$$1 :: join (2 :: nil , 3 ::: ints (3 + 1))$$

reduce the application of join using the general-case equation

$$1 :: (2 :: join (nil , 3 ::: ints (3 + 1)))$$

reduce the application of join using the base-case equation

$$1 :: (2 :: (3 ::: ints (3 + 1)))$$

The result is an infinite list with the first three elements evaluated. The applicative-order evaluation mechanism causes ints to be evaluated in the top-level application of join, but the resulting expression is not evaluated any further in the lower-level applications of join or :: because of the lazy constructor, which can only be removed by pattern matching. The primitive function <> behaves similarly. This observation has the important consequence that infinite lists may be incorporated safely into data structures. In some cases it may even be sensible to apply a strict function to such a data structure, for example:

```
length [ ints 2 , ints 3 , ints 4 ] ;
3 : num
```

8.10 Packaging infinity

Hope's applicative-order evaluation mechanism means that we must exercise care when programming with infinite lists, because applying a strict function to one will cause the Hope Machine to attempt to evaluate it fully. Common functions over lists must be modified for use with infinite lists to make them non-strict, and if a function cannot be so modified, we must take care never to apply it to an infinite list. This problem arises with functions which recursively process every element of a list, and can be minimised by using higher-order functions rather than explicit recursion. In particular, we may define a version of map which is safe to use on infinite lists:

```
dec map : ( alpha -> beta ) # list alpha -> list beta ;
--- map ( f , nil )     <= nil ;
--- map ( f , h :: t )  <= f h ::: map ( f , t ) ;
```

This differs from the version of map introduced in §6.4 only in constructing its result list lazily. The first equation is redundant if the new version of map is only used on infinite lists, but is retained for safe behaviour with finite lists. The result list is always lazy, however. In the following example we use map with square (from §2.6) to define an infinite list of perfect squares:

```
map ( square , ints 10 ) ;
100 ::: map ( square , ints ( 10 + 1 ) ) : list num
```

Programs which use the lazy version of map to perform iteration over lists are no longer explicitly lazy; the notion of laziness has been abstracted into the higher-order function along with that of recursion.

The lazy version of map immediately suggests the possibility of writing a lazy version of reduce. However, a little thought will soon convince us that this is not possible, because its essence consists of using the formal function to combine *all* the elements of the list together into a single value. We recollect from §6.10 that the formal function is applied to the list elements from *right to left*, which presents some difficulties with an infinite input list. This difficulty is fundamental; we developed reduce in §6.8 as an abstraction of functions like sum and length, so it is not surprising to find that we have effectively abstracted the notion of strictness. Lazy reduction is only feasible with normal-order evaluation and a given function which is non-strict in its second argument.

8.11 Saving space with infinite lists

The lazy version of until in §8.8 was intended to stop the Hope Machine trying to evaluate an infinite argument list, but a closer examination of the reduction sequence shows that it does more than this. The application of ints evaluates one element of the infinite list of integers, which is then *removed* by the application of until to form one element of its result list. Reduction stops when the lazy constructor is exposed and the final expression represents the infinite result list with one element evaluated. However, the term representing the infinite argument list once again contains *no* evaluated elements. When the top-level application of : : : (and its first operand) is eventually removed, the delayed application of until will be reduced in a sequence of steps identical to the above. It will be clear from this description that no matter how many elements are eventually evaluated, an expression representing an intermediate infinite list will never contain more than *two* terms. Paradoxically, infinite lists often have a much lower space cost than finite ones!

This observation enables us to write certain programs whose space cost might appear to make them incomputable in practice. If asked to construct the list of integers less than 100,000 and divisible by 1001, our first instinct might be to write:

```
choose ( fix ( factor , 1001 ) , nats 99999 )
```

since the problem is formulated to suggest a finite candidate list. Unfortunately, applicative-order evaluation will cause the entire list of 99,999 natural numbers to be created before choose is applied. Even though the result list is not large, the candidate list may exceed the capacity of a particular Hope Machine. The following solution uses an infinite candidate list:

```
let l == choose ( fix ( factor , 1001 ) , ints 1 )
   in until ( fix ( nonop > , 100000 ) , l )
```

The space cost of this solution depends only on the size of the result list (99 elements) and is within the capacity of a quite modest Hope Machine.

8.12 Approaches to a limit

Lazy lists can simplify many recursive functions which produce sequences of values by separating the issues of generating the values and terminating the recursion. The definition of nats in §3.10 contains two equations, one to specify the next value and one to control the recursion. In contrast, that of ints contains only one equation, to specify the next value. Termination is controlled by the function which *uses* the lazy list, which need not concern itself with how the values are generated.

As a more realistic example, consider the problem of calculating square roots from exercise 4 of chapter 4. Given a number n and an approximation to its square root r, a better approximation is given by the expression $1/2 \, (r + n/r)$. The algorithm familiar from high school (usually known as Newton's method) evaluates this calculation repeatedly, starting with the approximation $n/2$, until the difference between two successive values is sufficiently small. We can sidestep the subtle problem of how small this should be by noting that to obtain the result correct to the maximum precision of our floating-point numbers, it must be too small to affect any of the representable digits, so successive approximations will become equal. The following function repeatedly calculates a better approximation until the new value does not differ from the old one:

```
dec better : float # float -> float ;
--- better ( n , r )
    <= let b == ( r plus n over r ) over norm ( 2 , 0 )
       in if b = r
          then b
          else better ( n , b ) ;
```

`plus` and `over` are the functions from exercise 3 of chapter 4 for finding the sum and quotient respectively of two floating-point numbers. The term `norm ( 2 , 0 )` represents the normalised floating-point version of the constant value 2. The square root is now calculated by applying `better` to a suitable initial approximation:

```
dec root : float -> float ;
--- root n
    <= better ( n , n over norm ( 2 , 0 ) ) ;
```

An alternative approach is to produce an infinite list of approximations, and use a separate function to determine when two successive elements of the list are equal:

```
dec roots : float # float -> list float ;
--- roots ( n , r )
    <= let b == ( r plus n over r ) over norm ( 2 , 0 )
       in r ::: roots ( n , b ) ;
```

The new function `roots` illustrates the recurrence relationship between the successive approximations without regard to termination. This can be dealt with by the following function which returns the first element of a list which is the same as its predecessor (to the accuracy of our floating-point numbers):

```
dec same : list float -> float ;
--- same ( h :: ( i :: t ) )
    <= if h = i
       then i
       else same ( i :: t ) ;
```

`same` expresses the termination condition without regard to the recurrence relationship between the elements. The two occurrences of `::` in the pattern force *two* elements of the lazy input list to be evaluated on the first application of same. The list argument of the recursive application is constructed using : : and represents a partially lazy list like the one in §8.6. For recursive applications of same, the first : : in the pattern removes this previously evaluated element and the second forces the evaluation of the next list element. Using the new functions, the value of root would be defined by the equation:

```
--- root n
    <= same ( roots ( n , n over norm ( 2 , 0 ) ) ) ;
```

8.13 Visualising infinite lists

Although a program will normally evaluate only a finite part of an infinite list, we often need to examine an arbitrary number of elements, perhaps to satisfy ourselves that the function producing it works correctly. We can instruct the Hope Machine to do this using the special *command* show. For example, we can study the behaviour of the second square root program of §8.12 by examining the list of approximations produced by the auxiliary function roots:

```
show ( roots ( norm ( 2 , 0 ) , norm ( 1 , 0 ) ) ) ;
[ flo ( 10000 , -4 ) , flo ( 15000 , -4 ) , flo ( 14166 , -4 ) ,
  flo ( 14142 , -4 ) , flo ( 14142 , -4 ) , ...
```

We may imagine that show uses a special rewrite rule for applications of the lazy constructor which reduces an expression of the form n : : : e to e and displays the normal form of n on the screen before discarding it. The program above is evaluated as follows (omitting the reductions of the qualified expression in roots):

```
               roots ( norm ( 2 , 0 ) , norm ( 1 , 0 ) )
                                ↓
                   roots ( flo ( 20000 , -4 ) ,
                           flo ( 10000 , -4 ) )
                                ↓
       flo ( 10000 , -4 ) : : : roots ( flo ( 20000 , -4 ) ,
                                        flo ( 15000 , -4 ) )
                                │
            reduce the application of : : : and display the flo ( 10000 , -4 )
                                ↓
                   roots ( flo ( 20000 , -4 ) ,
                           flo ( 15000 , -4 ) )
                                │
                          and so on ...
                                ↓
```

Since the top-level expression will never contain more than two terms (as after the second reduction step), it will never exceed the capacity of the Hope Machine and the reduction sequence will never terminate. Reduction must be forcibly terminated by typing a *break command*. This is normally done using the break key (sometimes labelled *interrupt*), but this may vary with different Hope Machines. After entering a break command, evaluation is abandoned and the >: prompt is displayed again.

Experimenting with show reveals that the values generated by roots do not always converge as rapidly as in this example. A little thought (verified by further experiment) suggests that a better initial approximation for large numbers is given by halving the exponent.

8.14 Unbounded problems

Many interesting problems are unbounded in the sense that a complete solution may require an infinite computation, but a useful partial solution can still be obtained by a finite computation. Rather than deciding the criterion for termination when writing the program, we would like to evaluate it until an interesting result appears, or until we get tired of waiting. We can do this by placing the results into an infinite list, and using show to display it on the screen as they are produced.

As an example of this kind of problem, suppose we want to investigate prime numbers (a prime number is an integer with no factors except for 1 and itself). We might make a start by listing as many primes as possible and examining them for interesting properties. Since there are infinitely many primes, and we have no idea at this stage what constitutes an interesting property, how long should the list be? We can avoid the problem by generating *all* the prime numbers, and deciding later if we have seen enough. First consider the (finite) list of natural numbers up to 20:

```
1 2 3 4 5 6 7 8 9 10 11 12 13 14 15 16 17 18 19 20
```

1 and 2 are clearly prime (by the definition), but there are no further even prime numbers, because an even integer is divisible by 2 as well as 1 and itself. We can immediately remove all higher multiples of 2 from the list, giving:

```
1 2 3 - 5 - 7 - 9 - 11 - 13 - 15 - 17 - 19
```

Similarly 3 is prime, but higher multiples of 3 cannot be. These can now be removed by making a second pass through the list:

```
1 2 3 - 5 - 7 - - - 11 - 13 - - - 17 - 19 -
```

After we have struck out multiples of a known prime, the next higher integer not struck out is then known to be prime and the process can be repeated, eventually creating a list containing only primes. This algorithm is known as "the sieve of Eratosthenes" after its inventor, and because the removal of non-primes is analogous to the physical process of grading particles using successively larger sieves.

A function to perform a single sieving operation on a list is easily defined using `choose` and `factor` (both from §8.1):

```
dec sieve : num # list num -> list num ;
--- sieve ( n , l )
    <= choose ( lambda x => not ( factor ( n , x ) ) , l ) ;
```

By applying `sieve` to a list of increasing integers whose first element is known to be prime, we generate a list from which all multiples of the first element have been removed, and whose first element will also be prime. For example:

```
sieve ( n , l )
  where n :: l == [ 2 , 3 , 4 , 5 , 6 ] ;
[ 3 , 5 ] : list num
```

If we have a list of integers whose first element is known to be prime, we can find all the primes in the list using the following recursive function:

```
dec primes : list num -> list num ;
--- primes nil <= nil ;
--- primes ( h :: t )
    <= h :: primes ( sieve ( h , t ) ) ;
```

The head of the input list forms the head of the result list (because it is known to be prime) and the tail of the result list consists of the prime numbers which are left in the tail of the input list after multiples of the head are removed with `sieve`. An application of `primes` is reduced like this (note that the initial list starts from 2; we must not attempt to sieve out multiples of 1!):

$$\begin{array}{c}
\text{primes } [\,2\,,\,3\,,\,4\,,\,5\,,\,6\,,\,7\,,\,8\,,\,9\,,\,10\,] \\
\downarrow \\
2 :: \text{primes } (\,\text{sieve } (\,2\,,\,[\,3\,,\,4\,,\,5\,,\,6\,,\,7\,,\,8\,,\,9\,,\,10\,]\,)\,) \\
\downarrow \\
2 :: \text{primes } [\,3\,,\,5\,,\,7\,,\,9\,] \\
\downarrow \\
2 :: (\,3 :: \text{primes } (\,\text{sieve } (\,3\,,\,[\,5\,,\,7\,,\,9\,]\,)\,)\,) \\
\downarrow \\
2 :: (\,3 :: \text{primes } [\,5\,,\,7\,]\,) \\
\downarrow \\
2 :: (\,3 :: (\,5 :: \text{primes } (\,\text{sieve } (\,5\,,\,[\,7\,]\,)\,)\,)\,) \\
\downarrow \\
2 :: (\,3 :: (\,5 :: \text{primes } [\,7\,]\,)\,) \\
\downarrow \\
2 :: (\,3 :: (\,5 :: (\,7 :: \text{primes } (\,\text{sieve } (\,7\,,\,\text{nil}\,)\,)\,)\,)\,)
\end{array}$$

```
       2 :: ( 3 :: ( 5 :: ( 7 :: primes ( sieve ( 7 , nil ) ) ) ) )
                                      ↓
            2 :: ( 3 :: ( 5 :: ( 7 :: primes nil ) ) )
                                  ↓
                 2 :: ( 3 :: ( 5 :: ( 7 :: nil ) ) )
```

To search for an unspecified number of primes we need only change the definition of `primes` so that it constructs its result list lazily. No change is needed to `sieve` provided that `choose` is the lazy version of §8.7. We need only supply an infinite list of integers (starting from 2) to search, and use a `show` command to see the result:

```
show ( primes ( ints 2 ) ) ;
[ 2 , 3 , 5 , 7 , 9 , 11 , 13 , 17 , 19 , 23 , 29 , ...
```

As the integers grow larger, primes become less frequent, the time taken to print each new one increases. We have developed a truly remarkable program. Not only does the recursion of `primes` never terminate, but *each* recursive application of `primes` applies `sieve`, which is itself a non-terminating recursive function! The use of lazy lists causes reductions of `primes` and `sieve` to alternate like those of `first` and `ints` in §8.6, allowing the Hope Machine to begin reducing a second application of `primes` before the previous application of `sieve` is in normal form. However, since an application of `sieve` never terminates, the new term which it introduces is never eliminated from the expression. Unlike the example of §8.11, the growing expression will eventually exceed the capacity of any finite Hope Machine.

8.15 Review
Here is a summary of the main points introduced in this chapter:

- The technique of searching a set of candidate values for the solution to a problem is introduced, and the need for infinite lists explained.

- The lazy list constructor evaluates its second argument in normal order, and may be used for constructing potentially infinite lists.

- Lazy lists may be decomposed by pattern matching; this removes the lazy constructor and allows its second argument to be evaluated.

- Composing a function producing a lazy list with one which consumes it causes the reduction of the producer and consumer functions to be interleaved.

- Non-strict functions do not require their arguments to be in normal form and may be safely applied to infinite lists.

- Laziness can be hidden by the use of higher-order functions. Applicative-order evaluation precludes the definition of lazy consolidation functions.

- Lazy lists may have a lower space cost than strict lists because they are evaluated on demand.

- Lazy lists simplify program design by separating the issues of repetition and termination.

- Infinite lists can be visualised by the show command.

- Unbounded problems can be investigated by visualising part of the infinite list of potential solutions.

8.16 Exercises

1. The following problem is due to W. R. Hamming. We wish to find all the multiples of 2, 3 and 5 and arrange them in ascending order of magnitude. Write an expression using factor from §8.1, ints from §8.6 and the lazy version of choose from §8.7 to produce the Hamming numbers as an infinite list. What is the cost of evaluating Hamming numbers this way?

2. Write expressions using ints from §8.6 and the lazy version of map from §8.10 to define *(a)* the list of all factorials (use fact from §3.15) and *(b)* the list of all Fibonacci numbers (use Fib from §3.17). The elements of both lists should be in ascending order of magnitude.

3. The products of the elements of the *columns* of the following triangular table defines the first five factorials:

```
1 2 3 4 5
  1 2 3 4
    1 2 3
      1 2
        1
```

Higher factorials can defined by increasing the lengths of the rows and adding more of them. Write a function infact to define the infinite list of factorials from a table containing an *infinite number* of rows of infinite length. *Hints*: you do not need to construct a table. Use an infinite list (constructed with ints) to represent a row and combine the elements of *two* rows into a row of partial products using a lazy version of pairwise from §7.13.

4. The factorial-list programs of exercises 2 and 3 perform $O(n^2)$ multiplications to generate the first n factorials. Write an efficient function effact to define the list of factorials with $O(n)$ multiplications for the first n factorials. *Hint:* each factorial is the product of its position in the list and the previous factorial, so you might consider introducing parameters to carry these values forward between successive applications. These are called *accumulating parameters*.

5. The function Fib from §3.17 performs $O(2^n)$ self-applications to generate the nth Fibonacci number, hence the Fibonacci-list program of exercise 2 generates the first n Fibonacci numbers with $O(n.2^n)$ cost. Write an efficient function effib to generate the list, noting that each list element is the sum of the two previous elements.

6. Define a function iota which generates an infinite list of values by applying a given monadic function repeatedly to some starting value. iota (n , succ) defines the same list as ints n. Write expressions using iota to define *(a)* all multiples of 5, *(b)* all powers of 2, *(c)* alternating truth values (starting with true), *(d)* every third character (starting with 'a'), *(e)* all strings consisting of one or more '*' characters.

7. A more elegant solution to Hamming's problem (exercise 1) is to generate only the required multiples rather than testing every possible integer. The multiples of 2, 3 and 5 can be defined separately using iota from exercise 6. The final list is constructed by *merging* the three lists, eliminating any duplicates. Define a suitable lazy version of merge from §3.16 and write an expression using iota and merge to solve Hamming's problem. What is the cost of generating the Hamming numbers this way?

8. Redefine the second version of root from §8.12 so that it uses iota to generate the infinite list of approximations instead of roots.

9. Use iota (from exercise 6) to generate a list of numbers and their factorials (as pairs) with $O(n)$ cost for the first n elements. *Hint:* since number-factorial pairs will be supplied as parameters, the accumulating parameter technique of exercise 4 can be used.

10. The proportions of a *Golden Rectangle* are such that cutting off a square from one end leaves a smaller golden rectangle. Its æsthetic qualities were prized by the Ancient Greeks, who built their temple porticos in these proportions. The ratio of the sides (denoted by τ) is an *irrational* number, and cannot be represented as an exact fraction. However, the ratio of two successive Fibonacci numbers forms an increasingly good approximation to τ as the numbers get bigger. Write a program to generate an infinite list of pairs of Fibonacci numbers and calculate τ to the maximum accuracy allowed by the floating-point numbers of §4.6.

11. The ratio of the circumference of a circle to its diameter (denoted by π) is also irrational, but can be calculated to any desired accuracy by adding up sufficient terms of the following infinite series:

$$\frac{4}{1} - \frac{4}{3} + \frac{4}{5} - \frac{4}{7} + \frac{4}{9} - \ldots$$

Write a program to generate the series. Is it feasible to calculate π to the maximum accuracy of the floating-point numbers of §4.6 in this way?

12. Assuming that infinitely many integers exist (not quite true in Hope), how many rational numbers (exact fractions) exist? Georg Cantor demonstrated the rather surprising result that there are *the same number* of each by devising a way of using the integers to count all the rationals. At first sight this seems impossible, since there are an infinite number of fractions with numerator 1 alone:

$$\frac{1}{1} \quad \frac{1}{2} \quad \frac{1}{3} \quad \frac{1}{4} \quad \frac{1}{5} \quad \frac{1}{6} \quad \ldots$$

without even considering those with numerators of 2 and above. Cantor's trick was to arrange the rationals into a table, and then to count them *diagonally* rather than row-wise. This is illustrated in the following diagram:

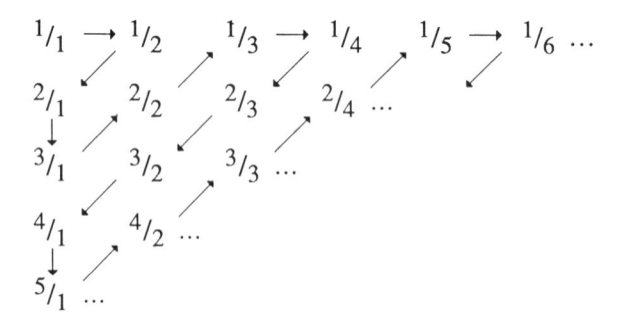

$$\begin{array}{cccccc}
\frac{1}{1} \rightarrow & \frac{1}{2} & \frac{1}{3} \rightarrow & \frac{1}{4} & \frac{1}{5} \rightarrow & \frac{1}{6} \ldots \\
\frac{2}{1} & \frac{2}{2} & \frac{2}{3} & \frac{2}{4} \ldots & & \\
\frac{3}{1} & \frac{3}{2} & \frac{3}{3} \ldots & & & \\
\frac{4}{1} & \frac{4}{2} \ldots & & & & \\
\frac{5}{1} \ldots & & & & &
\end{array}$$

Write an expression using the lazy version of map from §8.10 and iota from exercise 6 to define an infinite table (*i.e.* an infinite list of infinite lists) of rational numbers (represented as pairs of integers). Now write a polymorphic function Cantor which will flatten any infinite table using the diagonalisation technique, and use it to generate the infinite list of all rational numbers. *Hint:* try writing out the table with the rows staggered as in the diagram accompanying exercise 3. The (finite) sublist corresponding to each vertical column can be constructed in an analogous manner to a factorial.

Chapter 9

Input and Output

9.1 Saving the results of programs

A common problem is that a program produces too much output to examine on the screen at one time. In cases like this we would like to put the results in a safe place (perhaps printed on paper) and examine them at our leisure. A related problem is that we may wish to use the results later as input data for another program. This is easy if the first program and its original input data are available, for we can simply compose the two programs together, reevaluating the first one. This may be undesirable if the first program has a high computational cost, or impossible if the program or its data are no longer available. Although input data in examples has always been typed into the Hope Machine as part of the top-level expression to evaluate the program, the payroll examples of chapter 4 show that this is unrealistic for large data structures.

Both problems are solved by allowing the output of a program to be saved without displaying it on the screen. A saved data object is called a *file*, and can be retrieved later to be used as input to a second program. The collection of all files is called the *filestore*; exact details of the way files are held in it vary between different Hope Machines and need not concern us. Within the filestore each file is identified by a unique label so that it can be retrieved later. This *filename* is a character string and is attached to the file when it is first saved. This is done using a special command:

```
put ( [ 1 , 2 , 3 , 4 ] ,"numbers" ) ;
```

This causes the Hope Machine to save the list of numbers [1 , 2 , 3 , 4] in the filestore and label it numbers. If the filestore already contains a file labelled numbers, the new version *replaces* the old one. Some Hope Machines restrict the form of filenames; sequences of up to 8 letters or digits are usually acceptable. The argument pair is considered to have the type list char # alpha (allowing the file to contain any type of object), and can be specified by any valid expression. Here we save the ordered binary tree of numbers generated in §6.11:

```
put ( t , "tree" )
    where t == reduce ( insert , null , l )
        where l == [ 4 , 2 , 5 , 1 , 3 ] ;
```

The argument pair is evaluated in applicative order, so the result of any program can be saved by supplying the top-level expression to evaluate it as the second element.

Superficially, put resembles a dyadic function; however, it does not return any result, and may *not* be used as a term in a larger expression. The Hope Machine treats put as a *command* which instructs it to create a file. Creating a file where none existed before (or replacing an existing file) may also change the subsequent behaviour of the Hope Machine, giving put some of the properties of a declaration. When the put command is applied to a list, it replaces occurrences of the ::: constructor with :: which causes lazy lists to be fully evaluated, hence we should not attempt to save an *infinite* list using a put command.

9.2 Retrieving the results

Objects can be retrieved from the filestore of the Hope Machine using the command get. This takes a single parameter, which is the character-string filename. Here we retrieve the ordered tree of numbers saved in §9.1:

```
get "tree" ;
node ( 4 , node ( 2, node ( 1 , null , null )
                      node ( 3 , null , null ) )
            node ( 5 , null , null ) ) : tree num
```

In this example, the get command behaves like a function of type list char -> tree num. Unlike put, we can use a get command as a term in a larger expression; when we do this the retrieved object must have the correct type for the context. This is deduced in the usual way, treating get initially as a function of type list char -> alpha. For example, in the expression:

```
choose ( odd , get "numbers" )
```

the arguments of choose are an alpha -> truval and a list alpha. odd has the type num -> truval (*cf.* §2.4), so alpha is taken to be a num and get must return a list num. The type-checking mechanism retrieves the object from the file and checks that it has the correct type before evaluating the expression. If it has the wrong type for the context, the Hope Machine will report a type error:

```
flatten ( get "numbers" ) ;
Evaluation error: wrong operand type for flatten
Expression    : flatten ( get "numbers" )
Expected type: tree num
Actual type   : list num
```

It is important to note that `get` is *not* a function, because it is effectively evaluated by the type-checking mechanism and not by the evaluation mechanism. For this reason, its argument is restricted to a *constant* character string. A `get` command is best considered as a convenient representation of an object in a file. Also, `get` can only be used in top-level expressions, and not in recursion equations. This protects against accidentally invalidating a correct program by subsequently changing the types of objects in a file to which it refers (*e.g.* using a `put` command).

The possibility of changing the contents of a file restricts our ability to reason about programs which use `get`, because identical uses may represent different values on separate occasions. For example, the program:

```
sum ( nats 10 ) ;
```

always evaluates to 55. In contrast, we can make no statement about the program:

```
sum ( get "numbers" ) ;
```

and even if we know its value today, we cannot predict its value tomorrow. This is because the `get` command lacks the critical property of referential transparency (*cf.* §1.3) possessed by conventional functions. Changing the contents of a file which a program refers to effectively creates a *different* program, which is not guaranteed to behave like the original. However, since the `put` command can only change the contents of a file *after* a program has been executed, we can be confident that identical uses of `get` in a top-level expression represent identical values. The following program always evaluates to `true`:

```
( get "numbers" ) = ( get "numbers" ) ;
```

An important feature of the `get` command is that the `::` constructor of lists retrieved from the filestore is replaced by `:::` to yield a *lazy* version of the list:

```
get "numbers" ;
23 ::: <<get "numbers">> : list num
```

The symbol `<<get "numbers">>` is a representation of the unevaluated tail of the list; it is not a valid Hope expression and may not be used in expressions. This property allows files to contain lists which would exceed the capacity of the Hope Machine if fully evaluated.

Finally, we note that `get` and `put` can be used to specify simple manipulations on the filestore without evaluating a Hope program at all. For example:

```
put ( get "tree" , "TreeCopy" ) ;
```

will create a new file `TreeCopy` whose type and contents are the same as the existing file `tree`.

9.3 Special files

Although details of the way files are held in the filestore can usually be ignored, there are certain cases when we would like to specify exactly where a file is located. The Hope Machine provides special commands for this purpose. The most useful of these is `show` (introduced in §8.13) which causes the contents of the file to be sent to the screen, evaluating lazy lists fully. The `show` command can be applied to any type of object, including a strict list, for example:

```
show "Where there's life there's Hope" ;
"Where there's life there's Hope"
```

The object is displayed in the same format as if the expression defining it had been typed at the top level, except no type annotation is shown.

The command `display` will output a list of characters to the screen, but without the quotation marks or the type annotation; for example:

```
display "Hunt it with forks and Hope" ;
Hunt it with forks and Hope
```

We are only allowed to use `display` to output lists of characters. Supplying any other type of object as its actual parameter will cause a type error. Like `show` and `put`, `display` evaluates lazy lists fully.

Some versions of the Hope Machine provide a command `print` which behaves exactly like `show` except that the contents of the file are printed on paper. The data object is printed in the same format as the screen display (sometimes longer lines are allowed), without the type annotation and with lazy lists fully evaluated. Printing infinite lists is not recommended unless a large supply of paper is available! Files which have been displayed on the screen or printed on paper are not placed in the normal filestore, and cannot be subsequently retrieved using `get`.

9.4 Delaying the input

The use of `show` allows us to observe the initial results of a program before the evaluation is complete, but we must still provide all the input data which the program requires before evaluation begins. In many cases this is not convenient, because we cannot always decide exactly what the input data should be until we have seen some of the results. In cases like this we would like to enter enough data to allow the program to produce its initial results, and decide what data should be entered next after we have examined them. This will require the results to be displayed on the screen, and the input data to be typed in at the keyboard, resulting in a program which *interacts* with the user. We can specify that the contents of a file are to be typed in as the program is evaluated using the command `input`. This has a single parameter which is a constant character string to be displayed as a prompt. For instance:

```
square ( input "--" ) ;
```

As in the case of `get`, the type of object required from `input` is deduced from the context. Here, it forms the argument of `square`, so a num is required. However, unlike `get`, the type-checking mechanism does not check that `input` represents the correct type of object before evaluating the program. Instead, the correct type is *assumed* and the program is evaluated until the object is actually required. At this point, evaluation is *suspended*, the specified prompt (-- in this case) is displayed, and a valid num (in this case) must be entered from the keyboard. The `input` command effectively behaves as a function applied in normal order. If the wrong type of value is entered, an error is reported and `input` is *reapplied* until a correct value is entered; program evaluation then continues. This is illustrated in the following example (for clarity, the convention of showing prompts, underlining input and indicating input newlines by ® will be used for interactive program examples):

```
>: square ( input "--" ) ;®
-- '3'®
Evaluation error: wrong operand type for square
Expression   : square ( input "--" )
Expected type: num
Actual type  : char
-- 3®
9 : num
```

Data entered from the keyboard is not processed by the Hope Machine until a newline is entered, allowing it to be corrected by backspacing and overtyping like program text. As with `get`, the `input` command constructs lists read from the keyboard lazily, so the whole list need not be entered immediately. If we enter an `input` command at the top level we obtain the following effect:

```
>: input "==" ;®
== [ 43 , 44 , 45®
43 :: <<input "==">> : list num
>:
```

The [and the first value are sufficient to allow the Hope Machine to deduce that the partial object is a list of numbers. The result is printed as a lazy list, with its tail represented by the symbol <<input "==">>. Since top-level evaluation does not force the lazy constructor, no further input values are requested, and the normal prompt is displayed immediately without requiring the final].

If the lazy constructor is forced by pattern matching, further values will be read from the keyboard. If insufficient values are supplied, the specified prompt will be output again to indicate that further input is required. For example:

```
>: first ( 5 , input "==" ) ;®
== "You®
== ngest®
"Young" : list char
>:
```

Here, the number of elements required is determined by first, so the final " is not required and the extra characters are ignored. If the function requires the whole list, elements will be read until the appropriate closing symbol is entered:

```
>: sort ( input "==" ) ;®
== [ 5 , 3 , 2®
== , 6 , 4 , 1 ]®
[ 1 , 2 , 3 , 4 , 5 , 6 ] : list num
>:
```

If the input list is supplied to a show command, the lazy constructor will be forced as before. All the elements on the first line can be printed as soon as the newline has been entered; the attempt to obtain the next will cause the specified prompt to be redisplayed, giving truly interactive behaviour:

```
>: show ( input "--" ) ;®
-- [ 1 , 2 , 3 , 4 ,®
[ 1 , 2 , 3 , 4
-- 5 , 6 , 7 , 8 , 9 ]®
5 , 7 , 8 , 9 ] : list num
>:
```

The end of the input list is indicated by] in the usual way and causes evaluation to complete, as indicated by the normal prompt. Program evaluation can be forcibly terminated at any time by entering a break command instead of the expected input.

This program behaves this way because show is *eager* and forces the constructors of the lazy input list; the program is said to be *output-* (or *demand*) *driven*. However, the way in which the input and output are intermingled (or *interleaved*) on the screen is actually determined by the behaviour of the input command. To obtain the first element of the output list, show will force the constructor, causing input to display the prompt and read the *entire input line*. Only then is the head of the input list returned to show. Subsequent elements are obtained from the remainder of the line, allowing a whole line of output to be printed without further input. After the input line has been completely consumed, the next attempt to force the constructor causes the input command to redisplay the prompt and read the the next input line.

As in the case of get, we may only use the input command in a top-level expression, and not in a recursion equation. Multiple data objects can be entered interactively by using multiple input commands in the top-level expression. When doing this, distinct argument strings should be specified to help the user enter the correct data in each case. For example:

```
first ( input "Sublist length ?" , input "List ?" ) ;
```

Note particularly that *both* input commands are redexes in this example. The Hope Machine may reduce them in either order, and we cannot assume that the leftmost prompt will appear first. One possible sequence of interactions is as follows:

```
List ? [ 1 , 2 , 3 ,®
Sublist length ? 4®
List ? 4 , 5 , 6 ,®
[ 1, 2 , 3 , 4 ] : list num
```

Evaluation of this program terminates when sufficient elements of the lazy input list have been entered to allow the output list to be constructed; it is not necessary to enter the closing bracket of the input list. The use of input restricts our ability to reason about programs even more than get. Not only can we can make no assumptions about the result of:

```
( input "--" ) = 10 ;
```

but we cannot even assume that:

```
( input "--" ) div ( input "--" ) ;
```

evaluates to 1! Although the two input commands have identical arguments, they are evaluated independently and can represent *different* values depending on what the user chooses to enter. However, we can can safely make multiple references to the input stream by abstracting its value in a qualified expression:

```
i div i where i == input "?" ;
? 26®
1 : num
```

9.5 Controlling the output layout

Using `input` and `show`, a Hope program can interactively read and write any data object that could be written directly in the program. This is simple and convenient, but we often need more control over the output; a list of lists can be clarified by laying it out it as a table, or a binary tree as a diagram. Pleasing output is especially important when a program is used by someone with no knowledge of computers or of Hope. This kind of user wishes treat the computer as a "black box" to process data typed in at the keyboard, and has no desire to see constructor names on the screen.

All objects displayed on the screen or printed on paper are represented ultimately as sequences of characters. Thus, when we output a `list num`, the Hope Machine first produces a *character-string* representation of each number from its internal form (probably the binary representation of §4.2), inserts spaces and commas between the individual character strings, and adds brackets to produce the familiar representation. Normally this conversion is done automatically, but we can obtain complete control over the output by performing it ourselves, returning a `list char` as the final result of the program. The Hope Machine provides a number of primitive functions to assist with this. A number can be converted to a character string using the function `digits` of type `num -> list char`. For instance:

```
digits 426 ;
"426" : list char
```

By applying `listify` (from §7.10) to `digits`, we can generate an equivalent function over lists of numbers:

```
( listify digits ) [ 426 , 427 , 428 ] ;
[ "426" , "427" , "428" ] : list ( list char )
```

This is not yet quite what we want, because the result is a two-level list, with the commas and brackets added by the built-in layout mechanism. We can flatten it into a one-level list by concatenating the component strings, inserting appropriate separator strings between. This can be done using `condense` from §6.12:

```
condense ( lambda ( x , y ) => x <> " " <> y , id , l )
   where l == ( listify digits ) [ 426 , 427 , 428 ]
```

The first given function concatenates its arguments with a blank between. The second given function (`id`) is applied to the final element. A simpler way of achieving the same effect is:

```
condense ( lambda ( x , y )
              => digits x <> " " <> digits y ,
          digits , l )
   where l == [ 426 , 427 , 428 ]
```

In this solution we avoid creating an intermediate list of character strings by simply applying `digits` to each list element as it is selected by `condense`. In both cases the result is the following list of *characters*:

```
"426 427 428"  :  list char
```

The only remaining feature of the standard output layout is the presence of the quotation marks, indicating that the output is a list of characters. These can be removed by using the `display` command (*cf.* §9.3) instead of `show`.

It will be clear from this example that the list can be output in a variety of other layouts by varying the string which is inserted during the flattening process. The following function generalises the idea by abstracting both the separator string and the function which converts an individual list element to a character-string:

```
    dec format : list alpha # ( alpha -> list char ) #
                 list char -> list char ;
--- format ( nil , f , s ) <= nil ;
--- format ( l , f , s )
      <= condense ( lambda ( x , y ) => f x <> s <> y ,
                    f , l ) ;
```

Using `format`, the effect of the previous example is easily obtained by writing:

```
format ( l , digits , " " )
  where l == [ 426 , 427 , 428 ] ;
"426 427 428"  :  list char
```

whilst to obtain the conventional layout we need only write:

```
"[ " <> format ( l , digits , " , " ) <> " ]"
  where l == [ 426 , 427 , 428 ] ;
"[ 426 , 427 , 428 ]"  :  list char
```

By supplying an appropriate conversion function, we can use `format` to output lists containing any type of object, for instance:

```
format ( l , lambda true => "Yes"
              | false => "No" , "; " )
  where l == [ true , false , true , true , false ] ;
"Yes; No; Yes; Yes; No"  :  list char
```

This definition of `format` is not quite general, because it uses `condense`, and we recollect from §8.10 that reduction functions can only be defined over finite lists. In §9.10 we shall define a version which can be applied safely to infinite lists.

9.6 Control sequences

We can control the layout of text output by the `display` command by inserting special *control characters* into the character string. Control characters are not actually printed, but affect the screen in various ways. For example, inserting the character corresponding to the newline key causes subsequent characters to appear on the next line. The actual characters required to control the screen vary among Hope Machines, and must be generated using primitive functions. These *layout functions* have a result type of `list char` (rather than `char`) because more than one control character may be needed to get a particular effect. This is convenient, because we can always use `<>` to insert a control sequence, simplifying the use of functions like `format`.

The effect of control sequences is best understood by considering the screen to be a rectangular grid whose size depends on the particular Hope Machine we are using. The screen size can be discovered by using the standard nulladic function:

    `screen`   *of type*   `num # num`

The result pair gives the maximum number of lines which can be displayed on the screen and the maximum number of characters on a line respectively.

The linenumber and horizontal position of the next character to be displayed on the screen are called the *current position*. The top line on the screen and the leftmost character on a line are always numbered 1. Characters are displayed at successive horizontal positions until the current line is full, after which the linenumber is incremented by 1 and the horizontal position set to 1, starting a new line of output.

When the current line is the last on the screen, the new line causes the screen display to scroll up in the usual way. When this happens, the lines on the screen are renumbered, and the new top line is considered to be line 1. Other control sequences cause the `display` command to alter the current position in a similar way. The following standard layout functions are provided:

    `nl`   *of type*   `num -> list char`

The control sequence increments the linenumber by the given value and sets the horizontal position to 1 (*i.e.* it displays the specified number of newlines).

    `tab`   *of type*   `num -> list char`

The control sequence sets the horizontal position to the given value (*i.e.* tabs to the specified position). Specifying a position to the left of the current horizontal position or beyond the maximum line width has the same effect as `nl 1`. Finer control over the current position is achieved with the following two layout functions:

    `clear`   *of type*   `list char`

The control sequence erases the screen and sets both the linenumber and the horizontal position to 1, so that subsequent characters are displayed at the top of the screen.

goto   *of type*   num # num -> list char

The control sequence sets the linenumber and horizontal position to the given values. Any character which is already displayed at this position is overwritten. Specifying values beyond the maximum screen size has the same effect as clear.

The following program uses the format function defined §9.5 to flatten a list (list num) into a character string, using control sequences as separators:

```
format ( l , f , nl 2 )
   where l == some list ( list num )
      where f == lambda x
                 => format ( x , digits , tab 9 )
```

The lambda expression formats each sublist into a character string by inserting tab sequences between the representations of the individual numbers. The top-level application of format converts this list into a string by inserting newline sequences between each component string. The embedded layout characters will cause the final string to be displayed as a two-dimensional table.

9.7 Analysing the input

In the same way that we may wish to choose the layout for printing results, we may also wish to choose our own representation for input data. Input data can be entered in any convenient form by treating keyboard input as an unstructured list of characters; it is then the responsibility of the program to analyse the input character string and construct appropriate data objects for further processing.

The normal input processing can be bypassed by using the command keyboard, which returns all characters typed in as an infinite lazy list. Unlike the input command, keyboard does not display a prompt string and evaluates each character as it is entered without waiting for a newline, hence no correction is possible. If we enter a keyboard command at the top level, we obtain the following effect:

```
>: keyboard ;
XX ::: <<keyboard>> : list char
>:
```

The result is an infinite lazy list of characters whose unevaluated tail is represented by the symbol <<keyboard>>. As with input, only one item is read (*i.e.* a single character), because top-level evaluation does not force the lazy constructor. Further, since keyboard does not require a newline to be entered, the result appears on the same line as the input. Although we have become accustomed to seeing program output on a new line, this is a result of the newline normally used to enter the preceding *input* line, and is not a property of the output mechanism. To read further characters, it must be forced by pattern matching. Here we apply `first` to the result of `keyboard` to request 20 characters of input:

```
sort ( first ( 20 , keyboard ) ) ;
Hope springs eternal" aeeegilnnopprrsstH" : list char
```

Unlike the `input` command, `keyboard` will cause the Hope Machine to wait without displaying a prompt if fewer than 20 characters are supplied.

More complex data structures must be constructed by *analysing* the input list. As an example, suppose we wish to enter a sentence (a list of words). Using `input`, we can type a `list ( list char )` in conventional Hope layout. However, using `keyboard`, we must choose the representation for ourselves and convert the input character string appropriately. Fortunately a well-known representation already exists: a word is a sequence of letters; a sentence is a sequence of words delimited by blanks and punctuation marks and terminated by a period. The following sentence:

```
"Hunt it with forks and Hope."
```

can be considered to be a representation of the following `list ( list char )`:

```
[ "Hunt" , "it" , "with" , "forks" , "and" , "Hope" ]
```

We can use the following predicate to recognise delimiting characters (non-letters):

```
dec delimiter : char -> truval ;
--- delimiter c <= ( c < 'a' or c > 'z' ) and
                   ( c < 'A' or c > 'Z' ) ;
```

The following function removes the initial word from a list of characters, returning the word and the remaining list of characters (for further processing):

```
dec initial : list char -> list char # list char ;
--- initial ( S & h :: t )
    <= if delimiter h
       then ( nil , S )
       else ( ( h :: w , r )
              where ( w , r ) == initial t ) ;
```

`initial` must only be applied to a non-empty list whose first character is a letter, and terminates when a delimiter is found. For instance:

```
initial keyboard ;
Ho!"Ho" , '!' ::: <<keyboard>> : list char # list char
```

The following function uses `initial` to construct a list (`list char`) which contains all the words in a sentence:

```
dec sentence : list char -> list ( list char ) ;
--- sentence "." <= nil ;
--- sentence ( S & h :: t )
       <= if delimiter h
          then sentence t
          else ( ( w :: sentence r )
                 where ( w , r ) == initial S ) ;
```

`sentence` removes all punctuation from the input before applying `initial`, ensuring safe behaviour for the latter; however, we must not apply `sentence` to a finite string which does contain a period. This is not a problem with keyboard input, since the function simply fails to terminate until the required period is entered:

```
display ( sentence keyboard ) ;
Here's®
Hoping.[ "Here" , "s" , "Hoping" ]
```

No terminating newline is needed; the result is evaluated as soon as `keyboard` has returned the full stop, and is displayed on the same line as the input string. The simple-minded criterion used to distinguish delimiters has caused the possessive 's to be recognised as a separate word.

9.8 Discovering the input layout

In the example above, the analysis function `sentence` ignores newline sequences along with other non-letters, making the program insensitive to the layout of its input data. However, in many cases we need to know the layout of the input data in order to analyse it correctly. Thus, to find the length of an input line, we must recognise the end of the line. Fortunately, `keyboard` returns *all* characters entered, including the newline sequence. Although we do not know what characters are used to represent it, we can manipulate it using the following primitive functions:

```
isnl       of type    list char -> truval
skipnl     of type    list char -> list char
```

`isnl` yields `true` if its argument starts with a newline sequence (otherwise `false`, including the case when the argument is `nil`). `skipnl` removes a single newline sequence from the *start* of its argument (leaving it unchanged if there is none). Notice that there is nothing to stop us examining individual input characters and discovering how a newline sequence is represented; however, a program using `isnl` and `skipnl` will always work correctly on any Hope Machine, whereas a program which relies on a specific known representation may not.

The following function uses `isnl` to remove a line delimited by a newline sequence from the start of a longer character string:

```
dec line: list char -> list char ;
--- line ( L & h :: t )
    <= if isnl L
          then nil
          else h ::: line t ;
```

Notice that we cannot use `until` (from §8.8) to find a newline, because the given predicate is applied to a single list element, and a newline may may be represented by more than one character. Using `line`, the line-length reporting program is simply:

```
length ( line keyboard ) ;
```
<u>The long and short of it</u>®
24 : num

9.9 Controlling interleaving

In §9.4 we combined lazy input (using `input`) with eager output (using `show`) to give a simple interactive program which "echoed" its input. The interleaving of input and output on the screen was controlled by the `input` command, which reads the keyboard one line at a time. When using `keyboard`, input is not organised into lines automatically, and we must control the interleaving ourselves.

The interactive dialogue can be viewed as a sequence of *messages*, consisting of *requests* from the user alternating with *replies* from the program. When the input and all intermediate data structures are lazy, the program is output-driven, and evaluation will not occur unless it forms the argument of eager output command such as `show` or `display`. In such a program, the lengths of requests and replies are determined only by the amount of input needed to evaluate the next reply. Here is the simplest possible example:

```
display ( keyboard ) ;
```

The input and output are both lists of characters, and each output character requires a single input character for its evaluation. Requests and replies are each one character long, resulting in the following interleaving:

<u>t</u>t<u>h</u>h<u>i</u>i<u>n</u>n<u>k</u>k ...

In the following example, the output string depends upon all the characters of the input line (including the final newline):

```
display ( sort ( line keyboard ) ) ;
thin®
hint
>:
```

The behaviour of this program is at the opposite extreme to the first example, because *all* its input must be supplied before any output can be produced. Unfortunately, `sort` is a special case because the "lowest" character might be entered last, so every input character must be examined before the result can be returned. In many cases this kind of dependency does not exist; for example, we might try to read a line from the keyboard and echo the first word on the screen with:

```
display ( until ( delimiter , line keyboard ) ) ;
```

The problem here is that the output string does not logically depend on the whole of the input line; worse still, individual output characters depend only on a single input character. The actual result is:

```
FFiirrsstt.
>:
```

The reason for this behaviour is that both `until` and `line` construct their results lazily (refer to §8.8 and §9.8 respectively). Although `until` is forced by `display`, it terminates when the delimiter is found and `line` is not evaluated further. Because output characters can be evaluated immediately they are input, interleaving is at the character level.

One solution to the character-interleaving problem is to construct the reply using a *strict* function, ensuring that no characters are available to `display` until the entire string has been evaluated. Using the original strict version of `until` from §8.8 would give the following interleaving:

```
First.First
```

An analogous solution to the line-interleaving problem is to construct the *input* line using a strict function. This can be done by simply replacing the lazy list constructor in `line` by the normal one, and ensures that no characters are available to `until` before the whole line has been read.

The program above processes only a single request. To obtain correct interleaving of multiple messages, we must arrange the strictly-constructed requests into streams using suitable analysis functions. The following function uses `isnl` and `skipnl` to recognise a line delimited by a newline sequence in a longer list of characters. It discards the newline sequence and returns the opening line and the remainder of the input list for further processing:

```
dec opening: list char -> list char # list char ;
--- opening ( L & h :: t )
    <= if isnl L
       then ( nil , skipnl L )
       else ( ( h :: l , r )
              where ( l , r ) == opening t ) ;
```

Strict behaviour is enforced by the qualified expression which defines the components of the result tuple. This is always evaluated in applicative order, hence `opening` will always be evaluated recursively until a newline is found. Constructing the first element of the tuple lazily would not change this behaviour.

The following function uses `opening` to construct an infinite list of lines from a list of characters:

```
dec text : list char -> list ( list char ) ;
--- text ( c :: cs )
    <= l ::: text m
       where ( l , m ) == opening ( c :: cs ) ;
```

Although the individual lines are strict, the list of lines is constructed lazily. Both `opening` and `text` assume an infinite input stream, hence they are not defined over empty lists.

We can now construct the corresponding stream of replies by applying a suitable function to each element of the request stream, perhaps using (a lazy version of) `map` and displaying the resulting list eagerly. Evaluation of the program might look like this on the screen:

```
show ( map ( length , text keyboard ) ) ;
First line®
[ 10 ,
Second line®
11 ,
The third line®
14 ,
and so on®
9 ,
...
```

The use of `show` causes the output stream to be printed in the standard layout for lists, with brackets and commas. The appearance of the interactive dialogue can be improved by flattening the output stream into a list of characters and using `display` to visualise it. This requires a version of `format` (from §9.5) which is suitable for infinite lists, and in the next section we shall address this problem.

9.10 Formatting infinite lists

To see how we might develop a version of `format` for infinite lists, let us first examine the "obvious" recursive definition:

```
--- format ( h :: t , f , s )
    <= f h <> s <> format ( t , f , s ) ;
```

Again, `f` represents the given function to generate the character-string representation of a single list item, and `s` the given separator string. This version is also unsuitable for infinite lists, because the Hope Machine will attempt to reduce the recursive application of `format` in applicative order before applying the second `<>` operation, leading to a strict infinite reduction sequence.

To avoid this, we must arrange that the evaluation of `format` is suspended before the recursive application, but *after* the preceding characters of the result (defined by the term `f h <> s`) have been evaluated, so that they are available for display. One way of suspending the recursive application is to make it the second argument of a lazy constructor. For example, if the term `f h <> s` evaluates to `"1 ,"`, the right-hand side expression should evaluate to:

```
'1' :: ( ' ' :: ( ',' ::: format ( t , f , s ) ) )
```

To obtain this effect, we must replace the second `<>` operation by a list-concatenation function which applies `:::` in the base case, and also prevents its second argument (the recursive application of `format`) from being evaluated. In §6.11 we saw that two lists could be concatenated by using `reduce` to reconstruct the first list (using `::` as the given function) and replace its final `nil` by the second list. In this case we must replace the `nil` by the (unevaluated) term `format ( t , f , s )` and replace the final `::` by `:::` as well. Once again `condense` solves the problem neatly, because (as shown in §6.12) an application such as:

```
condense ( nonop :: , g , [ e₁ , e₂ , e₃ ] )
```

is equivalent to the expression:

```
e₁ :: ( e₂ :: ( g e₃ ) )
```

As well as reconstructing the original list, `condense` also applies the second given function `g` to its final element. Notice that although we may not apply `condense` to an infinite list, the term `f h <> s` represents a finite list. If we now supply the following lambda expression for `g`:

```
lambda c => c ::: format ( t , f , s )
```

the application of `condense` will be equivalent to the required expression:

```
    e₁ :: ( e₂ :: ( e₃ ::: format ( t , f , s ) ) )
```

By "packaging" the recursive application of `format` into the lambda expression, we have effectively delayed its evaluation. A possible lazy version of `format` is thus:

```
--- format ( h :: t , f , s )
    <= condense ( nonop :: ,
                  lambda c
                      => c ::: format ( t , f , s ) ,
                  f h <> s ) ;
```

To make `format` suitable for finite lists as well, we must add base-case equations to cover empty and singleton lists:

```
--- format ( nil , f , s ) <= nil ;
--- format ( [ a ] , f , s ) <= f a ;
```

It is left as an exercise to the reader to rewrite an application of `format` and verify that it works correctly. Note that since `:::` needs a character for its first argument, the term `f h <> s` must not evaluate to an empty string. If we supply an empty separator string (quite likely), we must be sure that f never produces an empty string as the representation of any list element (relatively unlikely).

We can improve the interactive example of §9.4 by using the new version of `format` to flatten the infinite list of replies (inserting newlines) and visualising the results with `display`:

```
display ( format ( l , digits , nl 1 ) )
         where l == map ( length , text keyboard ) ;
First line®
10
Second line®
11
The third line®
14
and so on®
9
...
```

9.11 Review

Here is a summary of the main points introduced in this chapter:

- The results of programs can be saved in the filestore of the Hope Machine using the `put` command.

- Files saved using `put` may be retrieved using the `get` command.

- Results can also be directed to the screen using the eager `show` and `display` commands or to the printer using the `print` command.

- Data may be entered interactively from the keyboard using the lazy `input` and `keyboard` commands.

- Techniques are introduced for formatting output strings and modifying the layout of output on the screen using control sequences.

- Techniques are introduced for analysing input strings, including the use of special predicates for recognising control sequences.

- The problem of input-output interleaving is discussed, and techniques introduced for controlling it.

9.12 Exercises

1. Write the function `digits` referred to in §9.5. The straightforward solution has $O(n^2)$ cost for an n-digit number, but it can be done with $O(n)$ cost using an auxiliary function with an accumulating parameter. Is it worth the extra trouble of writing the $O(n)$ version?

2. Write a function `real` to generate the canonical representation of a floating-point number, with the mantissa adjusted to lie in the range $1 \leq m < 10$. For example, the decimal fraction 0.125 has the normalised form `flo ( 1250 , -3 )` and the canonical representation 1.25×10^{-1}. A linear representation such as `1.25 E -1` is often used when the screen or printer cannot display superscripts.

3. Write a function `large` to produce a character-string representation of a long number from §4.10. Assume that the individual components of the long number represent single decimal digits (*i.e.* they are less than 10). The conventional representation of large numbers is to mark off groups of three digits from the right-hand (least significant) end with commas. For example, the long number `~1.2.3.4.5.6.7` would be represented as `"1,234,567"`.

4. Write a function `number` to convert the character-string representation of an integer into a `num`. Assume that the string contains only the valid character-string representation of a number which is small enough to represent in your Hope Machine. Your function should be capable of converting *negative* numbers, represented by a leading – sign.

5. Modify `number` from exercise 3 so that it also returns any characters following the representation of the number in the input string for further processing. For example, `number "3--xyz"` should evaluate to the pair 3 , `"--xyz"`.

6. Use `number` from exercise 5 to define a function `numlist` which will construct a list of numbers from a character string. Numbers must be separated by one or more blanks, but these are optional before a negative number. For example, `numlist "  -1 2-3"` should evaluate to the list [-1 , 2 , -3].

7. Modify `numlist` from exercise 6 so that it also returns any characters following the representation of the list of numbers; `numlist "  -1 2-3--xyz"` should evaluate to the pair [-1 , 2 , -3] , `"--xyz"`.

8. Modify `numlist` from exercise 6 so that it constructs an *infinite* list of integers from an infinite list of their character representations. You will not need to return the remainder of the input list in this version!

9. Is it possible to modify `numlist` from exercise 7 to construct a lazy *finite* list of integers from an infinite list of their character representations, and also return the remainder of the input list for further processing? Would such a function actually be useful?

10. Write a higher-order function `analyse` which given a function of type `list char -> alpha # list char`, will analyse an infinite list of characters representing objects of type `alpha`, and return an infinite `list alpha`. Thus `analyse ( number , "1-2-3 ... etc )` yields [1 , -2 , -3 ... *etc*, and `analyse ( opening , keyboard )` assembles keyboard input into a stream of strictly constructed lines (`opening` was defined in §9.9).

11. Write a function `unlist` of type `list ( list alpha ) -> list alpha` to flatten a list of lists into an one-level list. The component lists are finite (and may be empty), but the top-level list and the result list are *infinite* lists. Hint: consider the technique used to write `format` in §9.10.

12. Write an expression using `unlist` from exercise 11) and `format` to print the infinite list of rationals from exercise 11 of chapter 8. Rationals should be printed in the form a/b without embedded blanks, and be separated from each other by blanks and commas, as in the standard layout for lists and tuples.

Appendix 1
Solutions to Exercises

Chapter 1

1. (a) `-5 : num`
    (b) `3 : num`
    (c) `5 : num`
    (d) ***error***

    This result occurs because the parenthesised term evaluates to 0.

    (e) `true : truval`
    (f) `'b' : char`
    (g) `-2147483647 : num`
    (h) `0 : num`

    The last two results occur because of integer overflow, and may be different on another Hope Machine, depending on the number of bits used to represent integers in the real computer which simulates it.

2. (a) `( 0 - 100 ) div 3`
    (b) `100 div ( 0 - 3 )`
    (c) `2 div 3 div 4`
    (d) `2 div ( 3 div 4 + 1 )`

3. (a) 123 mod 10
   (b) 456 div 10 mod 10
   (c) chr (ord 'a' + 7)
   (d) chr ((ord 'Z' - ord 'A' + 1) div 2)
   (e) 823 div 13 + 1

4. (1000 * 24) + (50 * 24 * 24) div 2

5. (98 - 32) * 5 div 9   (See also §2.1)

6. (a) 100 mod 10 = 0
   (b) 22 mod 2 = 0
   (c) (139 div 10 mod 10) /= (55 mod 10)
   (d) (ord 'z' - ord 'a' + 1) = 26
   (e) ((ord 'c' - ord 'a' + 1) = 1) or
       ((ord 'c' - ord 'a' + 1) = 3)
   (f) not (((ord 'b' - ord 'a' + 1) = 1) or
       ((ord 'b' - ord 'a' + 1) = 3))
   (g) ((ord 'b' - ord 'a' + 1) /= 1) and
       ((ord 'b' - ord 'a' + 1) /= 3)
   (h) (100 > 50) and (100 < 200)
   (i) not ((10 > 50) and (10 < 200))
   (j) (10 =< 50) or (10 >= 200)

7. (a) Correct; interpreted as: (2 * 3) = 6; evaluates to true.
   (b) Incorrect; interpreted as: (6 = 2) * 3.
   (c) Incorrect; interpreted as: 2 + (3 = 5).
   (d) Incorrect; interpreted as: ((not 2) * 3) = 10.
   (e) Correct; interpreted as: (3 = 4) = true; evaluates to true.
   (f) Incorrect; interpreted as: (true = 3) = 4.
   (g) Correct; evaluates to 98.
   (h) Incorrect; interpreted as: ord (if 3 = 4 then 'b' else ('a' + 1)).

8. (b) 6 = (2 * 3)
   (c) (2 + 3) = 5
   (d) not (2 * 3 = 10)
   (f) true = (3 = 4)
   (h) ord (if 3 = 4 then 'b' else 'a') + 1

9. (a) if 0 /= 0 then 2 + 1 else 2 - 1   (b) 3 + 4 + 5 + 6
        ↓   ↓
    if false then 2 + 1 else 2 - 1   7 + 5 + 6
        ↓   ↓
        2 - 1   12 + 6
        ↓   ↓
        1   18

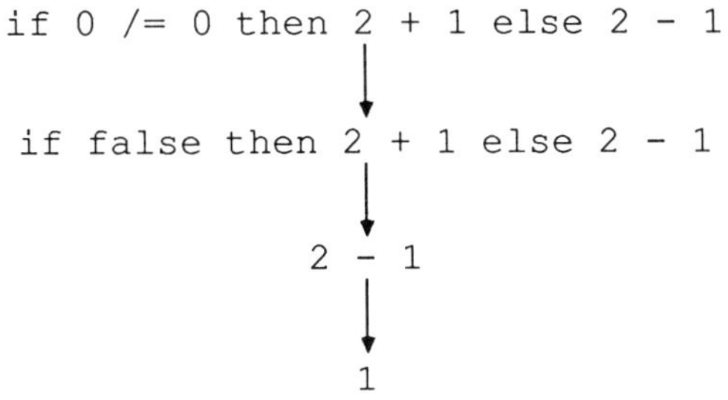

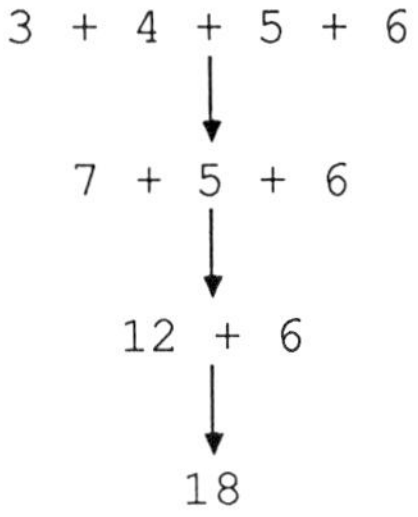

(c)   ord 'x' + ord 'y'
           ↙   ↘
    120 + ord 'y'   ord 'x' + 121
           ↘   ↙
                120 + 121
                   ↓
                  241

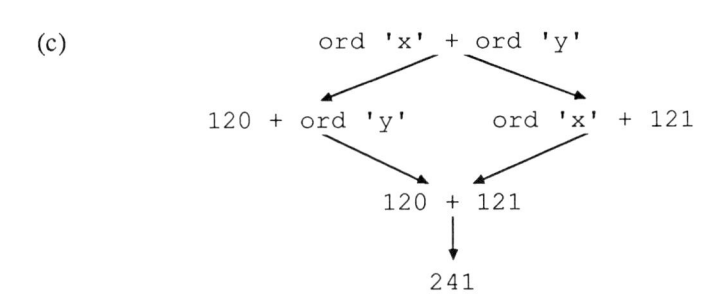

(d)   (3 = 4) = (4 = 5)
           ↙   ↘
    false = (4 = 5)   (3 = 4) = false
           ↘   ↙
                false = false
                    ↓
                   true

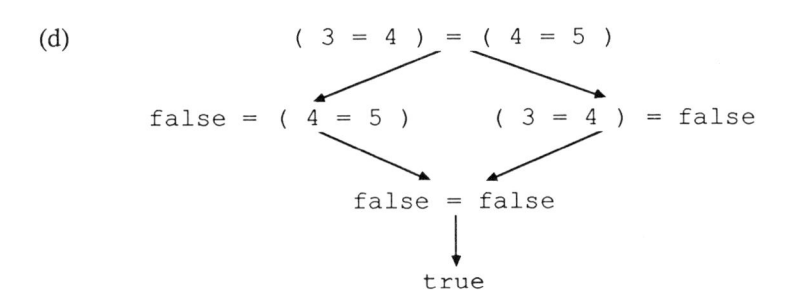

(e)   ord 'a' = (ord 'b' - 1)
           ↙   ↘
    97 = (ord 'b' - 1)   ord 'a' = (98 - 1)
           ↓   ↓
    97 = (98 - 1)   ord 'a' = 97
           ↘   ↙
                  97 = 97
                    ↓
                   true

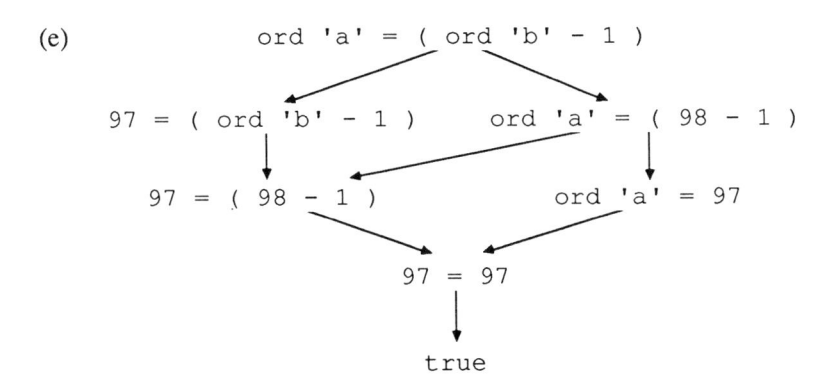

Chapter 2

1. ```
   dec add : num # num -> num ;
   --- add ( i , d ) <= 10 * i + d ;
   ```

2. ```
   infix cat : 4 ;
   dec cat : num # num -> num ;
   --- i cat d <= 10 * i + d ;
   ```

3. See §3.15

4. See §3.5

5. See §3.5

6. ```
   dec gcd : num # num -> num ;
   --- gcd ( m , n )
       <= if r = 0
             then n
             else gcd ( n , r )
          where r == m mod n ;
   ```

7. ```
   dec BinOf : num -> num ;
   --- BinOf n
       <= if n = 0
             then 0
             else BinOf ( n div 2 ) cat n mod 2 ;
   ```

    You might need parentheses round the final term if you defined cat in exercise 2 to have a priority greater than that of mod. Using add, the alternative expression will be:

    ```
    add ( BinOf ( n div 2 , n mod 2 )
    ```

8. ```
   dec NewBase : num # num -> num ;
   --- NewBase ( n , b )
       <= if n = 0
             then 0
             else NewBase ( n div b , b ) cat n mod b ;
   ```

    The remarks of solution 7 also apply here. Using add, the alternative expression will be:

    ```
    add ( NewBase ( n div b , b ) , n mod b )
    ```
    ```

9.  ```
    infix base : 4 ;
    dec base : num # num -> num ;
    --- n base b
        <= if n = 0
              then 0
              else n div b base b cat n mod b ;
    ```

    The operator priorities cause the alternative expression to be interpreted as:

    ```
    ( ( n div b ) base b ) cat ( n mod b )
    ```

    Explicit parentheses will be needed if cat has a higher priority than base, or if either cat or base has a higher priority than div or mod respectively. User-defined infix operations can render programs very obscure, and it is good practice to add extra redundant parentheses to help the reader understand what is intended.

10. ```
    infix P : 7 ;
    dec P : num # num -> num ;
    ```

    This simple solution follows directly from the second definition of ^nP_r:

    ```
    --- n P r <= fact n div fact ( n - r ) ;
    ```

    The recursive solution is derived from the first definition:

    ```
    --- n P r
        <= if r = 0
              then 1
              else n * ( n - 1 ) P ( r - 1 ) ;
    ```

11. ```
    infix C : 8 ;
    dec C : num # num -> num ;
    ```

    Again, a non-recursive solution from the second definition:

    ```
    --- n comb r <= fact n div fact ( n - r ) div fact r ;
    ```

    and a recursive solution from the first:

    ```
    --- n C r
        <= if r = 0
              then 1
              else n * ( n - 1 ) C ( r - 1 ) div r ;
    ```
    ```

240 APPENDIX 1

The order of terms is important here. The natural way to derive the expression from the first definition of ^nC_r is to pair off the first top and bottom term and multiply their quotient by the value of the remainder of the expression (evaluated recursively): n div r * (n - 1) C (r - 1). However, since div truncates its result, this gives the wrong answer (try $^5C_3$), unless all multiplications are performed before any divisions.

(a) Interpreted as (4 P 3) C 2; evaluates to 276.
(b) As for (a).
(c) Interpreted as 4 P (3 C 2); evaluates to 24.

Chapter 3

1. The full definition requires *four* equations (2 arguments × 2 constructors):

```
dec sum : num # num -> num ;
---  sum ( 0       , 0      ) <= 0 ;
---  sum ( succ x , 0      ) <= succ x ;
---  sum ( 0       , succ y ) <= succ y ;
---  sum ( succ x , succ y ) <= succ ( sum ( x , succ y ) ) ;
```

In the first, third and fourth equations, the second argument (whether succ y or 0) always appears unchanged on the right-hand side, so we do not need to check its constructor. The equations can thus be simplified to:

```
---  sum ( 0       , y ) <= y ;
---  sum ( succ x , 0 ) <= succ x ;
---  sum ( 0       , y ) <= y ;
---  sum ( succ x , y ) <= succ ( sum ( x , y ) ) ;
```

The third equation is now the same as the first, and can be removed. The second equation can also be removed because it is just a special case of the third equation with y having the value 0.

2. ```
   dec larger : num # num -> num ;
   ---  larger ( x , 0 ) <= x ;
   ---  larger ( 0 , y ) <= y ;
   ---  larger ( succ x , succ y )
          <= succ ( larger ( x , y ) ) ;
   ```
   ```

3.  ```
    dec chop : num -> ( num # num ) ;
    --- chop n
        <= if n < 10
             then ( 0 , n )
             else ( ( 1 + q , r )
                    where ( q , r ) == chop ( x - 10 ) ) ;
    ```

    Note that we must use a conditional to select the case when x is less than 10, as pattern matching only distinguishes between zero and non-zero arguments. Note also the high cost of chop: O(n) where n is the magnitude of the argument.

4.  ```
    dec concat : num # num -> num ;
    --- concat ( m , 0 ) <= 0 ;
    --- concat ( m , succ n )
        <= add ( concat ( m , q ) , r )
           where ( q , r ) == chop ( succ n ) ;
    ```

    concat performs one self-application and one application of chop for each digit in its second argument, so its cost is $O(n.\log_{10} n)$.

5. See §6.8.

6.  ```
    dec shout : list char -> list char ;
    --- shout nil <= nil ;
    --- shout ( h :: t ) <= fold h :: shout t ;
    ```

    fold is the function for converting lower-case characters to upper-case which was defined in §2.6.

7.  ```
    dec precedes : list char # list char -> truval ;
    --- precedes ( l , nil ) <= false ;
    --- precedes ( nil , h :: t ) <= true ;
    --- precedes ( h1 :: t1 , h2 :: t2 )
        <= if h1 = h2
             then precedes ( t1 , t2 )
             else h1 < h2 ;
    ```

    Notice that the alternative expression h1 < h2 evaluates directly to the required truval-valued result. We should never write expressions like:

    ```
    if h1 < h2
       then true
       else false
    ```

8.  ```
    infix before : 5 ;
    dec before : list char # list char -> truval ;
    --- 1 before nil <= false ;
    --- nil before ( h :: t ) <= true ;
    --- ( h1 :: t1 ) before ( h2 :: t2 )
        <= if h1 = h2
              then t1 before t2
              else h1 < h2 ;
    ```

    To make before case-insensitive, the general-case equation can be changed to:

    ```
    --- ( h1 :: t1 ) before ( h2 :: t2 )
        <= if f1 = f2
              then t1 before t2
              else f1 < f2
              where ( f1 , f2 ) == ( fold h1 , fold h2 ) ;
    ```

9. A more general solution appears in §5.14.

10. See §5.14.

11. See §5.15.

12. ```
    dec right : char # list char -> list char ;
    --- right ( c , nil ) <= [ c ] ;
    --- right ( c , h :: t ) <= h :: right ( c , t ) ;
    ```

13. ```
    dec reverse : list char -> list char ;
    --- reverse nil <= nil ;
    --- reverse ( h :: t ) <= right ( h , reverse t ) ;
    ```

    Alternatively, the general-case equation can be written as:

    ```
    --- reverse ( h :: t ) <= reverse t <> [ h ] ;
    ```

14. ```
    dec into : char # list char -> list char ;
    --- into ( c , nil ) <= [ c ] ;
    --- into ( c , h :: t )
        <= if c < h
              then c :: ( h :: t )
              else h :: into ( c , t ) ;
    ```

15. ```
    dec order : list char -> list char ;
    --- order nil <= nil ;
    --- order ( h :: t ) <= into ( h , order t ) ;
    ```

Chapter 4

1. ```
   data light == red ++ redamber ++ green ++ amber ;

   dec change : light -> light ;
   --- change red      <= redamber ;
   --- change redamber <= green ;
   --- change green    <= amber ;
   --- change amber    <= red ;
   ```

2. ```
   dec both , either : switch # switch -> switch ;

   --- both ( on  , on  ) <= on ;
   --- both ( off , s   ) <= off ;
   --- both ( s   , off ) <= off ;

   --- either ( on  , s   ) <= on ;
   --- either ( s   , on  ) <= on ;
   --- either ( off , off ) <= off ;
   ```

3. ```
   infix plus , minus : 5 ;
   infix over : 6 ;

   dec plus , minus , over : float # float -> float ;
   ```

   The simplest function is `over`, which is analogous to `mult` from §4.5, except that the precision is increased by scaling the mantissa of the dividend to double the number of digits, with the exponent reduced accordingly. This is safe because the division will reduce the number of digits. The arguments are assumed to be in normalised form, and the result is renormalised using `norm` from §4.5.

   ```
   --- flo ( m1 , e1 ) over flo ( m2 , e2 )
       <= norm ( m1 * 10000 div m2 , e1 - e2 - 4 ) ;
   ```

   Floating-point numbers with identical exponents can be added directly, otherwise the mantissa of the smaller must be scaled to make its exponent the same as that of the larger. Scaling reduces the number of digits in the mantissa and cannot cause overflow, but accuracy will be lost:

```
--- flo ( m1 , e1 ) plus flo ( m2 , e2 )
    <= if e1 = e2
         then norm ( m1 + m2 , e1 )
         else if e1 > e2
                 then flo ( m1 , e1 ) plus
                      flo ( m2 div 10 , e2 + 1 )
                 else flo ( m1 div 10 , e1 + 1 ) plus
                      flo ( m2 , e2 ) ;

--- flo ( m1 , e1 ) minus flo ( m2 , e2 )
    <= if e1 = e2
         then norm ( m1 - m2 , e1 )
         else if e1 > e2
                 then flo ( m1 , e1 ) minus
                      flo ( m2 div 10 , e2 + 1 )
                 else flo ( m1 div 10 , e1 + 1 ) minus
                      flo ( m2 , e2 ) ;
```

4. See §8.12.

5.
```
dec younger : staff # staff -> staff ;
--- younger ( st ( n1 , a1 ) , st ( n2 , a2 ) )
    <= if a1 < a2
         then st ( n1 , a1 )
         else st ( n2 , a2 ) ;
```

Change the the general-case equation for junior to:

```
--- junior ( h :: ( i :: t ) )
    <= younger ( h , junior ( i :: t ) ) ;
```

6. calc is declared first, because it will be used by operand:

```
dec calc : list item -> num ;

dec operand : item -> num ;
--- operand ( int x )    <= x ;
--- operand ( term s )   <= calc s ;

dec operator : char # num # num -> num ;
--- operator ( '+' , x , y ) <= x + y ;
--- operator ( '-' , x , y ) <= x - y ;
--- operator ( '*' , x , y ) <= x * y ;
--- operator ( '/' , x , y ) <= x div y ;
```

The equations for calc appear last, because they use operand and operator:

```
--- calc [ x ] <= operand x ;
--- calc ( x :: ( op c :: ( y :: t ) ) )
    <= calc ( int r :: t )
        where r == operator ( c , operand x ,
                                  operand y ) ;
```

7. ```
   dec minor : payroll -> staff ;
   --- minor ( record s ) <= s ;
   --- minor ( pair ( p1 , p2 )
       <= youngest ( minor p1 , minor p2 ) ;
   ```

8. ```
   dec cut : num # list num -> ( list num # list num ) ;
   --- cut ( 0 , r ) <= ( nil , r ) ;
   --- cut ( succ n , h :: t )
       <= ( h :: l , r )
           where ( l , r ) == cut ( n , t ) ;
   ```

9. ```
   dec build : list num -> bin ;
   --- build [ n ] <= end n ;
   --- build ( L & h :: ( i :: t ) )
       <= let ( l , r ) == cut ( length L div 2 , L )
          in limb ( build l , build r ) ;
   ```

10. ```
    dec ends : bin -> list num ;
    --- ends ( end n ) <= [ n ] ;
    --- ends ( limb ( l , r ) ) <= ends l <> ends r ;
    ```

11. ```
    dec swap : bin -> bin ;
    --- swap ( end n ) <= end n ;
    --- swap ( limb ( l , r ) )
        <= limb ( swap l , swap r ) ;
    ```

    In general, ends (swap (build *somelist*)) reverses *somelist*.

12. A sequence of calculations is represented by a list item, hence the declaration of improve will be:

    ```
    dec improve : list item -> expression ;
    ```

    The following useful auxiliary function can be used to convert a single item which is not an operator into an expression:
    ```

```
dec convert : item -> expression ;
--- convert ( int x   ) <= rand x ;
--- convert ( term s ) <= improve s ;
```

The operations in the list of items associate to the left, so we must arrange to convert the list rather as we evaluated it in exercise 6, passing on the result of converting the first subexpression (operand-operator-operand) to a function which converts the rest of the list of items. We cannot place the converted expression back on the head of the input list (as we did with the result in exercise 6) because it has the wrong type. We therefore introduce an auxiliary function to perform all conversions after the first:

```
dec rest : expression # list item -> expression ;
--- rest ( e , nil ) <= e ;
--- rest ( e , ( op c :: ( x :: t ) ) )
    <= rest ( rat ( c , e , convert x ) , t ) ;
```

The required improve function now only converts the first term:

```
--- improve [ i ] <= convert i ;
--- improve ( x :: ( op c :: ( y :: t ) ) )
    <= rest ( e , t )
       where e == rat ( c , convert x ,
                                convert y ) ;
```

13.
```
data expression == rand num ++
                   rat ( char # expression #
                                expression ) ++
                   monop ( char # expression ) ;

--- eval ( monop ( '\' , x ) ) <= 0 - eval x ;
```

14. A more general solution is given in §5.20.

Chapter 5

1.
```
dec elements : seq alpha -> num ;
--- elements ( one i )              <= 1 ;
--- elements ( two ( i , s ) )  <= 1 + elements s ;
```

2.
```
dec reverse : list alpha -> list alpha ;
--- reverse nil <= nil ;
--- reverse ( h :: t ) <= reverse t <> [ h ] ;
```

If the second version of reverse is to be made polymorphic, then we require a polymorphic version of right; just change its declaration to:

```
dec right : alpha # list alpha -> list alpha ;
```

3. ```
   dec palindrome : list alpha -> list alpha ;
   --- palindrome nil <= nil ;
   --- palindrome ( L & h :: t )
       <= L <> u
           where ( _ :: u ) == reverse L ;
   ```

4. ```
   dec CatSeq : seq alpha # seq alpha -> seq alpha ;
   --- CatSeq ( one i , S ) <= two ( i , S ) ;
   --- CatSeq ( two ( i , s ) , S )
       <= two ( i , CatSeq ( s , S ) ) ;
   ```

5. ```
   dec RevSeq : seq alpha -> seq alpha ;
   --- RevSeq ( one i ) <= one i ;
   --- RevSeq ( two ( i , s ) )
       <= CatSeq ( RevSeq s , one i ) ;
   ```

6. ```
   dec SeqToList : seq alpha -> list alpha ;
   --- SeqToList ( one i ) <= [ i ] ;
   --- SeqToList ( two ( i , s ) ) <= i :: SeqToList s ;
   ```

7. ```
   dec ListToSeq : list alpha -> seq alpha ;
   --- ListToSeq [ i ] <= one i ;
   --- ListToSeq ( h :: t ) <= two ( h , ListToSeq t ) ;
   ```

   ListToSeq cannot be completely general because sequences must contain at least one element, so there is no sequence corresponding to the empty list. The base case is therefore the *singleton* list.

8. ```
   dec nodes : tree alpha -> num ;
   --- nodes null <= 0 ;
   --- nodes ( leaf v ) <= 1 ;
   --- nodes ( node ( v , l , r ) )
       <= 1 + nodes l + nodes r ;
   ```

   The second equation is only needed if tree alpha has been defined to have a leaf constructor. It is arguable that since the the question asks for *nodes*, the result in this case should be 0! The solutions to the remaining exercises assume a version of tree alpha with no leaf constructor.

248 APPENDIX 1

9. ```
dec depth : tree alpha -> num ;
--- depth null <= 1 ;
--- depth (node (v , l , r))
    <= greater (depth l , depth r) ;
```

greater is the function defined in §2.9 for finding the larger of two numbers.

10. ```
dec twist : tree alpha -> tree alpha ;
--- twist null <= null ;
--- twist ( node ( v , l , r ) )
    <= node ( v , twist r , twist l ) ;
```

11. ```
dec BinToSeq : bin alpha -> seq alpha ;
--- BinToSeq (tip v) <= one v ;
--- BinToSeq (fork (l , r))
    <= CatSeq (BinToSeq l , BinToSeq r) ;
```

The comments on exercise 8 also apply here.

12. ```
data NaryTree alpha ==
        none ++
        branch ( alpha # list ( NaryTree alpha ) ) ;
```

13. The data declaration of §5.5 suffices. If we do not require error handling, then the index function of §5.5 is also suitable, provided its type is changed to make it polymorphic:

    ```
    dec index : num # vector alpha -> alpha ;
    --- index ( n , vec ( b , h :: t ) )
        <= if n = b
           then h
           else index ( n , vec ( b + 1 , t ) ) ;
    ```

    The access functions bound and size are straightforward:

    ```
    dec bound : vector alpha -> num ;
    --- bound ( vec ( b , l ) ) <= b ;

    dec size : vector alpha -> num ;
    --- size ( vec ( b , [ ] ) ) <= 1 ;
    --- size ( vec ( b , h :: t ) )
        <= 1 + size ( vec ( b + 1 , t ) ) ;
    ```

    Alternatively, given length over lists from §3.11, we can just write:

```
--- size ( vec b , l ) <= length l ;
```

The access function `update` is less straightforward, because we require an auxiliary function which will replace a selected element of a list:

```
dec replace : num # alpha # list alpha -> list alpha ;
--- replace ( 1 , a , h :: t ) <= a :: t ;
--- replace ( succ ( succ n ) , a , h :: t )
    <= h :: replace ( succ n , a , t ) ;

dec update : num # alpha # vector alpha ->
             vector alpha ;
--- update ( n , a , vec ( b , l ) )
    <= vec ( b , replace ( n - b + 1 , a , l ) ) ;
```

We could not write a recursive definition of `update` directly, because vectors are not defined recursively, so we cannot write an expression involving vectors analogous to the general-case equation of `replace`. If the elements of a vector are represented using a binary tree (*e.g.* replacing the `list alpha` by a `bin alpha` of §5.8), a version of `index` can be written which is analogous to `locate` of §4.14 and which has $O(\log_2 n)$ cost. We can also write an $O(\log_2 n)$ cost version of `update` by using an auxiliary function analogous to `replace` (and `locate`) to replace a single `tip` of a `bin alpha`. To make vectors usable in practical programs, we also need functions to create and visualise them. Typically we might provide functions to interconvert vectors and lists:

```
dec ListToVector : num # list alpha -> vector alpha ;
dec VectorToList : vector alpha -> list alpha ;
```

The `num` parameter of `ListToVector` is to allow the lower bound of the new vector to be specified. Other possible access functions are discussed in §6.17.

Chapter 6

1. map (change , *some list light*)

2. increment (map (flip , *some list switch*))

250 APPENDIX 1

3. *(a)*
```
dec MapSeq : ( alpha -> beta ) # seq alpha ->
                                seq beta ;
--- MapSeq ( f , one x ) <= one ( f x ) ;
--- MapSeq ( f , two ( x , y ) )
     <= two ( f x , MapSeq ( f , y ) ) ;
```

(b)
```
dec MapBin : ( alpha -> beta ) # bin alpha ->
                                bin beta ;
--- MapBin ( f , tip v ) <= tip ( f v ) ;
--- MapBin ( f , fork ( l , r ) )
     <= fork ( MapBin ( f , l ) ,
               MapBin ( f , r ) ) ;
```

4. See §8.1 for the definition of choose.

   To eliminate even numbers:

   ```
   choose ( odd , some list num ) ;
   ```

   To count lower-case letters:

   ```
   length ( choose ( LowerCase , some list char ) ) ;
   ```

5.
```
dec pairwise : ( alpha # beta -> gamma ) #
                list alpha # list beta -> list gamma ;
--- pairwise ( f , nil , nil ) <= nil ;
--- pairwise ( f , h1 :: t1 , h2 :: t2 )
     <= f ( h1 , h2 ) :: pairwise ( f , t1 , t2 ) ;
```

   To form the switch-by-switch conjunction of two accumulators:

   ```
   pairwise ( both , some list switch ,
                     some other list switch )
   ```

   To form the switch-by-switch disjunction of two accumulators:

   ```
   pairwise ( either , some list switch ,
                       some other list switch )
   ```

   A more robust definition of pairwise is obtained by adding equations to cover the cases where one list becomes empty before the other:

```
--- pairwise ( f , nil , l ) <= nil ;
--- pairwise ( f , l , nil ) <= nil ;
```

Both new equations overlap with the original base case, which can be omitted.

6. To test if any switch is on:

    ```
    reduce ( either , on , some list switch )
    ```

    To test if all switches are on:

    ```
    reduce ( both , on , some list switch )
    ```

7. ```
   dec RightInsert : alpha # list alpha -> list alpha ;
   --- RightInsert ( a , nil ) <= [ a ] ;
   --- RightInsert ( a , h :: t )
          <= h :: RightInsert ( a , t ) ;
   ```

   ```
   reduce ( RightInsert , nil , some list alpha ) ;
   ```

   The cost of evaluating this expression is $O(n^2)$ for an n-element list.

8. ```
   dec LeftAdd : list alpha # alpha -> list alpha ;
   --- LeftAdd ( l , a ) <= a :: l ;
   ```

   ```
   LeftRed ( LeftAdd , [ h ] , t )
       where ( h :: t ) == some non-empty list alpha
   ```

   The cost of evaluating this expression is $O(n)$ for an n-element list.

9. ```
   let s == MapSeq ( elements , some seq ( seq char ) )
       in ConSeq ( nonop + , id , s ) div elements s ;
   ```

10. First a given function of three arguments which returns a tree:

    ```
    dec assemble: alpha # tree alpha # tree alpha ->
                     tree alpha ;
    --- assemble ( a , l , r ) <= node ( a , r , l ) ;
    ```

    Using `assemble`, the required expression is then:

    ```
    RedTree ( assemble , null , some tree alpha ) ;
    ```
    ```

252 APPENDIX 1

11. The trick is to supply the value generated by reducing one subtree as the base-case value for reducing the other:

```
---   SquashTree ( f , b , node ( v , l , r ) )
      <= SquashTree ( f , f ( v , R ) , l )
           where R == SquashTree ( f , b , r ) ;
```

The given function f is used to combine the node value v and the "squashed" right subtree into a new base-case value. A symmetrical version uses the reduced left subtree as the base-case value for the reduction of the right subtree:

```
---   SquashTree ( f , b , node ( v , l , r ) )
      <= SquashTree ( f , f ( v , L ) , r )
           where L == SquashTree ( f , b , l ) ;
```

The base case is the same for both versions:

```
---   SquashTree ( f , b , null ) <= b ;
```

The first version consolidates the elements right-associatively, and the second, left-associatively. In both versions f is applied to a node value (an alpha) and a reduced subtree (a beta), allowing SquashTree to have the general type:

(alpha # beta -> beta) # beta # tree alpha -> beta

A less satisfactory solution consolidates the left and right subtrees separately, and combines the values using two applications of the given function f:

```
---   SquashTree ( f , b , node ( v , l , r ) )
      <= let ( L , R ) == ( SquashTree ( f , b , l ) ,
                            SquashTree ( f , b , r ) )
         in f ( L , f ( v , L ) ) ;
```

Here, the first argument of f is a consolidated tree value (a beta) in the outer application and a node value (an alpha) in the inner. The expression only has the correct type if beta is the same type as alpha, restricting the type of this version of SquashTree to:

(alpha # alpha -> alpha) # alpha # tree alpha -> alpha

12. SquashTree (nonop :: , nil , *some tree alpha*) ;

    The given function : : has arguments of different types, hence the expression is only valid if we are using the more general version of SquashTree. The cost of evaluating the expression is $O(n)$ for an n-item tree.

13. SquashTree (insert , null , *some tree alpha*) ;

    insert is the ordered tree insertion function from §5.10, hence SquashTree must be the more general version. The cost of evaluating this expression is $O(n.\log_2 n)$ for an n-item tree.

Chapter 7

1. (a) MapSeq (lambda n => 2 * n , *some seq num*)

   (b) MapSeq (lambda n => not (odd n) , *some seq num*)

   (c) MapSeq (lambda n => (n , if odd n
                                  then "odd"
                                  else "even") ,
               some seq num)

2. (a) ConSeq (lambda (x , y) => if x > y
                                     then x
                                     else y ,
                lambda x => x , *some seq num*)

   (b) ConSeq (nonop :: , lambda n => [n] ,
                some seq alpha)

3. (a) RedTree (lambda (a , b , c)
                       => node (a , c , b) ,
                  null , *some tree alpha*)

   (b) RedTree (lambda (_ , x , y) => 1 + if x > y
                                              then x
                                              else y ,
                  0 , *some tree alpha*)

   (c) The technique for avoiding two traversals of the tree is to collect both the sum of the node values and the number of nodes as a pair:

254 APPENDIX 1

```
         let ( s , n ) ==

         RedTree ( lambda ( v , ( ls , ln ) , ( rs , rn ) )
                   => ( v + ls + rs , 1 + ln + rn ) ,
                 ( 0 , 0 ) , some tree alpha )

         in norm ( s , 0 ) over norm ( n , 0 )
```

Here `norm` is the function for normalising a floating-point number defined in §4.5 and `over` is the function for finding the quotient of two floating-point numbers from exercise 3 of chapter 4.

4. `dec MapNary : ( alpha -> beta ) # NaryTree alpha -> NaryTree beta ;`

   The equations assume the constructor names from the definition of *n*-ary trees given in the sample solution to exercise 12 of chapter 5:

   ```
   ---  MapNary ( f , none ) <= none ;
   ```

   Using `map`, the general-case equation is simply:

   ```
   ---  MapNary ( f , branch ( v , l ) )
        <= branch ( f v , map ( lambda t
                                => MapNary ( f , t ) ,
                            l ) ) ;
   ```

   The lambda expression can be eliminated by using `fix`:

   ```
   ---  MapNary ( f , branch ( v , l ) )
        <= branch ( f v , map ( fix ( MapNary , f ) , l ) ) ;
   ```

5. The formal function must combine the value at a node with a (possibly empty) list of values resulting from consolidating each element of subtree list. Its type is therefore `alpha # list beta -> beta` and one possible definition of `RedNary` is:

   ```
   dec RedNary :  ( alpha # list beta -> beta ) # beta #
                  NaryTree alpha -> beta ;
   ---  RedNary ( f , b , none ) <= b ;
   ---  RedNary ( f , b , branch ( v , l ) )
        <= f ( v , map ( lambda t
                         => RedNary ( f , b , t ) ,
                     l ) ) ;
   ```

6. RedNary (lambda (n , l)
              => n :: reduce (nonop <> , nil , l) ,
       nil , some NaryTree alpha)

7. *(a)* `---` MapSeq (f , s)
         <= ConSeq (lambda (a , b)
                         => two (f a , b) ,
                     lambda a => one (f a) ,
             s) ;

   (b) `---` MapTree (f , t)
         <= ConTree (lambda (a , b , c)
                         => node (f a , b , c) ,
                      lambda a
                         => node (f a , null , null) ,
                  t) ;

   (c) `---` MapBin (f , b)
         <= ConBin (lambda (a , b)
                         => fork (a , b) ,
                     lambda a => tip (f a) ,
                 t) ;

8. choose (compose (p , not) , l)

9. compose (fix (transfer , null) , flatten)

   It is possible to dispense with `fix`, yielding a function of *two* arguments which can be applied as follows:

   compose (transfer , flatten) (null , some list num)

10. dec twice : (alpha -> alpha) -> (alpha -> alpha) ;
    `---` twice f <= compose (f , f) ;

    (a) lambda x => twice (twice x)
    (b) 4
    (c) 16

Chapter 8

1.  ```
    choose ( lambda x
                 => factor ( x , 2 ) or
                    factor ( x , 3 ) or
                    factor ( x , 5 ) ,
             ints 1 )
    ```

    The cost of evaluating this expression is $O(m)$ for the Hamming number with magnitude m, since we must test every integer up to m.

2. (a) `map ( fact , ints 1 )`
    (b) `map ( Fib  , ints 1 )`

3.  ```
    dec infact : list num -> list num ;
    --- infact ( h :: t )
        <= let p == pairwise ( nonop * , t , ints 1 )
              in h ::: infact p ;
    ```

    Here, p represents the infinite list of partial products formed by "merging" a new stream of integers into the tail of the original list. The top-level application is:

    `infact ( ints 1 )`

4.  ```
    dec effact : ( num # num ) -> list num ;
    --- effact ( n , p )
        <= n ::: effact ( p * n , succ p ) ;
    ```

    The top-level application is:

    `effact ( 1 , 2 )`

5.  ```
    dec effib : ( num # num ) -> list num ;
    --- effib ( a , b ) <= a ::: effib ( b , a + b ) ;
    ```

    The top-level application is:

    `effib ( 1 , 1 )`

6.  ```
    dec iota : alpha # ( alpha -> alpha ) -> list alpha ;
    --- iota ( a , f ) <= a ::: iota ( f a , f ) ;
    ```

    (a) `iota ( 5 , lambda n => n + 5 )`
    (b) `iota ( 2 , lambda n => n * 2 )`
    ```

(c) `iota ( true , not ) ) ;`
(d) `iota ( 'a' , lambda c => chr ( ord c + 3 ) )`
(e) `iota ( "*" , lambda s => '*' :: s )`

7. The following lazy version of `merge` also removes duplicates:

```
dec merge : list num # list num -> list num ;
--- merge ( h1 :: t1 , h2 :: t2 )
    <= if h1 = h2
       then h1 ::: merge ( t1 , t2 )
       else if h1 < h2
            then h1 ::: merge ( t1 , h2 :: t2 )
            else h2 ::: merge ( h1 :: t1 , t2 ) ;
```

The Hamming numbers can be generated by an expression such as:

```
merge ( mults 2 , merge ( mults 3 , mults 5 ) ) )
  where mults == lambda s
                 => iota ( s , lambda n => n + s )
```

This produces the first *n* Hamming numbers with O(*n*) cost.

8.
```
--- root n
    <= let g == iota ( n ,
                       lambda g
                       => ( g plus n over g )
                          over norm ( 2 , 0 ) )
       in same g ;
```

Notice that the value of n is bound in to the lambda expression supplied as the argument to `iota`, whereas `roots` required an additional parameter to carry this value forward between applications.

9. `iota ( ( 1 , 1 ) , lambda ( a , b )`
    `=> ( succ a , succ a * b ) )`

10. The technique is similar to that used to find square roots in §8.12. We can apply `same` to a list of successive approximations to τ to find the value to which they converge:

```
same taus
  where taus == ...
```

The infinite list of approximations (taus) can be defined in terms of an infinite list of pairs of Fibonacci numbers:

```
... map ( lambda ( d , n )
           => norm ( n , 0 ) over norm ( d , 0 ) ,
      Fibs )
      where Fibs == ...
```

Here norm is the function for normalising a floating-point number defined in §4.5 and over is the function for finding the quotient of two floating-point numbers from exercise 3 of chapter 4. The infinite list of pairs of Fibonacci numbers (Fibs) can in turn be generated by:

```
... iota ( ( 1 , 1 ) , lambda ( x , y )
                      => ( y , x + y ) ) ;
```

11. The following expression defines the terms of the infinite series as rational pairs:

```
let rats == iota ( ( 4 , 1 ) ,
             lambda ( n , d )
             => ( 0 - n , d + 2 ) ) in ...
```

and the following converts them to floating-point numbers:

```
... let terms == map ( lambda ( n , d )
                      => norm ( n , 0 ) over
                         norm ( d , 0 ) ,
                  rats ) in ...
```

If we have a function to sum the elements of the list until they become zero (*i.e.* too small to represent to the precision of floating-point numbers):

```
dec addup : list float -> float ;
--- addup ( h :: t )
    <= if h = norm ( 0 , 0 )
       then h
       else h plus addup t ;
```

we might hope to calculate π by writing:

```
... addup terms ;
```

but a little thought reveals a big problem. The first digit of the sum will stabilise when terms become smaller than 1, which occurs with the 3rd term

($^4/_5$). The second digit only stabilises when terms fall below 0.1, which does not occur until the 21st term ($^4/_{41}$). The third digit stabilises only after the 201st term ($^4/_{401}$), and so on. In general we must evaluate $O(10^n)$ terms to be confident that the nth digit is correct; to calculate π even to the 5-digit precision of our floating-point numbers requires the evaluation of around 10^5 terms! Since none of the applications of plus can be reduced until addup has been rewritten fully, the final expression representing π will itself contain 10^5 terms, exceeding the capacity of most Hope Machines.

The slow convergence is a fundamental problem of the series, and we cannot avoid the need to evaluate 10^5 terms. However, we can do something about the size of the final expression by defining an alternative to addup, which has an additional accumulating parameter:

```
dec accumulate : float # list float -> float ;
--- accumulate ( s , h :: t )
    <= if h = norm ( 0 , 0 )
       then s
       else accumulate ( s plus h , t ) ;
```

and applying it to terms like this:

```
... let ( s :: t ) == terms
    in accumulate ( s , t ) ;
```

Rewriting an application of accumulate in applicative order will generate an expression which contains at most two terms.

12. The left-hand column of the table is specified by using iota to generate the list of rationals with numerator 1 and successive denominators:

```
let l == iota ( ( 1 , 1 ) ,
                lambda ( x , y )
                => ( x , y + 1 ) ) ) in ...
```

The complete table is specified by using each element of l as the starting point for an application of iota which generates all the rationals with the same denominator and successive numerators:

```
... let t == map ( lambda ( x , y )
                   => iota ( ( x , y ) ,
                             lambda ( x , y )
                             => ( x + 1 , y ) ) ,
                  l ) in ...
```

If we write the table of rationals out in staggered form, it looks like this:

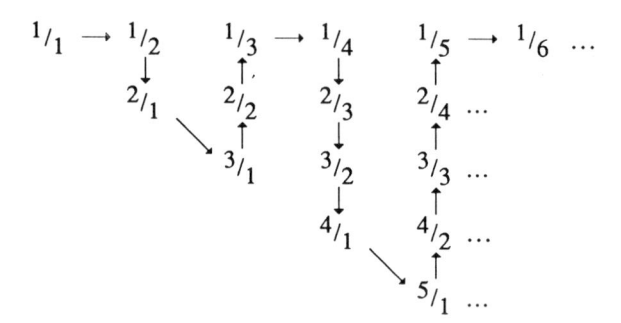

$$
\begin{array}{cccccc}
1/1 \rightarrow 1/2 & 1/3 \rightarrow 1/4 & 1/5 \rightarrow 1/6 & \cdots \\
\downarrow \nearrow & \uparrow \swarrow & \downarrow \nearrow & \\
2/1 & 2/2 & 2/3 & 2/4 & \cdots \\
& \uparrow \swarrow & \downarrow \nearrow & \\
& 3/1 & 3/2 & 3/3 & \cdots \\
& & \downarrow \nearrow & \uparrow \\
& & 4/1 & 4/2 & \cdots \\
& & & \uparrow \\
& & & 5/1 & \cdots
\end{array}
$$

Forming the columns into sublists is easy if we ignore the the arrows and treat each column identically. The solution is now similar to infact from problem 3, except that we "merge" in a new row of the table at each level of recursion (instead of the same list of integers each time) and form partial sublists using :: (rather than products using *). Type synonyms are used to clarify the definition:

```
type row    == list alpha ;
type table  == list row ;
type column == list alpha ;

dec Cantor : list column # table -> list column ;
--- Cantor ( h :: t , r :: s )
    <= let p == pairwise ( nonop :: , r , t )
       in h ::: Cantor ( p , s ) ;
```

The table appears as an additional parameter (so that successive rows can be obtained), and the arguments of pairwise are exchanged compared to infact, because :: is not commutative like *. The top-level application must be made to an infinite list of empty columns and the table t specified above:

... Cantor (iota (nil , id) , t) ;

id is the identity function from §6.12. This will generate the following infinite list of columns:

[nil , [$1/1$] , [$2/1$, $1/2$] , [$3/1$, $2/2$, $1/3$] , ...

The required list is obtained by reversing alternate sublists and concatenating them all together into a one-level list. Since the result represents a valid traversal as it stands (with each diagonal traversed from bottom left to top right), reversing alternate sublists is not strictly necessary. Concatenating an infinite list of finite sublists is discussed in exercise 11 of chapter 9.

Chapter 9

1. It is useful to define an auxiliary function yielding the character corresponding to a single-digit integer:

    ```
    dec digit : num -> char ;
    --- digit n <= chr ( n + ord '0' ) ;
    ```

    digit uses the property described in §1.11 that the characters representing numeric digits have consecutive ord values. Using digit, we can now write a version of digits suitable for positive numbers:

    ```
    dec digits : num -> list char ;
    --- digits n
          <= if n < 10
             then [ digit n ]
             else digits t <> [ digit b ]
             where ( t , b ) == chop n ;
    ```

    chop is the function which we wrote for exercise 3 of chapter 3 (for efficiency it should now be defined using div and mod).

    This version of digits has $O(n^2)$ cost for an *n*-digit number, because <> is applied *n* times (it also handles negative numbers incorrectly). An $O(n)$ version can be written using the following auxiliary function:

    ```
    dec auxdigits : num # list char -> list char ;
    --- auxdigits ( n , s )
          <= if n < 10
             then digit n :: s
             else auxdigits ( t , digit 1 :: s )
             where ( t , d ) == chop n ;
    ```

    auxdigits accumulates the character-string representation of the number n in the parameter s using : : instead of <>. The accumulating parameter must have the value nil initially. The following version of digits ensures this, and also takes care of negative integers:

    ```
    dec digits : num -> list char ;
    --- digits n
          <= if n < 0
             then '-' :: auxdigits ( 0 - n , nil )
             else auxdigits ( n , nil ) ;
    ```

Is it worth improving digits in this way? Converting a 100-digit number to a string requires 5,050 :: operations using the $O(n^2)$ version, but only 100 using the $O(n)$ version, a 500-fold improvement. However, the largest representable numbers have only 10 digits, requiring (at most) 55 and 10 :: operations respectively, so the maximum possible improvement is only 6-fold, and the average is much less (*e.g.* 3-fold for 5-digit numbers).

Improving the cost of digits is probably not a useful end in itself, and introducing auxdigits makes it harder to understand. However, the need to handle negative numbers at the top level makes an auxiliary function essential, so we might as well introduce the accumulating parameter at the same time.

2. There are some irritating complications here. The mantissa is a number between 32768 and 3276, but must be adjusted to lie between 1 and 10, and the exponent adjusted accordingly. We can use an accumulating-parameter auxiliary function to form the character-string representation of the mantissa as we did for digits in exercise 1, but we require an extra parameter to keep track of the exponent value:

```
dec auxreal : num # list char # num -> list char ;
--- auxreal ( m , s , e )
    <= if m < 10
       then digit m :: ( '.' ::
                         ( s <> ( " E " <> digits e ) ) )
       else auxreal ( t , digit b :: s , succ e )
            where ( t , b ) == chop m ;

dec real : float -> list char ;
--- real ( flo ( m , e ) )
    <= if m < 0
       then '-' :: auxreal ( 0 - m , nil , e )
       else auxreal ( m , nil , e ) ;
```

Ideally, trailing zeros should be removed from the character-string representation of the fractional part s; the following function performs this:

```
dec dezero : list char -> list char ;
--- dezero nil <= nil ;
--- dezero ( c :: s )
    <= if ( c , d ) = ( '0' , nil )
       then nil
       else c :: d
       where d == dezero s ;
```

However, there is yet another complication, because if there are no significant digits in s, a single zero must be generated to follow the decimal point. The complete processing of the fractional part is performed by this function:

```
dec trim : list char -> list char ;
--- trim s
    <= if d = nil
        then "0"
        else d
        where d == dezero s ;
```

3. The straightforward $O(n^2)$ solution is:

```
dec large : long -> list char ;
--- large ( ~ d )    <= [ digit d ] ;
--- large ( i . d )  <= large i <> [ digit d ] ;
```

Once again, the $O(n)$ solution uses an auxiliary function with an accumulating parameter:

```
dec auxlarge : list char # long -> list char ;
--- auxlarge ( s , ~ d ) <= digit d :: s ;
--- auxlarge ( s , i . d )
    <= auxlarge ( digit d :: s , i ) ;
```

large is now simply defined by the equation:

```
--- large i <= auxlarge ( nil , i ) ;
```

Once we have introduced auxlarge, it is simple to add an extra parameter to count off the digits and add commas:

```
dec auxlarge : num # list char # long -> list char ;
--- auxlarge ( n , s , ~ d ) <= digit d :: s ;
--- auxlarge ( 0 , s , i . d )
    <= auxlarge ( 2 , ',' :: ( digit d :: s ) , i ) ;
--- auxlarge ( succ n , s , i . d )
    <= auxlarge ( n , digit d :: s , i ) ;

--- large i <= auxlarge ( 2 , nil , i ) ;
```

As the definition of the data type stands, there is no representation for negative long numbers. An "obvious" representation would to extend the type definition to include extra constructors applied at the top level so that arithmetic functions could check them before performing any operations. `large` would then be defined by a pair of equations to check the sign and add a – to negative numbers.

4. First we define an auxiliary function to perform the inverse operation to `digit` from exercise 1, yielding the integer corresponding to a numeric character:

```
dec tigid : char -> num ;
--- tigid c <= ord c - ord '0' ;
```

Then an auxiliary function to accumulate each new digit in turn:

```
dec newdigit : num # list char -> num ;
--- newdigit ( n , nil ) <= n ;
--- newdigit ( n , c :: s )
    <= newdigit ( add ( n , tigid c ) , s ) ;
```

`add` is the function from exercise 1 of chapter 2 for adding a single digit onto the right-hand end of an arbitrary-size integer. The top-level function `number` takes care of a possible leading minus sign (indicating a negative number) and arranges that the accumulating parameter has the correct initial value:

```
dec number : list char -> num ;
--- number [ c ] <= tigid c ;
--- number ( c :: ( d :: s ) )
    <= if c = '-'
        then 0 - newdigit (tigid d , s )
        else newdigit ( tigid c , d :: s ) ;
```

5. First an auxiliary function to distinguish a numeric character:

```
dec isdigit : char -> truval ;
--- isdigit c <= ( c >= '0' ) and ( c =< '9' ) ;
```

`newdigit` must be modified to terminate on a non-numeric character as well as on the empty input string:

```
dec newdigit : num # list char -> num # list char ;
--- newdigit ( n , nil ) <= ( n , nil ) ;
--- newdigit ( n , c :: s )
    <= if isdigit c
        then newdigit ( add ( n , tigid c ) , s )
        else ( n , c :: s ) ;
```

```
dec number : list char -> num # list char ;
--- number [ c ] <= ( tigid c , nil ) ;
--- number ( c :: ( d :: s ) )
    <= if c = '-'
        then ( ( 0 - n , t )
                where ( n , t ) ==
                    newdigit ( tigid d , s ) )
        else newdigit ( tigid c , d :: s ) ;
```

6. First an auxiliary function to remove the blanks which separate the individual numbers in the list:

```
dec deblank : list char -> list char ;
--- deblank nil <= nil ;
--- deblank ( S & c :: s )
    <= if c = ' '
        then deblank s
        else S ;

dec numlist : list char -> list num ;
--- numlist nil <= nil ;
--- numlist ( S & c :: s )
    <= n :: numlist t
        where ( n , t ) == number ( deblank S ) ;
```

7. First an auxiliary function to see if a character string starts with a number:

```
dec isnum : list char -> truval ;
--- isnum nil    <= false ;
--- isnum [ c ] <= isdigit c ;
--- isnum ( c :: ( d :: s ) )
    <= if c = '-'
        then isdigit d
        else isdigit c ;
```

`numlist` must be modified to terminate on a non-number as well as on the empty input string:

```
dec numlist : list char -> list num # list char ;
--- numlist nil <= ( nil , nil ) ;
```

```
--- numlist ( S & c :: s )
    <= if isnum T
       then ( ( n :: l , u )
              where ( l , u ) == numlist t
              where ( n , t ) == number T )
       else ( nil , S )
       where T == deblank S ;
```

8. It is only necessary to substitute : : : for the : : constructor in the solution to exercise 5(b) and to remove the base-case equation and input pattern-match:

```
dec numlist : list char -> list num ;
--- numlist l
    <= n ::: numlist t
       where ( n , t ) == number ( deblank l ) ;
```

A different style of solution uses iota from exercise 6 of chapter 8 to construct a list of pairs, each of which contains a number and the rest of the input list:

```
iota ( number ( deblank l ) ,
       lambda ( n , t ) => number ( deblank t )
   where l == the input list ;
```

We can then "filter out" the required numbers from the pairs using the lazy version of map (from §8.10), leading to the following definition for numlist:

```
dec numlist : list char -> list num ;
--- numlist l
    <= map ( lambda ( n , t ) => n ,
             iota ( number ( deblank l ) ,
                    lambda ( n , t )
                        => number ( deblank t ) ) ) ;
```

The solution appears to have a high space cost at first sight, but since lazy evaluation interleaves the applications of map and iota, the result expression only ever contains one evaluated pair. Further, the copy of the remaining input stream which it contains will only have a single input character evaluated.

9. We cannot solve this problem by simply substituting : : : for : : in the solution to exercise 7 because the tail of the result list and the pair component which defines the remaining input are defined in a qualifying expression. Since these are evaluated in applicative order, this will cause all the elements of the list of numbers to be evaluated. We used this property to our advantage when we wrote opening in §9.9.

CHAPTER 9   267

It is arguable that the required function is not useful anyway, since it is not logically possible to know the value of the remaining characters until all the elements of the preceding list have been evaluated. Even if the function could be written, it would be applied at the top level in some context such as:

```
let ( l , s ) == numlist keyboard
   in program ;
```

Any attempt to use the value of s in *program* would simply cause evaluation to be suspended until the complete list of integers had been entered.

10.
```
dec analyse : ( list char -> alpha # list char ) #
                  list char -> list alpha ;
--- analyse ( f , l )
    <= a ::: analyse ( f , t )
         where ( a , t ) == f l ;
```

A solution using map and iota (*cf.* exercise 8) is also possible:

```
--- analyse ( f , l )
    <= map ( lambda ( a , t ) => a ,
             iota ( f l , lambda ( a , t ) => f t ) ) ;
```

11. In principle we need only append all the component lists together, but as in the case of format, we cannot simply write:

```
--- unlist ( h :: t ) <= h <> unlist t ;
```

because we must prevent the second argument of <> from being evaluated until all the elements of h have been placed in the result list. As with format, we can get this effect using condense, supplying a continuation for the base case:

```
--- unlist ( h :: t )
    <= condense ( nonop :: ,
                  lambda a
                      => a ::: unlist t ,
                  h ) ;
```

This does not quite solve the problem, because the elements of h are placed into the output list using : :, so the result is not fully lazy as required. It is not sufficient to supply : : : in place of : : as the actual parameter of condense, because we recollect from §6.12 that it is applied in the expression:

```
---  condense ( f , g , a :: ( b :: t ) )
  <= f ( a , condense ( f , g , b :: t ) ) ;
```

In this context, the formal function f will be applied strictly, even if : : is supplied as the actual parameter. We can solve this problem by writing an auxiliary function which applies : : : explicitly:

```
dec delay : list alpha # ( alpha -> list alpha ) ->
            list alpha ;
--- delay ( [ a ] , f ) <= f a ;
--- delay ( h :: ( i :: t ) , f )
  <= h ::: delay ( i :: t , f ) ;
```

As in the case of compose in format, the sublist being copied lazily must be non-empty, so that it contains an element to form the argument of the continuation function. A separate equation is required for empty sublists so that delay is not applied. A safe definition will also include an equation for the empty input list:

```
dec unlist : list ( list alpha ) -> list alpha ;
--- unlist nil <= nil ;
--- unlist ( nil :: T ) <= unlist T ;
--- unlist ( h :: t :: T )
  <= delay ( h :: t , lambda a => a ::: unlist T ) ;
```

12. show (format (unlist l , f , " , "))
      where l == *the list of rationals*
        where f == lambda (n , d)
                   => digits n <> ('/' :: digits d) ;

Appendix 2

Language Summary

A2.1 Character classes
Hope programs are written using a set of characters divided into classes as follows:

letter	_ A B C D E F G H I J K L M N O P Q R S T U V W X Y Z a b c d e f g h i j k l m n o p q r s t u v w x y z
digit	0 1 2 3 4 5 6 7 8 9
sign	# $ % & * + - . / : < = > ? @ \ ^ ` | ~
punctuation	! " ' ( ) , ; [ ] { }
layout	space tab newline

A2.2 Words
The sequence of characters forming a Hope program is considered to be grouped into a sequence of distinct words. Adjacent words which are formed from the same class of non-punctuation characters must be separated by at least one layout character.

number

string literal

name

character literal

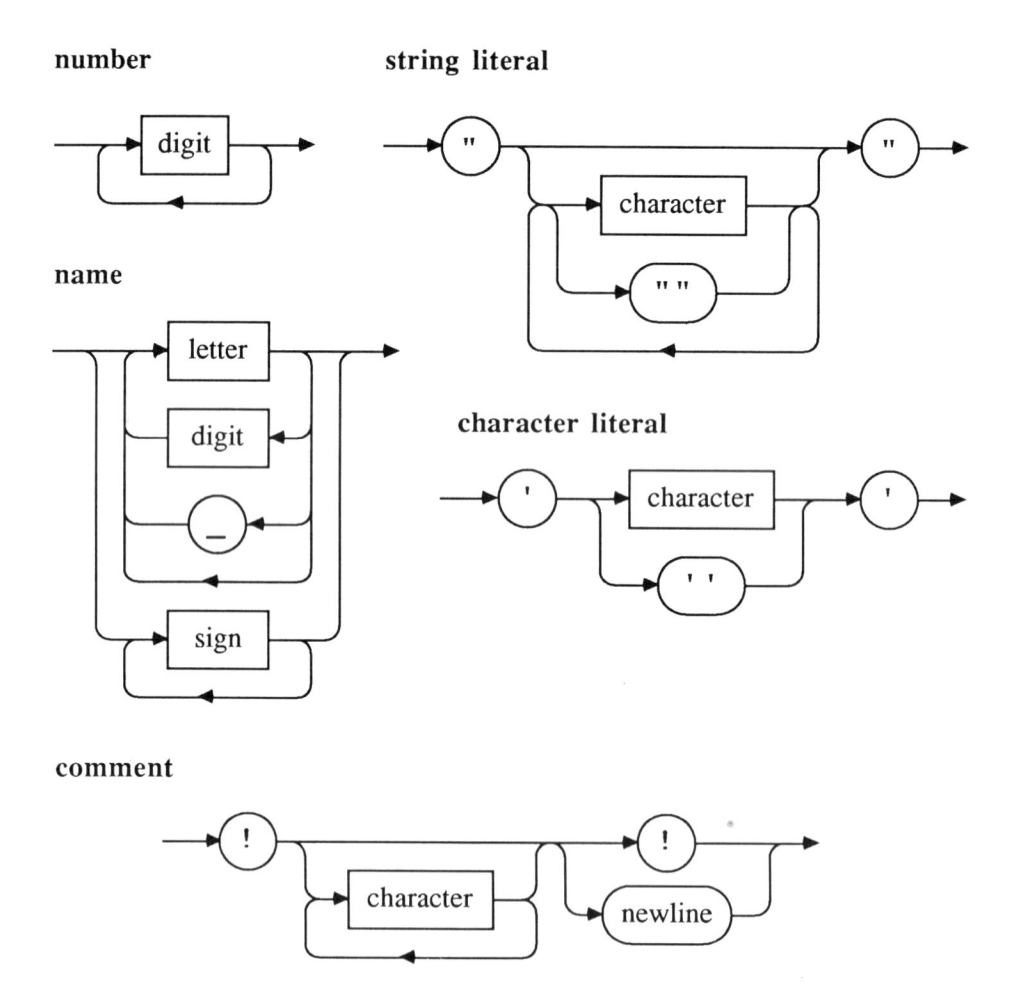

comment

Layout characters are not significant except in character and string literals, where newline is treated as a space. The character pair ' ' represents the single character ' in a character literal, whilst the character pair " " represents the single character " in a string literal. Comments are treated as layout and ignored.

A2.3 Program structure

In the remaining diagrams the objects in the boxes are words and must be separated from adjacent words according to the rules of §A2.2. Round-ended boxes represent predefined words. Boxes containing the word "name" or "synonym" as part of their title represent objects formed according to the **name** diagram of §A2.2. The term "operation" means either "constructor" or "function". The defining occurrence of a particular kind of name is indicated by double bars at the ends of the box. All other boxes represent objects defined in other diagrams.

LANGUAGE SUMMARY 271

constant

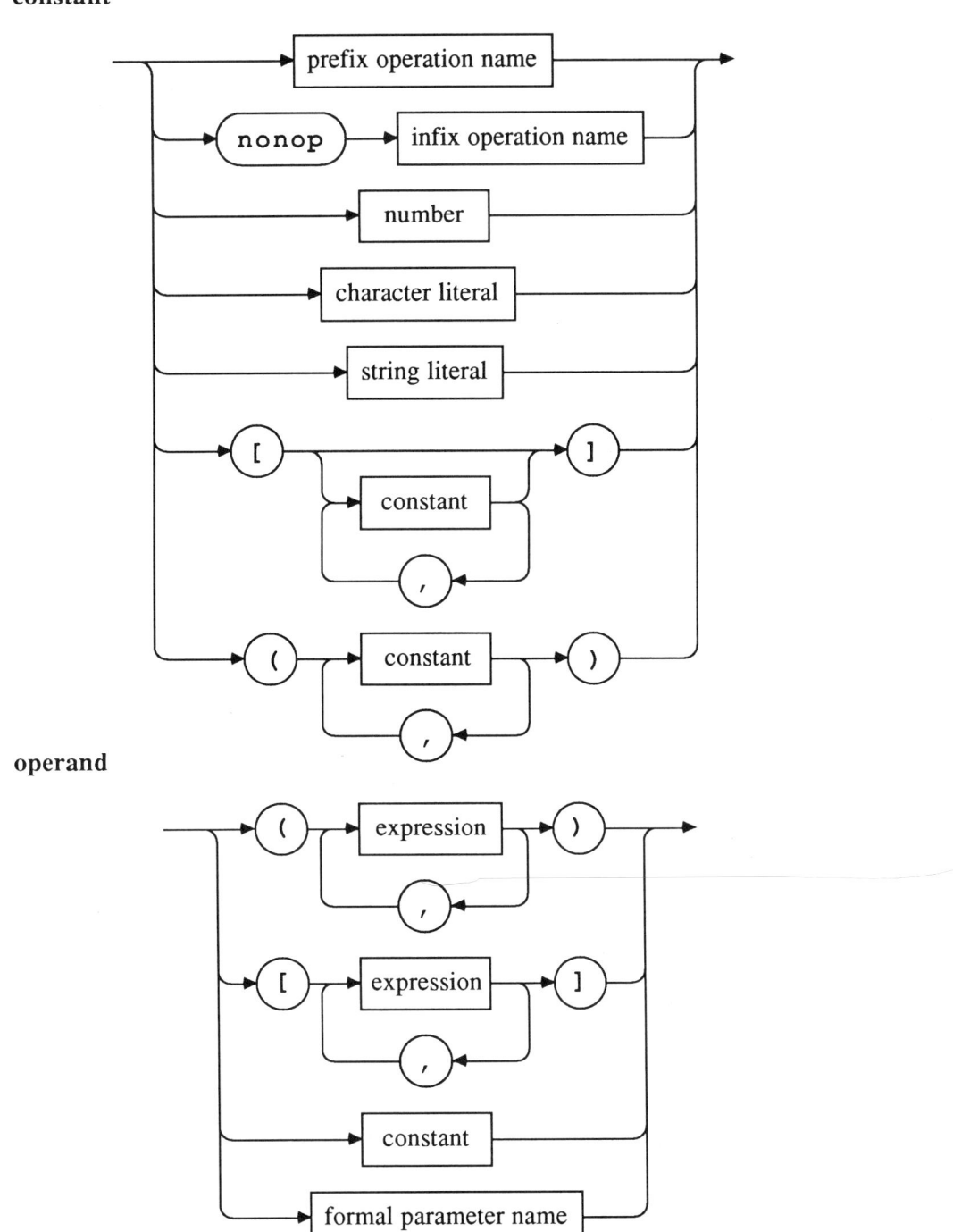

- → prefix operation name →
- → nonop → infix operation name →
- → number →
- → character literal →
- → string literal →
- → [→ constant (,) →] →
- → (→ constant (,) →) →

operand

- → (→ expression (,) →) →
- → [→ expression (,) →] →
- → constant →
- → formal parameter name →

272 APPENDIX 2

prefix operation

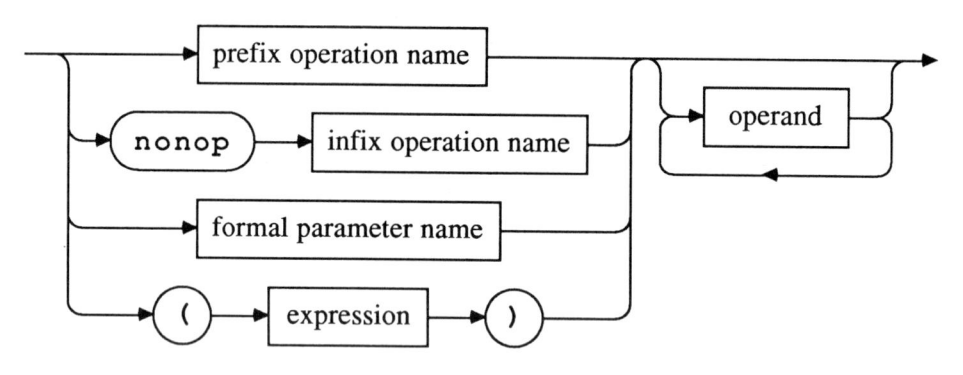

```
         ┌──→ prefix operation name ──┐
         │                            │
─────────┼──→ nonop ──→ infix operation name ──┼──→ operand ──→
         │                            │           ↖____↙
         ├──→ formal parameter name ──┤
         │                            │
         └──→ ( ──→ expression ──→ ) ─┘
```

expression primary

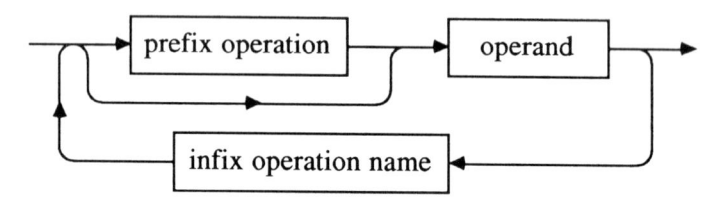

```
    ┌──────→ prefix operation ──→ operand ─────┐
────┤                                           ├──→
    └──←── infix operation name ←──┘
```

expression factor

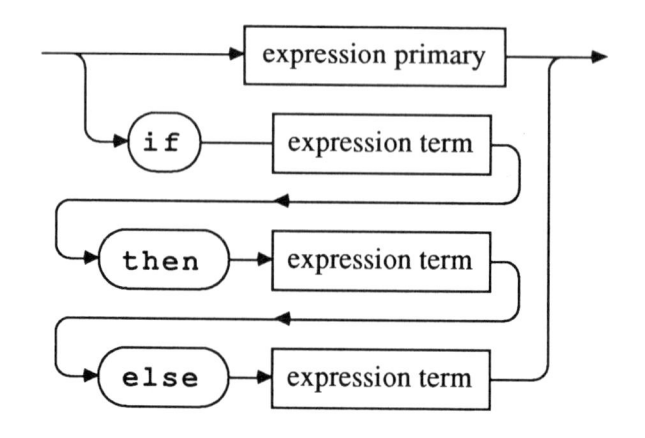

```
    ┌──────────→ expression primary ───────────┐
    │                                           │
    ├──→ if ──→ expression term ────────────────┤
    │                                           │
    ├──→ then ──→ expression term ──────────────┤
    │                                           │
    └──→ else ──→ expression term ──────────────┘
```

local definition

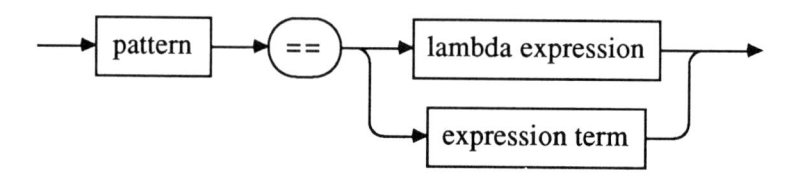

```
                       ┌──→ lambda expression ──┐
──→ pattern ──→ == ────┤                        ├──→
                       └──→ expression term ────┘
```

LANGUAGE SUMMARY 273

pattern term

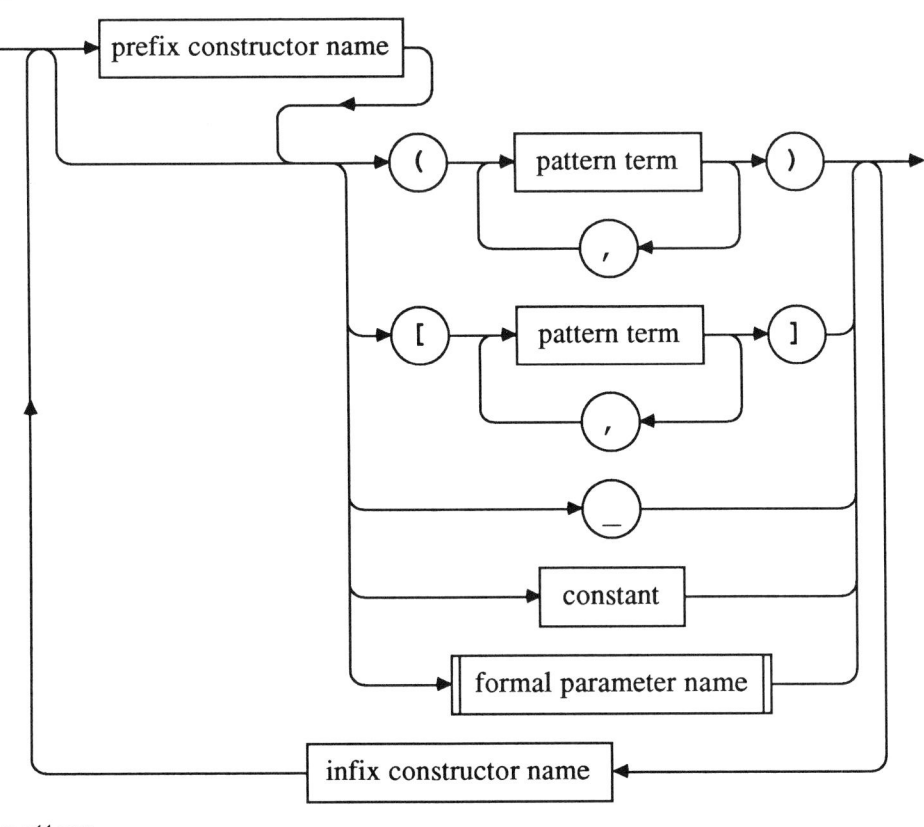

pattern

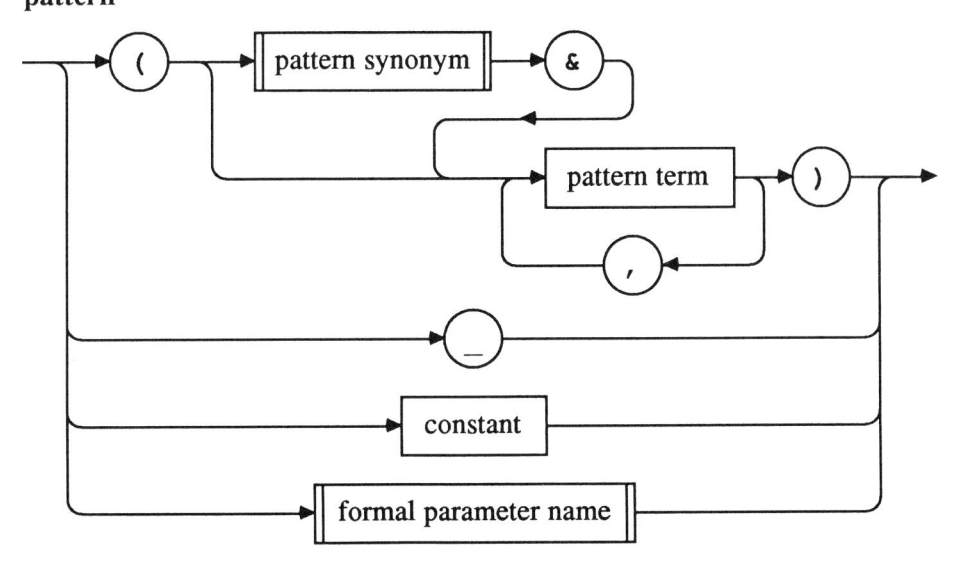

274 APPENDIX 2

let qualifier

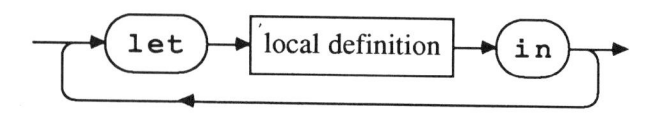

→─(**let**)─→[local definition]─→(**in**)─→

expression term

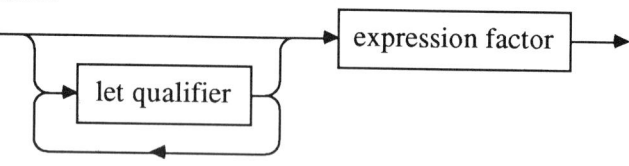

→─┬─→[let qualifier]─┬─→[expression factor]─→

lambda expression

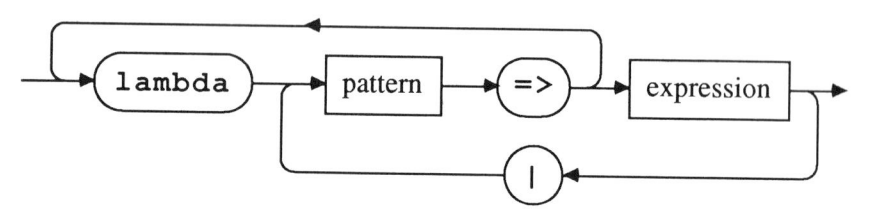

→─(**lambda**)─→[pattern]─→(**=>**)─→[expression]─→
                                    ↑
                                    (**|**)

expression

→─┬─→[let qualifier]─┬─→[lambda expression]──────────────────────→
  └─→[expression term]─→┬─→(**where**)─→[local definition]─┬─→

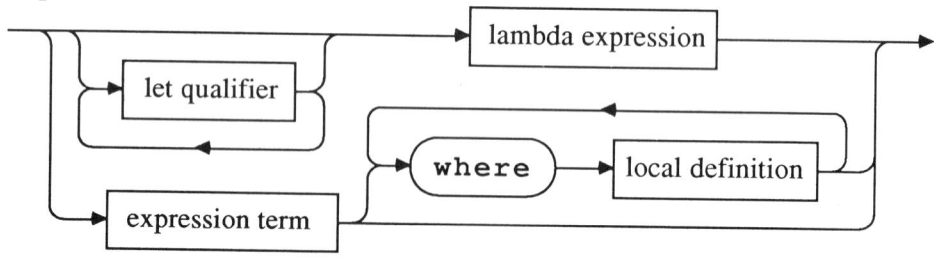

equation

→─(**---**)─→[prefix function name]─→[pattern]────────────────→
  └─→[pattern term]─→[infix function name]─→[pattern term]─┘
  └─→(**<=**)─→[expression]─→(**;**)─→

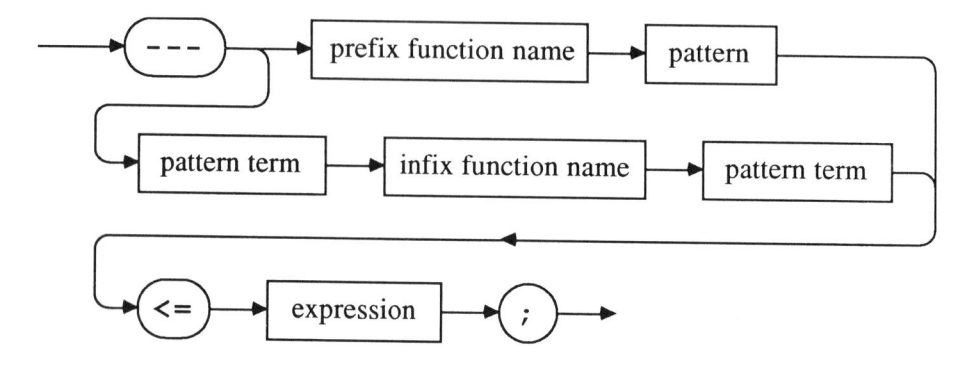

LANGUAGE SUMMARY

type factor

type term

type expression

type variable declaration

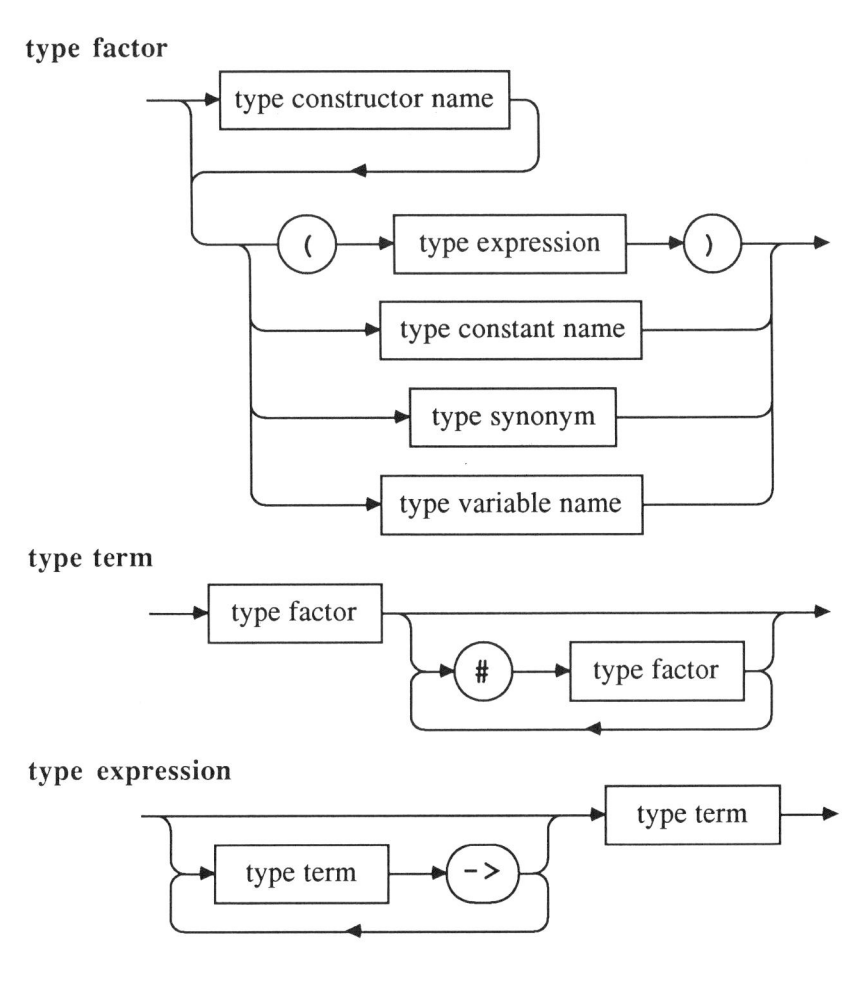

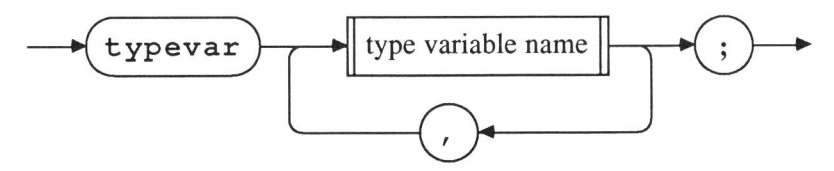

type synonym declaration

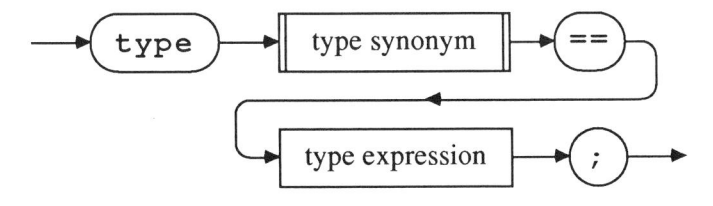

276 APPENDIX 2

data declaration

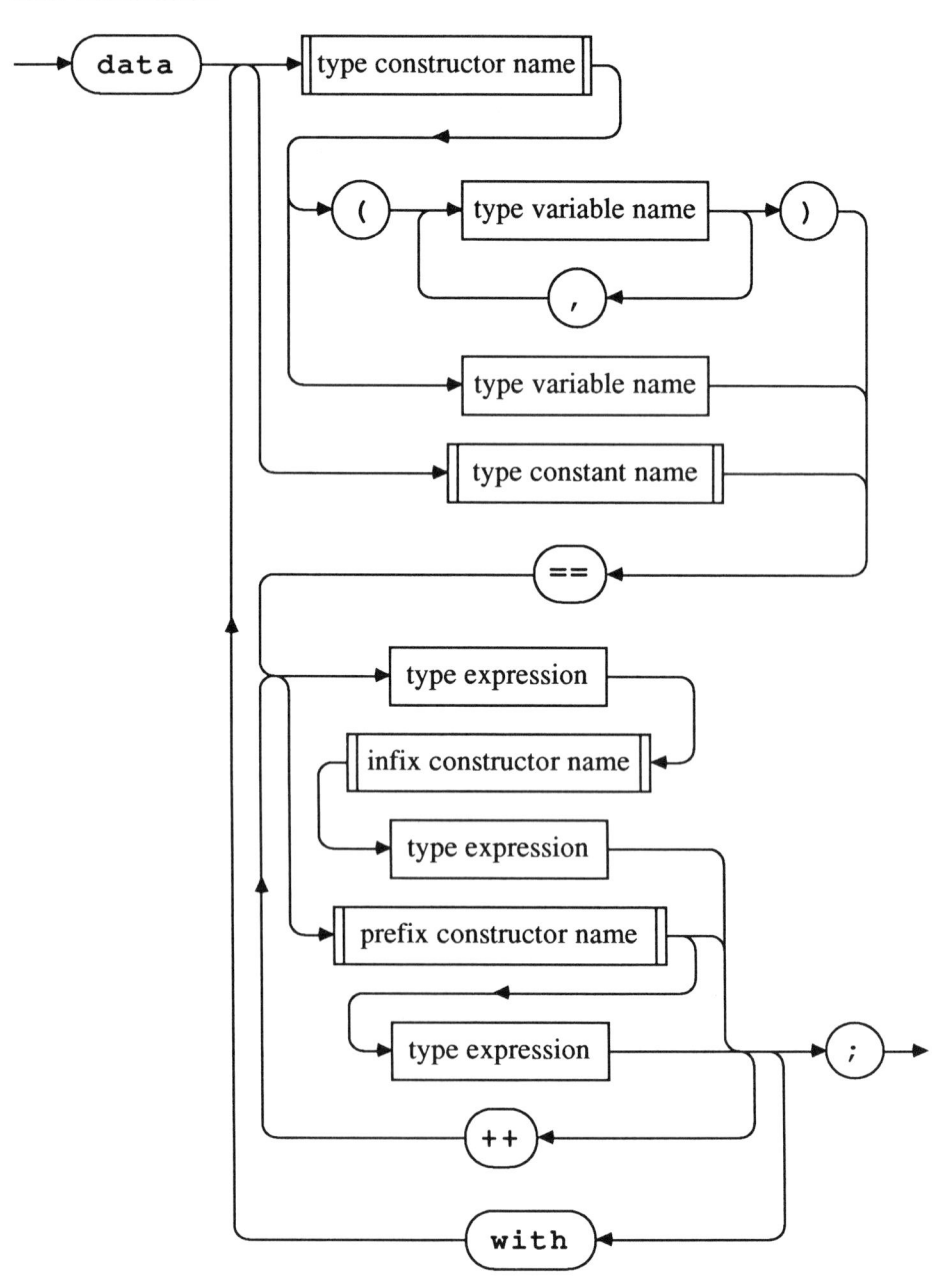

```
──▶( data )──┬──▶[ type constructor name ]──┐
             │                              │
             │   ┌──▶( ( )──┬──▶[ type variable name ]──┬──▶( ) )──┐
             │   │          └──◀──( , )──◀──┘                      │
             │   ├──▶[ type variable name ]──────────────────────  │
             │   └──▶[ type constant name ]───────────────────────┤
             │                                                    │
             │              ┌──◀──( == )──◀──────────────────────┘
             │              │
             │   ┌──▶[ type expression ]──┐
             │   │   ┌──▶[ infix constructor name ]──◀──┐
             │   │   └──▶[ type expression ]────────────┤
             │   ├──▶[ prefix constructor name ]──┐
             │   │       ┌──◀──────────────────┐  │
             │   │       └──▶[ type expression ]──┴──▶( ; )──▶
             │   │
             │   └──◀──( ++ )──◀──┘
             │
             └──◀──( with )──◀──┘
```

fixity declaration

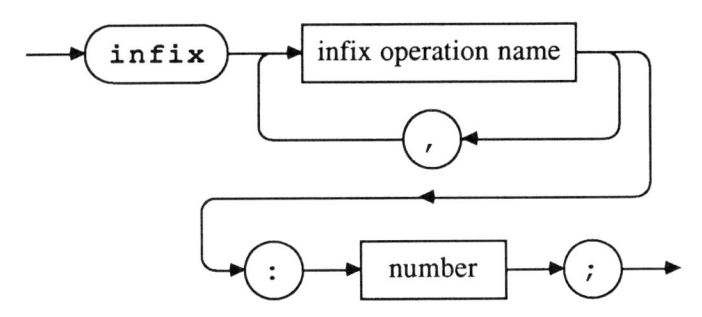

function declaration

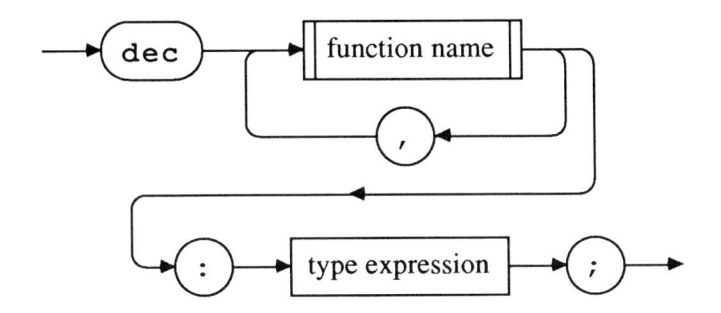

program

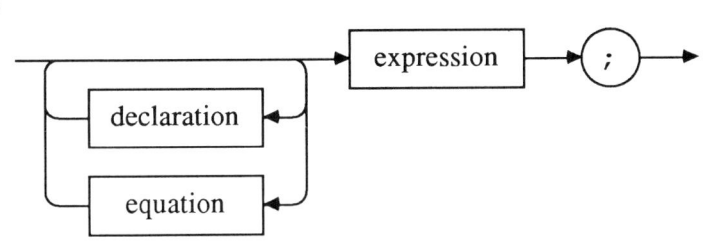

A2.4 Program order
Fixity declarations must appear before the operations are used in data declarations, recursion equations or expressions. Type variables must be declared before they are used in data or function declarations. Function declarations must appear before any of their recursion equations and before they are referred to in expressions. The recursion equations must appear before evaluating an application of the function. Provided these constraints are observed, the elements of the program can appear in any order.

Appendix 3

Standard Facilities

A3.1 Reserved words
The following words have predefined meanings in the language and cannot be chosen for a user-defined **name** (*cf.* appendix 2):

```
!  "  #  &  '  (  )  ++  ,  ---  ->  :  ;  <=  ==  =>  [  ]  _
data  dec  else  if  in  infix  lambda  let  nonop
then  type  typevar  where  with  |
```

A3.2 Predeclared names
The following declarations may be assumed and the type variables, data types, infix operations and functions which they introduce used without further formality. They cannot be chosen for a user-defined **name** (*cf.* appendix 2):

```
typevar alpha , beta , gamma ;

infix <> , :: , ::: , or : 4 ;
infix + , - , and : 5 ;
infix = , /= , < , > , =< , >= , * , div , mod : 6 ;

data num == 0 ++ succ num ;
data truval == true ++ false ;
data char == 'A'  ++ 'B' ++ 'C' ++ ... ;
```

The full set of constructors is the set of printable characters (*cf.* appendix 4).

```
data list alpha == nil  ++ alpha :: list alpha ++
                           alpha ::: list alpha ;

dec = , /= , < , > , =< , >= : alpha # alpha -> truval ;
```

The relational operators <, =<, >, >=, = and /= are overloaded over types num and char, with the latter ordered by their ordinal values (*cf.* appendix 4). Additionally = and /= are overloaded over all structured types.

```
dec + , - , * , div , mod : num # num -> num ;
dec and , or : truval # truval -> truval ;
dec not : truval -> truval ;
dec abs : num -> num ;
dec <> : list alpha # list alpha -> list alpha ;
digits , nl , tab : num -> list char ;
screen : num # num ;
clear : list char ;
goto : num # num -> list char ;
isnl : list char -> truval ;
skipnl : list char -> list char ;
```

A3.3 System commands behaving as functions

The commands described here are those introduced in chapters 8 and 9; they may vary slightly between different versions of the Hope Machine. The following commands may appear as an **operand** (*cf.* appendix 2) in a top-level expression:

```
get : filename -> object ;
```

filename is a **string literal** (*cf.* appendix 2) identifying a file in the filestore of the Hope Machine. The command returns copy of an *object* (of type alpha) held in the file with all lists lazily constructed.

```
input : prompt -> data object ;
```

prompt is a **string literal** (*cf.* appendix 2) to be displayed on the screen of the Hope Machine. The command returns a copy of an *object* (of type alpha) entered in the standard format from the keyboard with all lists lazily constructed.

```
keyboard : list char ;
```

The command returns a lazy list of all characters entered from the keyboard.

A3.4 Top-level system commands

The following commands can only be entered at the top level and cause the Hope Machine to perform some action:

```
put : object # filename
```

filename is a **string literal** (*cf.* appendix 2) identifying a file in the filestore of the Hope Machine. The command causes a copy of the *object* (of type `alpha`) to replace the original contents of the file with lazy list constructors forced.

```
show : object
```

The command causes a copy of the *object* (of type `alpha`) to be displayed on the screen of the Hope Machine in the standard format without type information and with lazy list constructors forced.

```
display : list char
```

The command causes the characters to to be displayed eagerly on the screen of the Hope Machine without enclosing quotes or type information.

Appendix 4

Ordinal Values of Characters

9	tab	48	'0'	65	'A'	78	'N'	97	'a'	110	'n'
13	newline	49	'1'	66	'B'	79	'O'	98	'b'	111	'o'
32	' '	50	'2'	67	'C'	80	'P'	99	'c'	112	'p'
33	'!'	51	'3'	68	'D'	81	'Q'	100	'd'	113	'q'
34	'"'	52	'4'	69	'E'	82	'R'	101	'e'	114	'r'
35	'#'	53	'5'	70	'F'	83	'S'	102	'f'	115	's'
36	'$'	54	'6'	71	'G'	84	'T'	103	'g'	116	't'
37	'%'	55	'7'	72	'H'	85	'U'	104	'h'	117	'u'
38	'&'	56	'8'	73	'I'	86	'V'	105	'i'	118	'v'
39	'''	57	'9'	74	'J'	87	'W'	106	'j'	119	'w'
40	'('			75	'K'	88	'X'	107	'k'	120	'x'
41	')'	58	':'	76	'L'	89	'Y'	108	'l'	121	'y'
42	'*'	59	';'	77	'M'	90	'Z'	109	'm'	122	'z'
43	'+'	60	'<'								
44	','	61	'='			91	'['			123	'{'
45	'-'	62	'>'			92	'\'			124	'|'
46	'.'	63	'?'			93	']'			125	'}'
47	'/'	64	'@'			94	'^'			126	'~'
						95	'_'				
						96	'`'				

Index

® character 6
π 214
τ (golden ratio) 213
... in description 14
symbol 8
   priority 138
& symbol 74
* operation 8
+ operation 8
++ symbol 78
, data constructor 27
- operation 8
--- symbol 22
-> symbol 7
   associativity 138, 176
   priority 138
. data constructor 89
/= operation 10, 12, 13
   over lists 61
   over tuples 50
0 data constructor 68, 69, 88
: symbol 22
:: data constructor 59, 123, 126

::: data constructor 197
; symbol 3, 4
< operation 10, 130
<<get ...>> symbol 217
<<input ...>> symbol 219
<<keyboard>> symbol 225
<= symbol 22, 24
<> operation 61
= operation 10, 12, 131
   over tuples 50
   over lists 61
=< operation 10, 24
== symbol 38, 40, 78, 127
   in type synonym declaration 92
=> symbol 167
> operation 10
>: prompt 6, 209
>= operation 10
_ pattern 33, 161, 169
| symbol 174
~ data constructor 89

INDEX

abbreviated form of `let` and `where` 41
`abs` operation 9
absolute
   program cost 102
   value 9
   zero 24
abstract
   data type 103, 189
      and higher-order function 162
      (exercise) 107
   expression 20, 21, 33, 167
abstracting
   operation 140
   ordering operation 159
   recursion 146, 148
   subexpression 38
abstraction 21, 34, 52, 136, 172
access function 103, 162
   polymorphic 131-2
   for lookup table 103
   for queue 131
   for vector 162
      (exercise) 135
accumulating parameter 213, 233
accumulator 1, 79, 88, 165, 166
accuracy
   of integer division 85
   of floating-point number 213
actual parameter 24, 26, 28, 30, 48, 65, 137, 167, 177
   expression 66
`add` function 83
   (exercise) 46
add machine instruction 2
adding
   element to an ordered tree 102
   record to a tree 98
addition
   of integers 8
   of rational numbers 83
   of floating-point numbers 87
   of long numbers 89
age of an employee 86
`ageless` function 161

algorithm 106, 209
   Euclid's 46
   Quicksort 118
`allsort` function 160
alphabetical ordering 12, 13
`alternates` function 97
alternation of applications 200
alternative 14, 16
ambiguity in pattern 69, 71
anagram 76
`analyse` function (exercise) 234
analysing input 225, 226, 227
`and` operation 11
anonymous
   function 167
   type value 109
append function 61
application 26
   of operation 4
   of lambda expression 174
   of a list of functions 184
applicative
   language 4
   order reduction 31, 32, 38, 138, 196, 203, 204, 216, 230
      of qualified expression 39, 40
approximation for square root 206
arbitrarily large integer 88
argument 24
arithmetic
   mechanised 2
   operation, and mathematics 9
arrangement of objects 47
`arrive` access function 131
   (exercise) 107
Art of Computer Programming, The 46
assembly language 2
assertion 10
associativity 9, 29, 166
   left 4, 154
   right (of consolidation) 149
   of function application 177, 180
`at` function 125
   (exercise) 76

INDEX

auxiliary
  function 38, 39, 54, 99, 106, 116, 129, 158, 167, 170, 208, 233
  variable 40, 41, 41, 43, 45
    distinct 42, 43
average
  value of numeric tree (exercise) 193
  word length (exercise) 166
avoiding potential error 16

backspace 6, 219
`balanced` function 128-9
balanced binary tree 96, 106, 122
`base` operation (exercise) 47
base case 36, 62, 64, 67
  in consolidator 152
  of `at` 125
  of `calc` 82
  of `combine` 146
  of `compress` 152
  of `ConTree` 158, 186
  of `each` 138
  of `increment` 80
  of `index` (polymorphic) 127
  of `join` 67
  of `LongAdd` 89
  of `lookup` 104
  of `nats` 62
  of `order` 118
  of `place` 160
  of `power` 36
  of `RedTree` 156
  of `split` 117
  of `stan` 64
  of `until` 202, 203
  of `youngest` 86
base-case value 154, 155, 157
basic symbol 3
`before` operation (exercise) 76
`big` data type 88, 108
big-O concept of cost 102
`bin` data type 115
`binary` data type 93

binary
  arithmetic 79
  digit 79
  notation 165
  number 88
  tree 93
`BinaryOf` function (exercise) 47
`BinToSeq` function 135
bit 79, 166
blank character 6, 12
body of lambda expression 168
`both` function (exercise) 106
`bound` access function (exercise) 135
bound
  value 172
  variable 173, 177
bracketing, implicit in calculator model 101
branch instruction 1
break command 209, 220
`build` function (exercise) 106
building a balanced binary tree 97

C operation (exercise) 47
`calc` function 82
  (exercise) 106
calculator 6, 20
candidate solution 195, 206
canonical form of floating-point number 85, 233
Cantor, Georg 214
capacity of Hope Machine 34, 36, 88, 196, 209, 217
careful design 36
carry
  on integer addition 80
  on long number addition 89
`cat` operation (exercise) 46
`CatSeq` function (exercise) 134
`Celsius` data constructor 81
  function 21, 136
`CelsiusOf` function 81
`change` function (exercise) 106
`ChangeBase` function (exercise) 47

INDEX 285

changing the representation of an abstract data type 103, 104
`char` primitive type 8
character
 ordering 12, 24
 printable 12, 13
 representing numeric digit 13
character-string representation 222
choice
 of action 14
 operation, rewriting 16
`choose` function 194
 (exercise) 165
 (lazy) 201
`chop` function (exercise) 76
`chr` primitive operation 12
Church-Rosser Theorem 6, 16, 30
circular definition 34
clarity of program 38, 44, 57, 74, 86, 170, 178
`clear` function 224
`combine` function 146
 (polymorphic) 147
command 216
common pattern of recursion 146, 159
commutativity 154, 149
`comp` data constructor 86
comparison
 of characters 12
 of truth values n
 operation 10, 11
 type of 12
completeness of equations 71, 99
`complex` data type 86, 87
complex number 86
`compose` functional 188
composition
 functional 30, 137
 of programs 215
`compress` function 152
computational cost 36, 215
computer 51, 79
 cheapness of 102
`ConBin` function 159

`concat` function (exercise) 76
concatenation of lists 61, 67
conciseness of program 115
concrete data type 103
`condense` function 153
conditional
 expression 14, 69
  containing constant value 28
  nested 15
  normal order reduction of 28, 33
  rewrite rule for 15
  as term in larger expression 15
 instruction 1, 14
conjunction 165
 (exercise) 106
cons data constructor 59, 123, 126
`ConSeq` function 153
consequent 14, 16
consistent instantiation of type variable 61, 114, 123, 124, 126, 142, 160
consolidator 148, 162, 186
 (lazy) 205
constant
 character string 217
 function 173, 183
 value in pattern 73
 value in relation 11
`construct` function 116
constructed type 109
construction of large program 26
constructor function 68
 in pattern 78
 parametrised 80
 priority 81
 as a label 81
 disguising data with 82
 as an infix operation 87
`ConTree` function 158
control
 character 224
 of interleaving 228
 of recursion over infinite list 202

convention
    mathematical 40, 79
    typographical 3, 7, 219
`convert` function 81
converting
    a list to a tree 97
    a sequence into a list (exercise) 193
`convey` function 160
correct
    formation of expression 23
    program 57
    type of object in expression 12
correction of typing mistake 6
correctness proof 128
cost
    of applicative-order reduction 32
    of linear search 95
    of normal-order reduction 32
    of Quicksort 118
    of programmer's time
    of programs
        $O(2^n)$ 37
        $O(\log_2 n)$ 96, 101, 121, 163
        $O(n)$ 38, 95, 101, 102, 121, 132, 163, 164, 213
        $O(n.2^n)$ 213
        $O(n.\log_2 n)$ 102, 118, 122, 163, 164
        $O(n^2)$ 151, 163, 213
    of tree search 96
    of vector indexing 135
counter-intuitive expression 10
counting
    lower-case letters (exercise) 165
    rational numbers (exercise) 214
criterion
    for list partitioning 118
    for list selection 194
    for termination 209
`cube` function 33
`cubes` function 67, 137
current position on screen 224
`customer` type synonym 132
`cut` function (exercise) 106

dangerous behaviour of vector indexing 113
`data` symbol 78
data
    termination of definition 88
    item 1
    structure 48
        choosing the best 101
        with polymorphic component 111
`dec` symbol 22
decapitation of list 174
decimal point, implied 84
declaration 21, 22, 26, 28, 216
deficiency in Hope 127, 128
defining new operation 21, 22
    tuple (recursive) 53
delaying
    evaluation 203
    input 218
    representation choice 103
deliberate
    termination 113
    error 128
`delimiter` predicate function 226
demand-driven program 220
denominator of rational 83
dependency of output on input 229
`depth` function (exercise) 134
depth of a binary tree 96
    (exercise) 120, 158, 193
design error 128
diagonalisation technique 214
`dig` data constructor 88
digital computer 1, 14, 165
`digits` function 222
    (exercise) 233
digit of long number 88
disguising a primitive type 81, 85, 186
disjunction 165
    (exercise) 106
`display` command 218, 223
distfix operation 14, 49, 57, 175, 176
`div` operation 8, 9, 10
dividend 53, 85

INDEX

dividing
   a list in two 106
   floating-point numbers 85
   programming task 103
divisibility 195
   test 194
division
   integer 8
      remainder after 8
   of floating-point numbers 84
   by zero 7, 46
divisor 53
domain of a function 23
doubling a sequence of numbers
   (exercise) 192
`duet` data constructor 114
duplicated
   reduction 54
   subexpression 38
   term 31, 38
   value in ordered tree 116, 119
dyadic
   function 27, 146, 152, 165, 177
   operation 9
      in calculator model 83

`each` function 137
eagerness 220, 228
ease of understanding 79, 115
`either` function (exercise) 106
electrical switch 78, 79
elementary
   arithmetic 83, 89
   mathematics 4, 9
`elements` function (exercise) 134
ellipses to show operand position 14
`employ` function 97, 102
`empty` access function 104, 189, 190
empty
   list 57, 60, 66, 97
   lookup table 190
   subtree 120
`encode` function 49
encrypting character 48

`end` data constructor 93
`ends` function (exercise) 106
`entry` type synonym 104
enumerating rationals (exercise) 214
equal to 10
equal-priority operations 4, 9
equality 62
equation 25, 26
   order 66
   selection 66, 79
   overlapping 99
erasing screen 225
Eratosthenes' sieve 209
erroneous
   operation 17
   expression (deliberate) 127
   result 152, 154
   infinite list 196
error 16
   in evaluation 7
   message 6
      cryptic 128
   checking 135
   forcing 127
   handling 112, 113, 126-7
`error` value 7, 67
Euclid's algorithm 46
`eval` function 101
   (modified) 185
   (exercise) 107
evaluating expression using tree 99, 185
evaluation
   error in 7
   mechanism 217
   of functional 177
   order in calculator model 101
even number elimination (exercise) 165
`every` function 141
execution of program 1
`exp` data constructor 87
exponent 33, 34, 84
   negative 34
exponential growth of expression size 36
exposing constructor 197, 203

288   INDEX

expression data type 100
  (modified) 185
  (exercise) 107
expression
  evaluation (exercise) 18, 19
  evaluation in calculator model 106
expression
  layout of 6
  meaning of 3
  type of (exercise) 19
  yielding a function 173
  conditional 14
  manipulating 5
  constant-valued 25
  number of terms 34
expressions
  equivalent 24
  non-equivalent 9
extra data constructor 88

fact function 69
  (exercise) 46
factor function 195
factorial 46, 69
  (exercise) 211
factorials function 137
Fahrenheit data constructor 81
Fahrenheit to Celsius conversion 20
false data constructor 10
family of data types 122
Fib function 73
Fibonacci number 73
  (exercise) 211
Fibonacci, Leonardo 72
file 215
  location 218
  name 215, 216
filestore 215
  manipulation 218
find function 95
first access function 131, 199
  (exercise) 107
first-class object 183
first-order function 140

fix functional 179
fixed type synonym 93
fixed size
  accumulator 80
  data structure 57, 111
  list 64
flatten function 122
  (polymorphic) 129-30
flattening a tree 102, 118, 121, 135, 158
  by consolidation 157, 158
    (exercise) 166
  a balanced binary tree 98
  a two-level list 222
  an n-ary tree (exercise) 193
  an ordered tree 116
flip function 78
flo data constructor 84
float data type 84, 87
floating type synonym 93
floating-point number 84, 93, 233
  zero-valued 85
  difference from real number 106
fold function 26
forcing
  lazy constructor 200, 207, 208, 220, 226
  termination 209, 220
fork data constructor 115
formal
  function 137, 141, 147, 149, 154, 156, 157, 159, 160, 205
  constructor function 143
  parameter 21, 22, 25, 26, 28, 33, 38, 43, 45, 65, 68, 83, 136, 137, 167
    name scope 67
    substitution 24
  type parameter 109, 110
format function 223
  (lazy) 232
formatting infinite list 231
FourthPower function 26, 33
fraction 83
fractional part of div result 9

free variable 173, 190
fringe of a tree 98, 106, 115, 118, 120
function
    as a monadic operation 22
    as a result 176,
    as an alternative to data structure 189
    as a building block 26
    defining
        a list 62
        a tuple 51
    in a data structure 183
    over lists 64, 67
    generalising 178
    unsafe 174
functional 176, 178, 187
functional composition 26, 28, 122, 137, 150, 54, 187
    generalised 188
functional language 3, 22
funny function 73, 74

gcd function 84
    (exercise) 46
general equation 34
    as rewrite rule 25
    for processing tree 118
get command 216
global scope 27, 44
    of constructor 78, 81, 115
    of type constructor 110
Golden Rectangle 213
goto function 225
greater function 27
greater than 10
greater than or equal to 10, 24
greatest function 30
greatest common divisor 46
guessing square root 106

Hamming, W. R. 211
head
    of a list 65, 67, 137, 147, 156, 210
    of input list 220
high school 206

high-level language 2, 3
higher-order function 140, 167, 186, 205
    non linear 145
    fully-general 142
Hoare, C. A. R. 118
holds function 121
Hope Machine 6

id function 153
identity function 153
if ... then ... else symbol 14
imag data constructor 87
imaginary part of complex number 86
improve function 207
    (exercise) 107
improving approximation 207
in symbol 40
incomputable function 37
incr function 32
increment function 79
incrementing a number 79
index access function 112
    (polymorphic) 126-7
    (exercise) 135
indexing a vector 112
inefficiency, tolerable 102
infinite
    list 195, 216
        and non-strict function 203
        safe use of 202
        reduction sequence 6, 17, 35, 40, 196, 201, 231
        series 214
        table 214
infinitely large expression 196
infix symbol 29
infix
    constructor 89
        priority 87
    operation 14, 28, 30, 61
        as actual parameter 144
initial function 226-7
inject function 101
innermost evaluation 31

input command 219, 221
insecurity in Hope 128
insert function 119, 159
   (polymorphic) 130
insert machine instruction 2
insertion
   sort 121
   into an empty tree 120
instance of an expression 21
instantiation 24, 26, 28, 39, 172, 174
   in pattern 66
   of type parameter 111, 122, 109, 114
instruction 1
   conditional 14
int data constructor 82
integer 8
   division 8
      remainder after 8
   overflow 8, 9, 47, 46, 80, 84, 88
interactive program 219, 220, 222, 228
interleave function 99
   (polymorphic) 129
interleaving
   of applications 220
   of input and output 200
interpreter 6
interrupt 209
into function 151
   (exercise) 77
ints function 196
   (lazy) 198
intuition 29
inverse subtraction 155
inversion of truth value 11
invert function 145
iota function (exercise) 213
irrational number 213, 214
isnl predicate function 227
isomorphic data structure 93, 145
italics typographical convention 7
item data type 82
   (extended) 90
   in series 91

iterator 142, 162, 163, 182

join function 67, 204
   (polymorphic) 123
justification
   for error handling 128
   for user-defined type 79, 80, 86
   for complex program 102

keyboard 3, 219
keyboard command 225
kill function 36
Knuth, Donald E. 46

lambda
   expression 167
   multi-rule 174
   rule 168, 169
   -forming operation 175
language
   applicative 4
   assembly 2
   functional 3
   high level 2, 3
large function (exercise) 233
larger function (exercise) 76
layout
   character 8
      obligatory 6
   function 224
   of expression 6
   of equation 26
   of data expression 94
   of conditional expression 14
   of output 222
   of input 227
lazy
   cons 197
      removed by pattern matching 204
      exposing 206
      forcing 225
   evaluation 33, 196
   consolidation 205

lazy
    input 219, 228
        list 217
    list 197, 225
    output list 216
leading zero 90
`leaf` data constructor 119
leaf of tree 94
least significant digit 79
    of a long number 88
`leave` access function 132-3
left
    association 4, 9, 29, 44, 154, 155
        of , 49
        of application 180
        of consolidation 154
    subtree 94
left-to-right evaluation in calculator 82
left-hand side
    of equation 22, 29, 68
    of == 41
`LeftAdd` function (exercise) 166
`LeftRed` function 154, 155
`length` function 64
    (polymorphic) 123, 148
less than 10
less than or equal to 10
`let` operation 40
    qualifying conditional 40
    qualifying `let` 41
    as a term 40
letter 13
lexical ordering 12
`light` datatype (exercise) 106
`limb` data constructor 93
limit 206
`line` function 228
line-interleaving problem 229
linear data structure 108, 111, 151
linenumber 224
list 57
    as actual parameter 64
    as set 195

list
    concatenation by consolidation 150, 231
    equality 61, 131
    insertion sort 151
    of characters 58
    of functions 59, 183
    of lists 58
    of tuples 58
    size of 195
    undefined-length 59
`listapply` function 184
`listify` functional 180
    (modified) 181
`ListToSeq` function (exercise) 134
load machine instruction 2
`locate` function 96
logical
    conjunction (exercise) 106
    disjunction (exercise) 106
`long` data type 89
long number 88
    (exercise) 233
    representation 89
`LongAdd` function 89
`lookup` access function 104, 189
lookup table 103, 189
loop 1
lower bound 111, 112
`LowerCase` function 24
lower-case letter 13, 24, 26, 48
lowest terms of rational 84

machine state 2, 3
manipulating an expression 5
mantissa 84, 233
many-to-one mapping 69
`map` function 142
    (lazy) 205
`MapBin` iterator function (exercise) 165
    non-recursive (exercise) 193
`MapNary` iterator function (exercise) 193

mapping 21
   many-to-one 69
   one-to-one 69
`MapSeq` iterator function (exercise) 165
   non-recursive (exercise) 193
`MapTree` iterator function 145
   non-recursive (exercise) 193
`MapVector` iterator function 162
mathematical
   convention 40, 79
   correctness proof 128
   expression (exercise) 18
   meaning 2
   notation 29, 79, 84
maximum integer 84
meaning of an expression 3
mechanised arithmetic 2
median value 117
`merge` function 72
merging lazy lists (exercise) 213
minimum depth tree 120
`minor` function (exercise) 106
`minus` operation 87
   (exercise) 106
mirror image of a binary tree (exercise) 166
   (exercise) 193
misleading use of name 68
missing equation trick 113, 128
`mod` operation 8, 10
modelling
   a pocket calculator 82
   a sequence of calculations 91
   a computer 80
   a payroll 111
modification of program 103
modular arithmetic 8, 49
`monadic` functional 177
monadic
   operation 9
      priority of 9
         arithmetic 139
      function 213
         anonymous 171

monadic
   function
      in calculator model (exercise) 107
      over characters 12
`more` data constructor 91
most significant digit 80
multiple
   `input` commands 221
   qualification 41
      naturally-arising 42
         essential 56
   references to a stream 221
   type parameters 113
multiplication 8
   of floating-point numbers 84, 87
`multiplier` functional 176
`multiply` function 87
mutually recursive data types 90, 91, 111

name
   scope 42, 182
      in qualified expression 41
   undefined 42, 175
      choice of 178
naming
   expression 21
   list component 65
   pair component 54
   value 38
`NaryTree` data type (exercise) 135
`nats` function 62
natural number 62, 68
`negate` function 140
negation of truth value 11
negative number 8, 233
nesting
   of conditional 15
   of qualified expression 41
newline 219, 224, 226, 227
   character 6
   sequence 227
Newton's method for square root 206
`nil` function 60

nl function 224
nobody access function 131
 (exercise) 107
node data constructor 119
nodes function (exercise) 134
node of tree 94, 119
 holding data 99
non-empty list 65
non-equivalent expressions 9, 10
non-linear
 consolidator 156-7
 data structure 93
 polymorphic type 115
non-strict function 32, 148, 161, 190, 205
 and infinite list 203
non-strictness, explicit 33
non-termination 34
nonop symbol 144
norm function 85
normal form 16, 17, 27, 31, 36, 39, 62, 138, 208
 as value or meaning 5
 existence of 32
 of lambda expression 169
 of list 58, 59, 139
normal order 31, 32, 37, 138, 196, 198, 200, 219, 204, 205
normalised floating-point number 84, 207
not operation 11
not equal to 10
notation
 English-like 2
 Hope 3
notional declaration 88, 123, 124
 operation 131
null data constructor 119
nulladic
 constructor 68, 79, 80, 104
 distfix operation 57
 function 60, 104
num data type 8, 88
number function (exercise) 233

number
 base of 47
 negative 8
 non-integral 83, 84
 non-zero 88,
 representation 9
 size limit 8
 storage 8
numerator of rational 83
numeric function 129
numeric digit character 13
numerical function 99
numerical calculation 2, 83
numlist function (exercise) 234

obscure expression 44
odd function 24
odds function 141
off data constructor 78
on data constructor 78
one-to-one mapping 69
only data constructor 91
op data constructor 82
open parenthesis 8, 39
opening function 230
operand function (exercise) 106
operand 4
 in calculator model 82, 99
operation type synonym 93
operation 22
 application of 4
 comparison 10
 in calculator model 99
 inappropriate 7, 80
 monadic 9, 11, 12
 characteristic of data structure 103
 defining list 59
 equal-priority 4
 of calculator 82
 over lists 61
 over tuples 50
operator function (exercise) 106
operator 4
optimum partition 11

or operation 11
ord operation 12
order function 118
   (exercise) 77
ordered binary tree 115
   balanced 129
   constructing 121
      from an unordered list 116
      by consolidation 151
        (exercise) 166
ordering criterion 115, 116
   for trees 121
   for data objects 159
   for lists 63
   for queues 132
   predicate 161
   for staff records 131
   unimportant 195
outermost constructor 66
   evaluation 31
output mechanism 226
output-driven program 220, 228
over operation (exercise) 106
overflow 8, 9
overlapping
   equations 99
   patterns 71
overloading 130-1, 159
overtyping 6
overwriting the screen 225

P operation (exercise) 47
packaging
   expression 122
   recursion 146, 157
   infinity 205
pair 27, 41
   constructor 95
      in pattern 71
   representing a rational 83
pairs data type 114
pairwise function 184, (exercise) 165
palindrome function (exercise) 134

parametrised constructor 158
parentheses 4, 11
   insufficient 23
   missing 45
   obligatory 9, 25, 39, 40, 42, 49, 51, 52, 58, 81, 175
   in list 60
   in qualified conditional 55
   in type expression 83,
   unnecessary 51, 87, 176
parity of number in a sequence (exercise) 192
partial
   abstraction 33
   application 171, 172
   parametrisation 177
      for polymorphic sorting 172
   solution 209
partially lazy list 208
   polymorphic data 111
partitioning a list 116
pattern match 68, 81, 132, 168
   failure 74, 127
   ordering of 71
   infix constructor in 87
   in qualified expression 86, 73, 127
   of lazy constructor 198
   of tuple 70, 168
   of number 70
   of other data type 69
pattern
   of computation 136
   of data 136
pattern synonym 74, 98
payroll 85, 95, 102, 106, 111, 118, 130
payroll data type 95
perfectly balanced tree 120
permutation of objects 47
pick function 129
Pisa 72
pivot in partitioning 116
pivot value 117
place function 160

plus operation 87
   (exercise) 106
pocket calculator 90
polyadic
   function 30
   constructor 83, 85
polymorphic
   higher-order function 140, 147
   list constructor 108
   queue abstract data type 131-3
   sorting 130, 159-62
   vector abstract data type 162
   vector (exercise) 135
polymorphism 186
   as abstraction mechanism 136
pos function 125
   (exercise) 76
potential error 16
power function 33
power of lambda expression 172
   of list 108
power of two 179
precedes function (exercise) 76
precision, of floating-point number 207
predicate 14, 15, 195, 202
prefix operation 14, 30, 144
prime number 195, 209
primes function 210
primitive
   comparison operation 10
   constructor 87
   operation 22
   type 8, 10
print command 218
printable character 12
printing results 215
   infinite list of rationals 234
priority 4, 11
   declaration 28
   of -> and # 138
   of user-defined constructor 87
   of , 27
   of , and where 39
   of choice 15

priority
   of function application 22
   of lambda-forming operation 175
   of let 40
   of let and where 44
   of list construction 58
   of operation 4
      monadic 9, 22
   in calculator model 90
private name 26
processor 1
product function 146
   (exercise) 76 program 1
   clarity 92, 93, 146, 186 195
   complexity 57, 186
   order 26
programmer, careful 128
programming style 44, 56, 122, 170, 178,
   186, 187
prompt 6, 220
   user-defined 219
   string 225
pruning a tree 97
punctuation mark 4
put command 215, 216

qualified expression 38, 40, 41, 45, 52,
   56, 86, 127, 170, 174, 230
   as term 39
   as error-forcing mechanism 127
   lambda expression with let 176
   using where 175
   conditional expression with where
      39
queue type synonym 132
queue abstract data type
   (polymorphic) 131-3
   (exercise) 107
Quicksort 118, 122
quotation marks
   double 58
   single 12, 58
quotient function 53, 54
   (exercise) 46

quotient 53
    of floating-point numbers 106
QuotRem function 53, 54

rand data constructor 100, 185
randomly ordered data 122
    in list 117, 121
range error in vector 112
range of a function 23
rat data constructor 83, 185
rational data type 83, 87
rational number 83, 214
    problem with 84
    as triplet 84
    counting (exercise) 214
rator data constructor 100
raven 12
readability 26, 29
real function (exercise) 233
real
    number 84
    part of complex number 86
reasonable person 11
reasoning
    about get 217
    about input 221
    about types 138, 144, 147, 155, 156, 160, 188, 216
        of lambda expression 169
        mechanised 60
record data constructor 95
record 85
records function 98
recurrence relationship 33, 34, 54, 62, 64, 65, 207
recursion
    equation 22, 24, 25, 29
        multiple 66, 70
    explicit 146, 148, 205
recursive
    data type 88
    definition 36
    lambda expression 170, 181
redefining existing name 44, 57

redex 5, 16, 30, 42, 142, 143, 149, 221
RedNary consolidator (exercise) 193
RedTree function 156
reduce function 148
    lazy 205
    substituting for map 171
reduction 5, 16, 26
    example
        application 30
        expression 5
        choose 200
        each 138
        fact 70
        first 199
        greater 28
        ints 196
        join 204
        kill 36-37, 38, 42-43
        listify 180-181
        lookup 191
        map 142
        multiplier 177
        nats 63
        odd 25
        power 34, 35
        primes 210
        quotient 53
        QuotRem 55
        reduce 148
        roots 208
        scale 173
        square 31-32
        sum 19
        until 203
        update 190
    infinite 6
    normal order 31, 37
    number of steps 31
    of conditional 35, 196 reduction
    of qualified expression 39, 44
    postponing 16
    redundant 31
    rule 5
    sequence (exercise) 19

reduction
    strategy 16, 30
redundant
    effort in evaluating conditional 16
    computation 204
    equation 72
    reduction step 38
referential transparency 3, 217
relative priority of operation 29
reloading instructions 21
remainder function 54
remainder after integer division 8, 53
    (exercise) 46
renaming type 92
reordering by consolidation 151
repeat function 162
repeated
    calculation 20
    subtraction 53, 54
replacing a file 215
reply from program 228
representation
    of long number 89
    of calculation 82
    of lookup tabl 190
    of pair 27
    of decimal number in binary 79
    of floating-point number 85
    of list 58
    of newline sequence 227
    of object in file 217
    of abstract data type 131-2
    of expression in calculator model 90
    of vector
        as balanced binary tree 135
        as linear data structure 135
    type 163
request from user 228
reserved word 22 29
return character 6
reverse function
    (exercise) 77
    (polymorphic, exercise) 134
reverse lexical order 161

reversing a list by consolidation (exercise) 166
RevSeq function (exercise) 134
RevSub function 155
rewrite rule 5, 16, 25, 34 66 139, 149, 208
    for conditional expression 15
    for function application 24
rewriting 5, 34
    actual parameter expression 65
    to match a pattern 69
    choice operation 16
rewriting
    generating constant expression 11
right function (exercise) 77
right association 154
    of -> 176
right subtree 94
right-to-left consolidation 205
right-hand side
    of equation 22, 24, 26, 28, 30, 33, 43, 62, 65
    of == 41
RightInsert function (exercise) 166
root function 207, 208
    (exercise) 106
    using iota (exercise) 213
roots function 207
rule
    reduction 5
    rewrite 5
    lambda 168
run-time error 66, 74, 113

safe
    behaviour
        of CelsiusOf 81
        of first 199
        of power 36
        with finite list 199, 203, 205
    reduction strategy 16
    use of pattern 73
same function 207
sandwich function 157

INDEX

save machine instruction 2
saving
   results 215
   space with infinite list 206
school mathematics 106
scientific notation for number 84
scope of name 26, 45
   in qualified expression 56
   hole in 43
   limited, of auxiliary variable 42
   local 27, 168
`screen` function 224
screen 6, 215, 218, 224
   overwriting 225
   scrolling 224
   size of 224
searching
   binary tree 95
   large quantity of data 121
selection of objects 47
`sentence` function 227
sentence 166
   analysis 226
separation of issues 206
`SeqSand` function 158
`SeqToList` function (exercise) 134
sequence 111
`series` data type 91
`serve` access function 131
set 23, 24, 195
   of characters 12
shape
   of a data structure 136, 157
   of a function 137, 146
shorthand notation
   for tree 94
   for constant long number 89
`shout` function 140
   non-recursive 144
   (exercise) 76
`show` command 208, 209, 210, 218, 220
`sieve` function 210
sieve of Eratosthenes 209

sign
   of result 10
   character 29, 89
simplification 5
   of equation 72
simulation of computer operation 79
simultaneous declaration 91
single-element vector 112
`singleton` function 154
singleton list 63, 86, 97, 57, 116, 117, 152, 232
`size` access function (exercise) 135
`skipnl` function 227
smallest element of a sequence (exercise) 193
`solo` data constructor 114
`sort` function 122
   (polymorphic) 130
sorting 118, 121
   a list of staff records 161
   a list of words 161
   a list of numbers 118
   by consolidation 151
   by composition (exercise) 193
space cost 36
special file 218
specialised version of a function 172
specific
   equation 24, 83
   pattern 72
   type 109
`split` function 116-7
`SqrCons` function 150
`square` function 26
`squares` function 64
square root
   Newton's method for finding 206
   of −1 86
   of a real number (exercise) 106
`SquashTree` function (exercise) 166
`st` data constructor 85
`staff` data type 85
staff record 106, 130-1
`stan` function 64

Standardisation Theorem 6
state of a machine 2, 3
store 1
stored
   program 1
      computer 20, 79
   equation 22
stream 198, 229
strict
   function 205, 229
   list 197, 218
style of name 29
subexpressions in calculator model 90, 100
subscript 3
subtle error 45
subtract machine instruction 2
subtraction 8
   of floating- point numbers 87
subtree 94
subtype 81
`succ` data constructor 68, 88
   in pattern 70
`sum` function 67, 146, 197
   (exercise) 75
sum of floating-point numbers 106
superscript 3, 233
suspension of evaluation 219, 226
`swap` function (exercise) 107
switch 106, 166
`switch` data type 78
symbol
   basic 3
   confusion of 174
symbolic
   name 21, 28
   value 21
synonym
   type 92
   pattern 74, 98

`tab` function 224
tab character 6
`table` type synonym 104, 189

table abstract data type 189
tail
   of a list 65, 67, 137, 147, 156, 210
   of a lazy list 202
      unevaluated 217, 219
team of programmers 103
`temp` data type 81
temperature conversion 81
`term` data constructor 90
termination 64
   condition 207
   of `QuotRem` 54
`text` function 230
theorem
   Church-Rosser 6, 16, 30
   Standardisation 6
`time` function 52
time
   conversion 51
   cost of program 36
time-of-day clock 51
`times` operation 85, 87
`tip` data constructor 115
`tips` function 116
   (polymorphic) 129
top level
   expression 215, 216, 217, 219, 221
   application 89
      of `alternates` 97
      of `choose` 201
      of `LeftRed` 155
      of `power` 35
      of `transfer` 121
      of a lambda expression 170
`total` function 94
traffic lights (exercise) 106, 165
`transfer` function 121
   (polymorphic) 130
`transpose` function 126
   (exercise) 76
transposition of list elements 76,
`tree` type constructor 119
   (modified) 120

tree 93
   insertion sort 151
   flattening by consolidation 157, 158
   ordering preservation 118
   representation of expression 100
`treeify` functional 182
triadic operation 49
trick to trap error 113
triplet 49, 51, 56
tripling operation 49, 50
`true` data constructor 10
truncation towards zero 10
truth value 8, 10
   inverting 11
   combining 11, 12
`truval` primitive type 8, 10
tuple 49, 50
   equality 131
   construction priority 50
`twice` functional (exercise) 193
`twist` function (exercise) 135
two's complement 165
two-dimensional table 225
`type` symbol 92
type 7
   annotation 218
   constant 109
   constructor 109
   containing user-defined type 86
   declaration, hypothetical 88, 109, 122
   error 9, 12, 23, 216
   explicit 171
   expression 7, 109
      parentheses in 83
   of `nil` 60
   of conditional 14
   of consequent and alternative 14
   of comparison operation 12
   parameter 123
   synonym 109
   values, anonymous 109
   variable 110, 136
      instantiation 144

type-checking mechanism 58, 60, 81, 92, 109, 110, 114, 124, 128, 132, 175, 180, 216, 217
   as help 80
typeface in example 3
`typevar` symbol 110
typewriter-like keyboard 3
typing mistake 6
typographical convention 3, 7, 219

unbounded problem 209
undefined
   length list 59
   name 42, 175
`under` infix operation 28
unevaluated function 137
uninstantiated type variable 132
universal type declaration 109
unnatural example 11
   as a result of an earlier rewrite 16
unnecessary
   parentheses 51, 87, 176
   reduction step 31
unsafe function 174
`until` function 202
   (modified) 203
`update` access function 104, 189
   (exercise) 135
`upon` data constructor 87
upper-case letter 13, 26
user-defined
   data type 78
      in data structure 79
      polymorphic 110
   name 39

value
   absolute 9
   variable 20
      inappropriate 128
variable function 173, 183
`vec` data constructor 111, 112, 163

vector
    abstract data type 111, 112
    type constructor 163
vector 111
    abstract data type (exercise) 135
    as balanced binary tree 163
    as linear data structure 163
    element, non-existent 113
    iterator (optimal cost) 163
vertical bar symbol 174
visualising
    a tree 94, 102
    an infinite list 208

where operation 38
    qualifying 41
whole number 9
with symbol 91
word 166
word type synonym 92, 104
writing desk 12

younger function (exercise) 106
youngest employee 86
youngest function 86

zero division 7, 128
    error 113
    trick 113, 127

ELLIS HORWOOD SERIES IN COMPUTERS AND THEIR APPLICATIONS
Series Editor: IAN CHIVERS, Senior Analyst, The Computer Centre, King's College, London, and formerly Senior Programmer and Analyst, Imperial College of Science and Technology, University of London

Rubin, T.	USER INTERFACE DESIGN FOR COMPUTER SYSTEMS
Rudd, A.S.	PRACTICAL USAGE OF ISPF DIALOG MANAGER
de Saram, H.	PROGRAMMING IN MICRO-PROLOG
Savic, D. & Goodsell, D.	APPLICATIONS PROGRAMMING WITH SMALLTALK/V
Schirmer, C.	PROGRAMMING IN C FOR UNIX
Schofield, C.F.	OPTIMIZING FORTRAN PROGRAMS
Sharp, J.A.	DATA FLOW COMPUTING
Sherif, M.A.	DATABASE PROJECTS
Smith & Sage	EDUCATION AND THE INFORMATION SOCIETY
Smith, J.M & Stutely, R.	SGML
Späth, H.	CLUSTER ANALYSIS ALGORITHMS
Späth, H.	CLUSTER DISSECTION AND ANALYSIS
Stratford-Collins, P.	ADA
Tizzard, K.	C FOR PROFESSIONAL PROGRAMMERS
Turner, S.J.	AN INTRODUCTION TO COMPILER DESIGN
Wexler, J.	CONCURRENT PROGRAMMING IN OCCAM 2
Whiddett, R.J.	CONCURRENT PROGRAMMING FOR SOFTWARE ENGINEERS
Whiddett, R.J., Berry, R.E., Blair, G.S., Hurley, P.N., Nicol, P.J. & Muir, S.J.	UNIX
Xu, Duan-zheng	COMPUTER ANALYSIS OF SEQUENTIAL MEDICAL TRIALS
Yannakoudakis, E.J. & Hutton, P.J.	SPEECH SYNTHESIS AND RECOGNITION SYSTEMS
Zech, R.	FORTH

Computer Communications and Networking

Currie, W.S.	LANS EXPLAINED
Deasington, R.J.	A PRACTICAL GUIDE TO COMPUTER COMMUNICATIONS AND NETWORKING, 2nd Edition
Deasington, R.J.	X.25 EXPLAINED, 2nd Edition
Henshall, J. & Shaw, S.	OSI EXPLAINED
Kauffels, F.-J.	PRACTICAL LANS ANALYSED
Kauffels, F.-J.	PRACTICAL NETWORKS ANALYSED
Kauffels, F.-J.	UNDERSTANDING DATA COMMUNICATIONS
Muftic, S.	SECURITY MECHANISMS FOR COMPUTER NETWORKS